Black Feminist Writing

Black Feminist Writing

A Practical Guide to Publishing Academic Books

STEPHANIE Y. EVANS

SUNY PRESS

Published by State University of New York Press, Albany

© 2024 State University of New York

All rights reserved

Printed in the United States of America

No part of this book may be used or reproduced in any manner whatsoever without written permission. No part of this book may be stored in a retrieval system or transmitted in any form or by any means including electronic, electrostatic, magnetic tape, mechanical, photocopying, recording, or otherwise without the prior permission in writing of the publisher.

Links to third-party websites are provided as a convenience and for informational purposes only. They do not constitute an endorsement or an approval of any of the products, services, or opinions of the organization, companies, or individuals. SUNY Press bears no responsibility for the accuracy, legality, or content of a URL, the external website, or for that of subsequent websites.

For information, contact State University of New York Press, Albany, NY www.sunypress.edu

Library of Congress Cataloging-in-Publication Data

Name: Evans, Stephanie Y., author.
Title: Black feminist writing : a practical guide to publishing academic books / Stephanie Y. Evans.
Description: Albany : State University of New York Press, [2024] | Includes bibliographical references and index.
Identifiers: LCCN 2024000533 | ISBN 9781438499260 (hardcover : alk. paper) | ISBN 9781438499284 (ebook)
Subjects: LCSH: Womanism. | African American feminists. | African American women authors.
Classification: LCC HQ1197 .E936 2024 | DDC 305.48/896073—dc23/eng/20240411
LC record available at https://lccn.loc.gov/2024000533

To Gramms, Mary Edmonds.
Thank you for reminding me that writing is my birthright.

To Professor John H. Bracey, Jr. Rest in Peace.
Thank you for teaching me how to calm the tempest inside
so I can sit still, focus my energy, and write.

To mentors, colleagues, and students with whom
I have had the honor to WERK.
Thank you for inspiring me and for committing to your practice.

To Black women academics and those who support us.
Sistren, thank you for paying attention to the
narrative care of yourself and others.

And always,

To Dr. Curtis D. Byrd, my husband.
Thank you for sharing your abundant life with me.

Black women's ideas
Can help solve global problems
At least, they solved mine.

—Stephanie Y. Evans, 2010

Contents

Abbreviations of Books by the Author — ix

Preface: Time to Think — xi

1 Introduction: Academic Stress — 1

2 Regenerative Writing: Learn, Create, and Teach the Practice of Collective Self-Care — 23

3 Voice: Personal Practice — 47

4 Argument: Professional Practice — 73

5 Editing: Publishing Practice — 99

6 Community: Public Practice — 125

7 Institution: Political Practice — 157

8 Conclusion: Academic Wellness — 181

Coda: Feeling Good — 201

Acknowledgments — 207

Appendix A: List of Reflection Questions — 209

Appendix B: List of Practical Tasks — 213

Appendix C: Playlists — 217

Notes — 219

Select Bibliography — 233

Index — 239

Author Bio — 255

Abbreviations of Books by the Author

Sole Titles

Black Women's Yoga History: Memoirs of Inner Peace. State U of New York P, 2021. (BWYH)

Black Passports: Travel Memoirs as a Tool for Youth Empowerment. State U of New York Press, 2014. (BP)

Black Women in the Ivory Tower, 1850–1954: An Intellectual History. UP of Florida, 2007. (BWIT)

Coedited Titles

Evans, Stephanie Y., Stephanie Shonekan, Stephanie Adams, editors, with Johnetta Cole (Foreword), and Tracy Sharpley-Whiting (Afterword). *Dear Department Chair: Letters from Black Women Leaders to the Next Generation.* Wayne State UP, 2023. (DDC)

Evans, Stephanie Y., Sarita Davis, Leslie Hinkson, and Deanna Wathington, editors. *Black Women and Public Health: Strategies to Name, Locate and Change Systems of Power.* State U of New York P, 2023. (BWPH)

Evans, Stephanie Y., Andrea D. Domingue, and Tania D. Mitchell, editors. *Black Women and Social Justice Education: Legacies and Lessons.* State U of New York P, 2019. (BWSJ)

Evans, Stephanie Y., Kanika Bell, and Nsenga Burton, editors. *Black Women's Mental Health: Balancing Strength and Vulnerability.* State U of New York P, 2017. (BWMH)

Evans, Stephanie Y., Colette Taylor, Michelle Dunlap, and DeMond Miller, editors. *African Americans and Community Engagement in Higher Education.* State U of New York P, 2009. (AACE)

Preface

Time to Think

> The most important luxury we have on this planet is the time to think.
>
> —John H. Bracey, Jr. (2017)[1]

Black feminist writing is a wellness practice. While both writing and wellness can be solitary journeys, my healthy writing practice is the result of mentoring and academic community building that began at the start of my professional career. As a graduate student in the W. E. B. Du Bois Department of Afro-American Studies at UMass Amherst, I came of age intellectually in an environment where scholarly writing was taught as a practice to foster individual and collective mental health. As stressful and challenging as graduate school was, professional training in academic writing made me well in ways visible and invisible.

My doctoral advisor and faculty mentor, Professor John H. Bracey, Jr., was a teacher's teacher—a fifth-generation educator—and it showed. I was one of dozens of students he guided through the dissertation process and one of thousands that he mentored in the vast learning community he cultivated in his fifty-two years at UMass. A prolific writer, he was among a cadre of faculty in the department that trained graduate students to read widely and write regularly; he led by example. Most of his publications were collaborative volumes, as a number of mine have been, too. His extensive bibliography demonstrates his commitment to the academic writing process and he created a diverse writing community.

Above all, Professor Bracey modeled how to slow down enough to think—how to freeze time and be in the moment. He taught us how to sit still—alone or together—and think deeply for our own growth and in ways that benefit the world. And Professor Bracey taught us how to act in ways that made our thoughts come to life. He collaborated with UMass colleagues in feminist studies and demonstrated the powerful impact that Black feminist collaborations could have to empower students. Reading, teaching, and writing about Black feminist writers was central to my development as a scholar.[2]

Professor Bracey took Black feminist scholarship seriously enough to study and teach it with the same rigor that he taught history, literature, sociology, political philosophy, and other core components of Black studies. Reading Black women writers helped me slow down enough to listen to my inner voice. Reading about other educators who recounted their writing process, I recognized that slowing down and making time to think is the key to doing the scholarly work that means so much to me. Reading and writing were also ways I learned to care for my mental health. Time, like poetry, is not a luxury. Audre Lorde confirmed this revelation. In fact, time to think is essential to our ability to thrive. As Professor Bracey intimated, time to think is immeasurably valuable. Some habits of being unnecessarily busy die hard, but I have continually committed to recover, rest, and restore my right mind. Writing has become a healthy pathway for me to think more calmly and clearly.

Writing reflects self-determination. As Toni Morrison explains, "If all the publishers had disappeared in one night, I would have written anyway. I like the fact that other people like what I write. . . . But writing was a thing that I could not *not* do at that point—it was a way of thinking for me." At its best, writing is a way of thinking, independent of external compulsion or reward.[3]

Time to think means reflecting on those who have come before and, alongside clocking our own thoughts, contextualizing our ideas in relation to others in the present and future. Time to think means learning to appreciate the luxury of a quiet mind and the honor of learning to communicate with other human beings in mindful exchange rather than through ego-based lectures or WWF-style debate. Time is needed to think and write ourselves toward a better world. Academic monographs are often well received by smaller, more specialized audiences, proving books do not need to chart as best sellers or go viral in order to make an impact. None of us knows how much time we have to live, so it is best to use all the time we have as wisely as possible. Personally, I believe writing books has been the best use of my time. Books have been my gift—my way of trying to give myself and others time to think.

Letter to Gramms: My Lifelong Practice of Writing

Maya Angelou called her books "letters to my daughters." I am one of many beneficiaries of the letters, lives, and life writing of Angelou, Morrison, Lorde, and so many others. This book is my effort to share this legacy, and to help you situate yourself in this vast, multigenerational community of scholars.

The cover for this book features images from a letter I wrote to my grandmother, Mary Edmonds (whom I called Gramms), in 1972, when I was three years old. We had just moved from Washington, DC, where I was born, to Albuquerque, New Mexico, and I sent Gramms the letter to tell her about my travel adventures. She kept it and gave it back to me when I started graduate school. While Professor Bracey trained me to be a professional writer, that letter reminded me—and reminds me still—that writing is deeply embedded in my personal history.

I have always been certain that I want to write and, in the words of Toni Cade Bambara's *The Salt Eaters*, that I want to write and be well. While I firmly believe that Black feminist writing is a wellness practice, writing does not come easy for me. And even though I love to write, the process still hurts sometimes, emotionally and physically, whether in the form of professional anxiety, eye strain, or stiffness from sitting long hours. Although writing can be emotionally healing, writing is also stressful—and stress kills. But, despite the stress, I have found satisfaction in my chosen profession. Writing is work that takes lifelong commitment, but, unlike the work I did before entering college, writing for a living is work that feeds my soul.

All my life I've had to work. I started working early: babysitting at age eleven; McDonald's at age fifteen; the Good Earth health food restaurant at age sixteen. When I moved out of my mother's house at sixteen (because it was not physically safe to remain), I held down several jobs while finishing high school. During the eight years between high school and college, I worked in restaurants, from fast food to fine dining, movie theatres, retail, as well as health and fitness clubs. But, even then, I was writing—if only bad, rhyming poetry. A few years before I started college, I got a golden piece of advice: always work for yourself. Since then, no matter who happens to be my employer, I control my own time, energy, and labor (as much as possible). For me, who has had no choice but to work if I want to eat, travel, and enjoy some level of comfort, owning my own time and owning my own mind have been game changers.

I entered college in 1994, at age twenty-five, as a first generation, adult reentry student. I was on a quest for answers about my humanity and in search of community. I was desperate for tools to navigate the wild world—skills my experience as a Black girl confirmed I needed to survive personal, cultural, and structural violence. Whether surviving attacks on my body, on my self-image, or on my physical and material conditions, I came to understand that violence against Black women is a generational struggle. At no point in history have Black women's bodies or minds been universally valued, safe, or centered. Black women's time to think has always been under attack.

When I entered college, I knew books were one means to gain power, otherwise reading would not have been deemed illegal for those who were enslaved and certain books would not continue to be banned. I thought I wanted to teach high school, but loved college so much I quickly changed my career goals to remain in higher education. And remain I did—though eventually realizing the academy could neither affirm my humanity nor fully answer my questions. However, it did enable me to develop skills to do those things for myself within a community of like-minded learners.

In 1999, when I was flailing in my first year as a graduate student, I visited Gramms in DC, and she regifted me the letter I wrote to her decades before. The letter affirmed my purpose and her confidence in me allayed my doubts. Whenever I struggled in my career as a professor—my first year as tenure-track faculty, as a new department chair, or during my review for promotion to full professor for example—my letter to Gramms became a talisman that grounded me and reminded me that I could persevere. In times of doubt, it has reminded me that I have survived doing hard things and come out on the other side. Writing is hard work, but I write with the same sense of adventure I experienced as a child telling Gramms of my travels. Even academic writing and publishing can be adventurous. My lifelong adventure of writing has evolved into a way to foster agency for me and those with whom I write in community.

Mindfulness and Compassion:
Writing and Working for Freedom and Equality

My dissertation explored Black women's educational philosophies. As an undergraduate student I was most impacted by classes that had a community-service learning component, so I wanted to better understand Black women's traditions of applied learning. For me, thinking and acting were conjoined, as in the origins of "head, heart, and hand." This exposure to active learning had a lasting impact on my understanding that what we teach matters. I start all of my classes by assigning the 1948 United Nationals Universal Declaration of Human Rights (UDHR). Regardless of a student's background, beliefs, or goals, the UDHR places everyone on the same plane and underscores the imperative to work for justice, no matter what degree you seek to obtain. Article 1 of the declaration affirms that "all human beings are born free and equal," so, ultimately, Black feminist writing works to support—in theory and practice—universal human rights.

Given the stressors I encountered before and during enrolling in college, I was particularly drawn to practices that affirmed my desire to be free and be treated equally. It turns out that freeing my mind was the most effective strategy to begin to claim agency for myself and others. As such, meditation became an essential way I created time to think. Meditation led me to studies of stress reduction and compassion and those strategies fueled my ability to write with not only longevity but in a way that fed my soul.

As you read this guide, you may be just starting your dissertation, finalizing the manuscript for your first book, or revising your tenth for publication. Maybe you're working on a project that picks up where your previous one left off, or maybe you're trying to completely escape the confines of anything you have written before. Regardless of where you are on your path, this book models ways for you to persist and leave stress on the cutting-room floor. My hope is that this book can be a kind of talisman for you—a resource you reference and return to throughout your career when you need to recenter your practice and remind yourself why this work matters.

My writing is wellness work. This is a WORK-book, so get into the work sooner rather than later! The questions and tasks at the end of each chapter should help you evolve from work to WERK. When I werk, as on the runway, I aim to transform my labor into a creative style that reflects who I am. You can publish a book that not only gets you to your next professional goal, but that galvanizes, bends, and moves energy. I hope this guide helps you craft a tome for the ages that radiates your message far and wide. In essence, I propose that writing can give us life, not simply be another thing that drives scholars to an early grave. When I do my work, I don't want to "kill it," I want to make it live.

Black women's ideas solve problems, particularly the problem of dehumanization. If some in the world do not see the value of Black women's writing, "at least," as I surmise in the haiku for the epigraph of this book, I understand the positive impact that Black women's writing has had on my life. I have built a career writing about Black women's ideas. This work has given me life, provided a livelihood, and sustained me in purpose. Even in academe, my life ain't been no crystal stair. But my climb has been softened by those who have come before, and I share resources in the spirit of making the climb easier for you.[4]

    I invite you to locate a place where your body can sit still and a space where your mind has time to flow freely. I hope you can write yourself free or at least define what freedom and flourishing looks like for you. Writing is a practice—a gift my ancestors gave me. In turn, *Black Feminist Writing* is my gift to you. I hope it helps you. Breathe.

Stephanie Y. Evans
Atlanta, Georgia
February 10, 2024

1

Introduction

Academic Stress

> Though it is conventional wisdom in academe that faculty must either publish or perish, there is precious little discussion about either the process of academic writing or the development of healthy pathways to publication.... In short, *how do you publish and flourish?*
>
> —Kerry Ann Rockquemore and Tracey Laszloffy (2008)[1]

Black feminist writing is a mentoring practice. A year before I earned tenure, Kerry Ann Rockquemore and Tracey Laszloffy, two tenured professors, published a stellar mentoring resource: *The Black Academic's Guide to Winning Tenure—Without Losing Your Soul*. Even though I did not have the advantage of their guide for my own career, and would only come to read it years later, I found the book helpful. One question from that book drives *Black Feminist Writing*: "how do you publish and flourish?"

After earning tenure, I became increasingly productive as a writer. Even as I took on a long series of administrative roles, I continued to publish single-authored and coedited books in Black women's studies (BWST). My academic career is rooted in BWST. I earned my doctorate in Afro-American studies (2003) with a graduate certificate in advanced feminist studies (2002). My faculty appointments have all been joint appointments between the departments of African American Studies and Women's Studies with supplemental appointments in history.

I get asked—a lot—about how I have maintained a high degree of productivity while carrying a heavy administrative and service load. But the question I really want to answer is: How can we, *collectively*, publish and flourish? How can we—as Black women, as Black queer and trans women, as nonbinary feminists and womanists, as scholars in race and gender studies, as minoritized intellectuals, and as freedom-loving people—publish and flourish? Flourishing does not mean simply earning tenure, winning awards or book prizes, acquiring power as an administrator, or being recognized as distinguished faculty—though those things are nice. Flourishing is beyond material reward. The authors of *The Black Academic's Guide to Winning Tenure* identify the vapid, soul-crushing environment that is higher education. They define flourishing as "not losing your soul." I agree. But flourishing requires practice.

Writing and publishing a book does not have to be a soul-crushing experience. In *Keywords for African American Studies*, Emily Lordi defines the concept of soul as "capacious" and points to a broad tradition of African American cultural and political expressions of soul. From W. E. B. Du Bois during Reconstruction to James Brown in the Black Arts and Black Power eras, *soul* has an expansive meaning in Black life. Lordi focuses on women writers and artists, including Toni Cade Bambara, Toni Morrison, and Audre Lorde, as well as singers such as Aretha Franklin, Odetta, Nina Simone, and Miriam Makeba. Her work perfectly illustrates the ability to write about creative thinkers and art that feeds your soul. In the BWST anthology, *Soul Talk: The New Spirituality of African American Women* (2001) Akasha Gloria Hull explores the spiritual traditions of Black women's soulful writing. The soulful contributions of Black women educators have grounded my practice, enabling me to receive energy and joy from the writing process—despite the arduousness of tasks involved with academic writing and book publishing.[2]

This book connects the heart—and soul—to the brain and body, offering a model of holistic writing in a context—academia—that seldom takes the whole person into consideration. Developing a sustainable writing practice is a struggle, in any context. Ask most professional writers (especially those belonging to a union) and they will tell you that writing is work. My writing is joyous and I'm passionate about the pleasure writing offers. But, mostly, writing is challenging work. I view writing as volition but also vocation. It is both my calling and my profession. And it is hard.

Academic writing presents specific challenges. As a genre, it requires research that is validated by professionals in your field. Publishing books with an academic press requires professional peer review. In addition to the multitude of demands like teaching, campus service, and administrative responsibility, book publishing requires a focus that is constantly challenged by personal and professional stressors.

The publishing world, like everything else, is inherently political and stressful, especially for those in race and gender studies. Dynamic factors include the amount of money for-profit presses make from unpaid academic labor, resources allocated (or not) to university presses by their institutional sponsors, lack of diversity in academic publishing leadership, uneven peer review assessments, and whether academics should (or can) get an agent or a publicist. There are different kinds of scholarly publishers, to be sure. All of my own books have been published with university presses. University presses (UPs) are nonprofits with lots of moving parts. They all practice some form of peer review, which is what makes them reputable but also brings challenges. The undercompensated professional service required for peer review can not only extend the lengthy process but can also become a source of exhaustion for the scholars who stand to benefit most from publishing. The corporate model of publishing, like everything else, exploits labor. In addition to facing institutional bias, scholars who write about human rights and social justice issues are either actively dissuaded or can be discouraged by the long wait time to see a book in print. The splintering of BWST factions and cliques who seemingly cling to bitter disputes can make an already hostile terrain downright depressing.

In addition to unequal disciplinary and professional factors, there is the increased politicized public targeting of Black women academics specifically designed to induce stress. The white supremacist establishment is working hard to make Black feminist work impossible by using tactics like hypocrisy, extraordinary scrutiny, abuse (overwork, lies, and character assassination), or double standards. We witnessed these tactics with Nichole Hannah-Jones who was denied tenure in July 2022 (UNC Chapel Hill), the death of President JoAnne Epps at a university event in September 2023 (Temple), the targeting and bullying of President Claudine Gay until she resigned in January 2024 (Harvard), and the suicide of Dr. Antoinette Candia-Bailey in the same month (Lincoln University). These are just the highly publicized instances; writers like professors Monica A. Coleman and Lori Patton Davis note many other lesser-known examples of how Black women suffer uniquely from academic death dealing. But, in the words of Alexander Pope (studied by Eva Dykes in one of the first Black women's dissertation), "hope springs eternal."

Despite the negative aspects of this work, I have grown to love the practice of publishing academic books. It was a challenge for me to learn to navigate the publishing process. A good amount of work I have proposed in the past has been incomplete or inadequate, so my writing lessons are as much about my "failures" as my successes. Now that I have a general sense of the world of university presses, I flourish when I write book-length studies, and releasing books is an ever-exciting milestone. With each new book comes an opportunity to gather, celebrate, teach, and either tear down existing structures or build new ones.

If you work in higher education, chances are you feel at the mercy of too many others in decision-making roles. In addition, if you are an academic author from one or more marginalized communities (based on race, class, gender, religion, ability, nationality, or other identity markers), you may struggle with the imperative to "say the thing you came here to say" while operating in overlapping hostile environments. If you are reading this, you may desire to write beyond the constraints imposed upon you by tradition, convention, malice, or negligence. Identifying locations of your stress is the first step in effectively managing it.

Tragic Inevitability: Managing Stress as a Scholar of Race and Gender Studies

> If we are truly fashioned by fate
> And we are modeled by destiny
> Then surely we must concede
> To this tragic inevitability
>
> —Lalah Hathaway, "Tragic Inevitability"

Many things on this earth are designed to kill or oppress Black women. This is not hyperbole. As a Black woman academic, I have witnessed entire structures operate to cage my being, murder my spirit, and outlaw my ideas. I am indebted to Dr. Alexandrina Deschamps, an advisor and member of my dissertation committee, for showing me early on in my career how to challenge academic violence. Her pedagogical excellence and mentoring had an indelible mark on my conviction to move forward regardless of what came my way. So, I'm here to say, not only will I not let the stress of academic writing kill me, but I'm determined to make writing something that gives me life. At best, writing and publishing should give you a little life too. In her song "Tragic Inevitability," Lalah Hathaway laments that we must concede the tragedy of being human. Yet the rest of the songs on her album *Self-Portrait* confirm that the tragedies of grief, sorrow, and heartbreak are only a small part of our human experience. While some see writing as a tragic task, I refashion it as a harbinger of hope.[3]

At work, Black women are expected to perform a disproportionate amount of service and, at the same time, denied needed breaks because of the Black Super Woman myth.[4] At home, women are disproportionately charged with child or familial care, cleaning, meal preparation, and other gendered labor. Women and birthing people carry whole human beings in our bodies . . . and write books. Childcare, especially for children with disabilities, requires mental and emotional stamina unknown to child-free people or others not in charge of daily care. In the community, Black women create the infrastructure for change and perform the innumerable tasks that set the stage, lead, and sustain justice moments.

My first book, *Black Women in the Ivory Tower* (which was based on my dissertation), traced these historical patterns from the early generations of Black women academics. Mindful of these patterns, I began to fiercely defend my right to spend my time as I please . . . and will continue to do so. In full transparency, part of my privilege is the relative freeness of my time. Though I am a first-generation and adult-reentry college student, I am child free, did not marry until the age of forty, and am partnered with another higher education professional who values and affirms my writing time. Also, I don't cook. Once a week I'll make a light Sunday brunch, but that's it. I love to eat quality food, so before marriage I mostly ate out, and after marriage, we either share meal preparation (and he is a marvelous cook) or we order prepared healthy meals. Most recently, we rely on meals delivered to our door weekly. That matters. The space I have enjoyed is only the space I demanded. I am also a happy introvert. I enjoy my own company so I can write all day and night without feeling like I'm missing out on anything happening in the streets. I take great pride in teaching and mentoring but I also set clear boundaries.

Despite the privileges I have enjoyed, there are challenges that counterbalanced my relative freedom. Specifically, in my twenty years as a professor, I have not had a full semester on sabbatical or research leave (let alone a full year). I have applied three times for a professional break (at two separate institutions). Each request has been rejected. Additionally, during twelve of the twenty years I have spent as a faculty member, I served as department chair. For a dozen years, I prioritized the needs of faculty colleagues, staff, students, and upper-level administrators as I struggled to remain intellectually active. So, I had to learn to multitask, or I would have not gotten any writing done after my first "tenure book." Something so simple as learning to manage my email inbox was an act of desperation to secure more time to write while still ethically handling all my other responsibilities.

Black feminist writers have several distinct challenges. In addition to personal stressors and political stressors, our profession requires that we write in ways that challenge individual and systemic oppression. What is unique about writing in race and gender studies (whether in stand-alone departments or in other disciplines) is that we, generally, challenge systemic conditions while inevitably benefitting from those same conditions. Because we write to agitate for change, our work is often diminished, attacked, or even outlawed. Facing the regular stress of academic writing is compounded by the need to write despite additional burdens of knowing your writing will not always be valued. Producing an academic book takes courage; publishing in Black feminist studies requires absolute conviction.

Regardless of when you begin or complete a book, you will most likely be writing through stressful conditions. It may even seem like some forces conspire to keep you from writing. Challenge. Disappointment. Duress. Crisis. These stressors may be personal, professional, national, or global. To illustrate this point, below is a short list of stressors that I have worked through since I began college in 1994. Each event severely increased my stress level as I struggled to complete college, graduate school, the dissertation, or book projects—including this one:

Locating Stress: Layers of Challenge since 1994

1. Working while entering college (1994): Personal stress
2. Transferring schools to focus on BWST (1995): Professional stress
3. Proposition 209 outlawing diversity in CA (1996): Professional stress
4. CSU system strike (1999): Professional stress
5. September 11 (2001): Global stress
6. Iraq War (2003): Global stress
7. Economic recession (2007): National stress

8. Threats to cut African American studies (2007): Professional stress

9. Appointed department chair (2010–2022): Professional stress

10. Miscarriage (2013): Personal stress

11. Family deaths (2013–2015): Personal stress

12. Election of the 45th US president (2016): National stress

13. Denied application for research leave (2018): Professional stress

14. COVID-19 (2020): Global stress

15. Black Lives Matter protests (2020): National stress

16. Election of 46th US president (2020): National stress

17. Denied application for research leave (2022): Professional stress

18. Book bans, attack on BWST (2022): Professional stress

19. Spouse health issue (2022): Personal stress

20. Denied application for research leave (2023): Professional stress

21. Passing of Bracey (2023): Personal stress

22. Hair loss (2023): Personal stress

23. Human Rights crises in Ukraine, Gaza, Sudan, Congo, and Haiti (2023): Global stress

24. Threats to cut African American/women's studies (2023): Professional stress

These are mild stressors compared to what you may be going through—or, hopefully, this list is far worse than you might encounter. Either way, know that you cannot control circumstances but you can put them in context and manage your stress response while still moving forward with your writing.

Beyond crises that can impede writing progress, simply trying to navigate routine life events or joyous occasions can twist your emotions in knots. When you are facing deadlines, it can be difficult to fully be in the moment for birthdays, graduations, anniversaries, sports events, or other once-in-a-lifetime celebrations. Writing seems impossible when you have to face chores like doing laundry or dishes; caretaking for family; commuting or teaching classes; resisting oppressive institutional conditions; serving your community; agitating for justice; or offering direct service to support a worthy cause. All of these regular-degular activities can creep into your precious little writing time and exhaust you in ways that make it seem impossible for you to meet the demands required to complete a book-length project. Then there are era-defining stressors such as COVID-19 that shut everything down. And don't even get me started on high blood pressure or menopause or global warfare that can fill you with despair. But we do not have the luxury of despair. We got this. Breathe.

Placing your challenges in relation to others (historical and contemporary) might help you move forward with the tasks in front of you each day—even if only in small ways. For better or worse, you are not alone facing the task of writing in dire times. However, there is no need to create the mindset of "no pain, no gain," in order to push through personal, familial, national, or global pain. On the contrary, embracing more creative aspects of your scholarly expression and succumbing to gentleness—tenderness even—can move you further, if more slowly. Learning self-compassion might help you reframe your relationship to writing if it is now oriented in doom, despair, or displeasure. Self-compassion takes courage. It also takes courage to demonstrate compassion for coworkers in and beyond academe. Institutionalizing wellness requires that you have compassion for more than just yourself.

In my mind, flourishing means experiencing wholeness, kindness, professionalism, and wellness, as well as shouldering the responsibility to create space in academia for more people to experience the same. It also means using every possible resource to ensure academe reverses oppressive structures outside our gilded halls. This happens even as we do the hard work of fundamentally restructuring the profession to reflect progressive values, radical movements, and advocate for a less violent world.

I am not a deeply radical scholar. Given my extended time in administrative service, I think it would be disingenuous to claim that position. Yet, there is a role that even administrators can play to mentor, support, and serve the interests of radical faculty who are making necessary demands to fundamentally shift academe in ways that create conditions that do not abuse humans or other living beings. Not everyone has the same role to play in resistance movements, and being transparent about your role is important.

As a former administrator and now, with this book, I want to support progressive scholars who are invested in working together to institutionalize wellness. By institutionalize, I mean to find malleable ways to ensure the growth of race and gender studies that defy academic efforts to snuff us out. To be clear, Black feminist writing can never be truly institutionalized because higher education is a capitalist project and can therefore never fully affirm our humanity or answer our questions. Yet, here we are, teaching and grading, attending too many meetings, applying for tenure, getting promoted, conferencing, speaking, and publishing. Essentially, I want my writing to identify sustainable practices that allow us to handle the necessary rigor of scholarly work without making ourselves or other people sick. If our writing is not informed by multiple communities, then illness, irrelevance, and harm are sure to follow. I'm thinking here of Bernice Johnson Reagon's "Coalition Politics: Turning the Century" in Barbara Smith's *Home Girls: A Black Feminist Anthology*. When we write, we have to learn to create and navigate healthier home spaces and coalition spaces.[5]

I want to explore how scholars—especially marginalized scholars—can create a more abundant life and enjoy our profession as university educators. How can we do the hard work of creating measurable equity and not mere tokenism? This is not easy work, but BWST is a tradition of writing that facilitates structural transformation, and many people are committed to the cause.

Origins of This Book:
The Practice of "Everyday" Writing and Feminist Peer Review

> Black women's experiences, ideas, and practices can inspire contemporary educators to transform the academy.
>
> —Stephanie Y. Evans, *Black Women in the Ivory Tower*

I started this project as the result of a series of dialogues with colleagues in race and gender studies. Within one year, between February 2022 and 2023, I was invited to review twelve book drafts in BWST. Topics ranged from intellectual and educational history to biography and wellness traditions—all within the scope of my research. In addition to reviewing this large body of new research, I worked as a thesis and dissertation advisor, provided informal periodic mentoring for a few new faculty authors, reviewed several full professor tenure and promotion dossiers, and assessed multiple submissions in my role as a series editor for SUNY Press.

During this time, I was invited by three faculty fellowship writing programs to serve on book manuscript review panels (University of Notre Dame, Pennsylvania State University, and Syracuse University) in addition to a request from Spain to sit on a dissertation committee (which I could not accommodate due to scheduling). I was thrilled to be exposed to the work of so many emerging scholars at once and happy to share insights where they might help others. The fortuitous convergence of these meetings, consultations, and written reviews in a brief time span was transformational.

Sharing, as an act of giving and receiving, is fundamental to African feminist values. In short, we can publish and flourish by simultaneously focusing our attention on our own voice and harmonizing our voice with others who believe in fighting for human rights, mental health, and wellness. Black feminist writing is a peer review practice.

The energizing experience of speaking with authors about the publishing process in general, and their manuscripts in particular, was a pivotal moment in my career as a writer. Those closed meetings with new faculty who were substantively revising their dissertations to create manuscripts for submission to academic presses allowed me to reflect on my own journey and what I have learned since I undertook the same daunting exercise twenty years ago.

With each assessment, I began to formalize my feedback. I surveyed developmental editing resources to ensure my responses were detailed and complete. During these meetings, I was reminded of the thrill of graduate seminars and the beauty of critical exchange and interdisciplinary engagements. I was more than happy to add my two cents and appreciated learning about nuanced perspectives from other reviewers on those panels. Increasingly, I became clear about my desire to codify and share publicly the lessons I found myself repeating in each private session. I also wanted to apply what I was learning about developmental editing to my own writing process.

In May 2022, I was awarded a Georgia State University Humanities Center Faculty Fellowship to develop a proposal for another book project I was starting, about Black women and the history of tea. The four-week

"Maymester" program also included periodic meetings during the academic year to read and give feedback to participants. The tea research will take several years to complete, but I benefitted from participating in a formal sponsored writing group that shared short pieces for peer assessment. Unfortunately, during this time, my husband was diagnosed with a serious illness so I worked through tasks as effectively as possible, not able to fully be present, sometimes joining a call or online meeting from the car after doctor appointments. Nevertheless, being in a space of collective learning helped me focus on something other than the panic I felt at the time and helped remind me of how valuable community can be to managing the big and small stressors that inevitably interfere with all of our writing. The fellowship resulted in an accepted book proposal (SUNY Press) and an article, "'Take No Tea for the Fever': Tea in Black Women's Mental Health History and Traditions of Self-Care as Resistance" for the *Phylon* journal. I benefitted from pointed and thorough critique from some colleagues and kind encouragement from others, while sharing my bullet pointed responses to their work as well.

In spring 2023, I began to enroll in editorial training workshops so I could streamline my feedback to authors and make sure my responses were informed by standards set by professional consultants. What I discovered during this time was something I knew from years of work in BWST but hadn't quite solidified in my mind: writing is not extraordinary—it is an ordinary act of resistance.[6]

Black feminist writing is an everyday practice. In their *Signs* article, "Who's Schooling Who?: Black Women and the Bringing of the Everyday into Academe, Or Why We Started *The Womanist*," Layli Maparyan and Barbara McCaskill recall the impact of learning about the origins of BWST on their collaborative work. Referencing Michele Russell's chapter in *All the Women Are White, All the Blacks Are Men, but Some of Us Are Brave*, the authors published a newsletter to gather and disseminate information that places Black women at the center of "making history." They centered themselves and their perspectives, but also recorded their lives as active history makers. Unlike the top-down, exceptional individual model of history, Black women academics center the everyday, common, regular acts—acts of survival that contribute an alternate history to academic settings.[7]

My writing is intimately connected to this tradition. My contribution to Black feminist praxis is to offer a basic, practical "everyday" approach to writing: *write what you can every day*. No more, no less. I unpack the details of my writing practice throughout this book, but my takeaway message is that Black women's intellectual history shows academic writing is common. Normal. Plain. Mundane. Quotidian. Black women writers such as Beverly Guy-Sheftall and Patricia Hill Collins reflect on how they steal moments of time whenever they can find them. My everyday approach is not unique. It's ubiquitous. Black feminists understand the struggle for freedom is not completed in one day, but requires a commitment to a daily struggle, and writing is part of that struggle. Every day, whenever you find or make time, you can do one small thing to finish your book.

That small thing may be reading. I count reading as writing. I mean it. Discovering an article on social media, reading the work, then reaching out to the author to share appreciation of the most salient points—all that is writing. Being excited about a new book release, and reviewing that book is writing. Teaching foundational or cutting-edge publications and incorporating your analysis into a lesson plan, then citing those texts in an article counts as writing. Writing can mean researching, collecting data, sketching drafts, editing, taking care of administrative publishing tasks such as gathering permissions, or enjoying other forms of creative expression. While I was writing *Black Women's Yoga History*, I earned a two-hundred-hour certification in Kemetic yoga. That research counted as writing.

You may not be able to write words on a page every single day but developing a habit means making time to think, read, and write regularly. You may write only on weekdays, weekends, or certain days of the week—but without consistent practice you will not improve your writing and will certainly not complete a full manuscript. With regular everyday practice, you can and you will complete your book.

One technique I have used to increase my productivity is to understand the various stages of writing and publishing and identify what piece is at which stage. One article may be in draft form, one book project may be in proofs (the final stage of production before publication), and one book may be out for peer review or have reader reports that I must address. Each task requires a different amount of energy, so "writing" for me looks different at every stage of the publishing process.

You do not have to hold your breath and sit on your hands waiting for editorial responses. You can continue to work on the book manuscript or work on another manuscript adjacent to the one in progress. Not everyone can or should work on more than one project at once. However, if you clearly define your research agenda it can become easier to write (and write multiple things) regularly.

I write by the spirit. There are usually several options on my daily task list so each day I wake up and decide what I feel like doing or what I'm most excited to write that day. Often, I'll meditate, breathe, and stretch, until I decide an idea is clear enough to get me to the computer. Some days I determine what task I am dreading or least excited about and start there. Usually, I'll exercise (Peloton, yoga, or qigong) and play music to help motivate me for the writing day. Then, when I'm in front of the screen, before I know it, I'm tapping away at the keys like pianist Hazel Scott, who famously played two pianos at once. Most times I exercise at night to recover from a long writing day.

No matter how much you write, you won't finish a book in one day, one week, or even one year so going to the library, a bookstore, a colleague's talk, or a conference also counts as writing. When viewed this way, dancing, digging in a garden, working on a grant, attending a child's dance recital, going to a movie, or getting a massage can also free your mind enough to tackle the tasks when you get back to your desk. Resting is writing. In the end, though, you do have to put words on the page.

I am a writer, every day. I am an everyday writer. I write every day. In some small way I think every day and, for me, thinking is an essential element of writing. Even if I don't increase my word count every day, I advance a part of my writing project. Some days this means I have to reread something for clarity or edit what I have already put down. I am not exceptional. I take periodic writing breaks for much-needed rest. The break may be for a few days or even a few weeks. But I return. Writing is my default. For me, academic writing is not an elite activity or something to gain elite status. Writing is a common practice designed to create common-unity about ideas, positions, or actions. I write to help build and sustain community.

Of course, not everyone writes for pleasure and not everyone experiences pleasure while writing. I do experience pleasure when writing, but do not, generally, write for pleasure. I write for work. For me, academic writing is a choice—how I choose to spend my time in ways that advance my life work. Discussing my writing process with other writers has heightened my awareness of how uncommon pleasure is in the academy and how few people embrace the idea of claiming pleasure in the professional choices we make. When teaching, I have actively tried to create space for my students to experience writing as pleasure.

There is no singular right way to practice academic writing. Some scholarly projects will take three years to complete. Some book projects that will redefine a field can take many more years to research and won't see the light of day for a decade or more. Most faculty in the humanities and social sciences are required to produce a scholarly monograph to obtain tenure and promotion to associate or full professor. There is usually a six- or seven-year window for each step, though the second promotion may take longer due to additional service duties post tenure. But publishing academic books does not have to fulfill external goals. Writing is a practice that can stimulate the intellect and produce jewels for the expansive human library. Writing is a practice that can enliven the imagination and push individual boundaries. Writing is a practice that can serve communities and inform policies to advance social movements.

Writing is a practice that authors can define for themselves. But, like Toni Cade Bambara advised, "writing will cost you something." The practice of writing requires your attention . . . and attention to that practice is inevitably a struggle. You will have to sacrifice something. Writing is inherently stressful. Writing takes a toll and requires a tax. Only you can decide if it is worth the price.[8]

Whatever you pay attention to grows. Your attention is valuable. Reading and writing are ways to value your time. Literacy is an act of narrative care—care for self and others. When I started this book, I was awash in manuscripts for a full year and loved it. Of course, the workload and time crunch were sometimes distressing. But it was work I wanted to do with people whose time and energy I appreciated. That year of giving and receiving feedback solidified for me that I wanted to write a book about writing that stimulated collective gain. I hope that my year of peer review and developmental editing with authors eased their pathway to publication in some small way. That hope is the premise of this book.

Book Outline: *Sesa Wo Suban*—Change and Transformation

Black Feminist Writing is part intellectual history, part publishing memoir, and part resource guide. These three areas of historical wellness, learning from my own experience, and prioritizing the goal of community mental health drive the content of this book. Each chapter ends by posing a set of questions and proposing tasks to identify and alleviate a certain type of writing stress. In the course of each chapter, I answer the questions that I pose. Essentially, I demonstrate how approaching the tasks with a calm mind can result not only in a finished a book, but also an enhanced appreciation for the course you have charted. My story and the bookwork of other writers are central to charting a course in race and gender studies.

This book is longer than most writing guides for two reasons that are central to Black feminist writing: first, I include my personal writing journey; and, second, I offer expansive references to other relevant work. As a Black feminist writer, my personal writing journey is inseparable from those of the Black feminists I have always written about. Acknowledging my debts and influences via citation is a fundamental component of my practice and foundational aspect of the field of BWST.

The intro and outro of the book (Preface and Coda) pay homage to Professor Bracey and share a sentimental reflection of my affinity for writing, including my lifelong commitment to writing as a means of advocating for freedom and equality. Both sections demonstrate the power of mindfulness practices and the role that compassion (for self and others) plays in changing the academy and transforming the world around us. The introduction and conclusion outline some of the contours of personal and institutional stress that authors face in the writing and publishing process. Specifically, in this introduction (Academic Stress), I outline the mental challenges unique to publishing as marginalized faculty in higher education. In the concluding chapter (Academic Wellness), I advocate for the normalization of well-being in the academy, especially as those in race and gender studies struggle to secure more space in academe while simultaneously dismantling oppressive systems—including academe.

In chapter 2, "Regenerative Writing: Learn, Create, and Teach the Practice of Collective Self-Care," I develop the Black feminist notion of care that undergirds this entire project. I begin with Audre Lorde's call for care and honor her recognition that self-compassion is a political act. I then cite Rosalyn Terborg-Penn's African feminist values to define self-care (survival) and collective care (self-reliance in network) to identify ways Black women have used writing for self-determination. This approach to writing suggests moving beyond writing for an audience to use books as a means to create community.

In chapters 3 through 7, I identify and guide you through five different "locations" of stress. Each of these locations corresponds to an area, or type, of stress-management practice: personal, professional, publishing, public, and political. Each of these areas of stress is also an area where your writing can be transformed and areas where your work can impact change. In other words, each location of stress is also a location of self-care practice. My thinking about locations of stress and practice is shaped by Gwen Kirk and Margo Okazawa-Rey's social location theory. Social location captures the dynamic and interlocking experiences of disempowerment. For example, a personal illness can be exacerbated by the illness of a family member. If health care is not available due to economic or political restrictions, these stressors have a compounding effect. Stress happens in each of these locations, and stressors vary because they are largely influenced by the politics of social environments. So, it is essential to create culturally appropriate and comprehensive stress-management interventions. This especially holds true in the academy, where oppressive epistemologies are reified and often just reading, let alone writing about, established scholarship can be triggering.

As a guide, *Black Feminist Writing* aims to help you turn your writing into a practice whereby you are able to identify, assess, anticipate, manage, and reduce stress.

CHAPTERS: Five Locations of Practice:
Writing Every Day with the Morning Star

The West African Adinkra concept *Sesa Wo Suban* symbolizes change and the transformation of one's life. There are two concepts of applied learning embedded in the symbol: change and transformation. Change and transformation can happen each day with the morning star (the inner part of the symbol). Change and transformation are constant waves of movement (the outer part of the symbol). Together, the symbol summarizes the overarching message of BWST: each new day is a chance to rise and write in ways that improve the quality of life for self and others.

Figure 1. Sesa Wo Suban symbol, meaning "change and transform your life."
Source: Shutterstock.

Symbols have meaning, so I have chosen this symbol to indicate a point of pause in each chapter—a moment to breathe and embrace your choice to improve your practice on many levels.[9]

Writing is a way to transform your life, one day at a time. Think of the five locations of practice—and *praxis*—in terms of a star's five points. Each of the five locations of writing practice corresponds to an overarching writing objective:

- Personal Practice. FIND YOUR VOICE
- Professional Practice. STATE YOUR ARGUMENT
- Publishing Practice. EDIT AND ORGANIZE YOUR STRUCTURE
- Public Practice. ENGAGE YOUR COMMUNITY
- Political Practice. INSTITUTIONALIZE BWST

While voice, argument, and structure are common themes in writing guides, *Black Feminist Writing* links them to ancestor acknowledgment, community building, political engagement, and other motifs that are central to BWST. In detail, the chapter outline includes recognizable editorial subthemes.

> VOICE: Tone, Message, Reflexivity
> ARGUMENT: Thesis, Theory, Intervention
> STRUCTURE: Narrative Arc, Organization, Clarity
> COMMUNITY: Data, Citations, Peer Review, Audience, Impact
> INSTITUTION: Human Rights, Interdisciplinarity, Race and Gender Studies

The chapters show you five locations where you might encounter stressors and within each chapter I share context, insights, and possible solutions to remove any barriers to your writing and publishing processes.

THEMES: LEARN, CREATE, TEACH (THE GIFT, THE LESSON, AND THE WORK)

Historians mainly study change over time. Themes of past, present, and future reflect the second part of *Sesa Wo Suban*: change and movement. Within each chapter, there are three key subsections based on changes of time. Although the chapters are not all uniform, each chapter contains three constant themes: LEARN: Celebrate Black woman intellectuals (highlighting a historical scholar); CREATE: Care for your self-development (how I have created knowledge from my writing); and TEACH: Find the courage to continue your work despite barriers (tools that teach you how to incorporate wellness into your writing habits). These three sections represent the past, present, and future of Black feminist writing practices and the constant challenge to both measure change and make change.[10]

In the next chapter, I unpack the interconnectedness of these parts and show how individual mental health combines with collective well-being through an intellectual ecology. Basically, Black women's scholarly writing is one way to create a supportive environment that I identify as an academic family tree. Writing is a practice that we learn, create, and teach in order to develop and sustain communities. Black feminist writing is the practice of celebration, courage, and care. We honor the gifts bestowed upon us by elders and ancestors (The Gift), we make meaning from our own experiences (The Lesson), and we share our writing for the benefit of the next generation (The Work).

Developing a writing practice steeped in Black women's wellness helped me change and transform my life. And, as often stated by feminist scholars, the point of freeing oneself is to free others. In each of the five core chapters, I draw on my writing career to provide examples and offer tips for readers to develop sustainable practices of care to address and manage the stresses you face. Classifying particular characteristics of your stress can help you customize a writing plan based on your own specific experiences, skills, and goals.[11]

Reflection Questions and Practical Tasks

I offer key questions and prioritize tasks for a more focused, more balanced, less draining, and more energizing publishing process. These suggestions should be tempered by your own critical self-assessment though. For example, some practices, like exercise or mediation, can function to help you avoid the writing tasks you need to complete or prevent you from dealing with other types of stressors, so make sure you are honest with yourself when assessing what you need. As with any useful tip, one size does not fit all.

At the end of each chapter—including this one—I provide reflection questions and a list of practical tasks. The role of asking questions emerges from a long tradition of Black women asking questions to seek and share wisdom. While some call this approach to cognitive development the Socratic method, I consider the practice of questioning a Makedaic tradition. The tenth century Queen of Sheba, also known as Makeda, traveled to Jerusalem to discuss questions of wisdom with King Solomon. Questions are a part of the learning process central to African ways of learning and I am invested in making African epistemologies visible since they have often been erased, coopted, or maligned in the academy. Applying lessons—actual practice—is another required aspect of Black feminist writing. The questions and tasks are simply suggestions, not all of which may be relevant for you personally.

FINDING MY WRITING GROOVE WITH MUSIC

Black feminist writing is a soulful practice. Music is central to Black culture and, as evidenced by the very name *soul* music, feeds our mind and our spirit. Concerns like finding time to write, transforming a dissertation into a book project, or feeling intimidated about contacting an acquisitions editor are inevitable for the uninitiated. Art is an African pedagogical tool. Tapping into the creative part of your mind can help you find alternate ways to tackle mundane tasks. Music can help you find your groove and bolster your courage.

In addition to referencing actual writing resources, at the close of each chapter, I share a vignette for inspiration. These takeaway messages constitute a playlist that fulfills a part of the criteria for Anna Julia Cooper's definition of intellectual growth: that collective learning should be joyous. In the Coda, I explore how writing can be a radical act of joy. At its best, writing is liberatory in more ways than one; at its finest, writing becomes as much art as playing music, singing, or dancing.

Not everyone pays attention to Black women's ideas, but for those who do, the lessons learned can help address crises. And crises are never in short supply, whether issues of political injustice (global problems) or stress and mental health challenges (personal problems). This workbook is designed to help you define and solve problems that matter to you while also centering your own vitality. Healing happens in the liminal spaces— breaths we take in between the days, hours, minutes, and seconds where we are active. Care happens in moments of pause and repose. Remember, when you see the *Sesa Wo Suban* symbol, take a moment to breathe.[12]

As a Black woman, reading and writing has kept me from feeling "hopeless, as a penny with a hole in it." As in the 1990s neo-soul classic "Hopeless" by Dionne Farris, some days when I was a young woman I felt "no less than up to my head in it." But being introduced to Black feminist writing directed me toward a path of wholeness and fulfillment. Farris's *Wild Seed—Wild Flower* (1994) was my favorite album in my first year of college. I was driving from St. John's College in Santa Fe to work as a waitress in Albuquerque, New Mexico, so the album would be in rotation for the duration of the drive. Nonstop repeat. A no-skip record. The breakout hit, "I Know"; the bottom Chakra rocking "Passion"; the melancholy "Now or Later"; the playful "Audition." Her 2011 *Signs of Life* most closely resembles the range of her first album and the song "Every Day" affirms the continuity of her self-hood day in and day out. Like Farris, I have learned to be myself, every day.

Though I was raised in several places, I have made my home in books. In the early days of my career, learning to embrace myself as a "wild flower" was part of my healing and those reflections still elicit celebration. Back then, I began to understand that every day is another day I get to try to improve my writing. Every day for the past three decades, I have practiced the work of writing in order to be me, know me, and do me. And it has been work that has fed my soul.

Sankofa, a Ghanaian term meaning "go back and get it," is a way to connect the past and present to the future. The term "regeneration" is a reference to Anna Julia Cooper that also reflects the principals embedded in sankofa. Regeneration is the guiding principle that I have centered during my writing processes—a way to change and transform higher education. Thus, regenerative writing practice allows us to study both African and African American intellectual history and apply wisdom learned from elders in ways that benefit a diversity of young scholars in the diaspora.

Reflection Questions

Question 1: What does flourishing look like for you?

Question 2: What types of educational stress have you faced? What has been your main source of stress in the writing process?

Question 3: How do you want your writing to change institutions and policy and transform the quality of life for you and others around you?

Practical Tasks

- Assess your career path thus far. Decide which direction you would like to move after publishing your book. Identify campus, inter-campus, local, national, and international publics who might benefit from discussions about your work.
- What recurring questions do you want to explore in more depth? How are you creating a research plan in ways that are emotionally and intellectually sustainable?
- Read a book—from cover to cover—that takes your mindfulness practice to the next level.
- Review existing scholarship on your topic. Read historical research as well as new contributions. What are the patterns that have remained consistent or changed over time?
- Name a historical scholar who is a publishing inspiration. Identify gifts your intellectual ancestors granted you. Name a writing tradition you are carrying forward.

2

Regenerative Writing

Learn, Create, and Teach the Practice of Collective Self-Care

> In this country, black women traditionally have had compassion for everyone else except ourselves. We cared for whites because we had to for pay or survival; we cared for our children and our fathers and our brothers and our lovers. We need to also learn to care for ourselves.
>
> —Audre Lorde, "The Great American Disease" (1979)

Black feminist writing is a sankofa practice. We have much wisdom to recover that will spare our mental health. Black feminist writing emphasizes the need for Black women's self-care. Feminist Audre Lorde rightly claims that any liberation movement in which Black women participate must center our voices. She also notes that Black women must first practice peace in our own lives before we can teach healing practices to others. In a 1979 article entitled "The Great American Disease," published in *The Black Scholar*, Lorde unapologetically argues for Black women centering ourselves as a necessary step toward Black (and ultimately universal) liberation. As seen in the preceding epigraph, she also notes the racial and gendered politics of compassion, arguing that Black women must care for ourselves to effectively deal with the "diseases" of both racism and sexism.

A decade later, while battling cancer, Lorde famously wrote in *A Burst of Light and Other Essays* (1988), "Caring for myself is not self-indulgence, it is self-preservation, and that is an act of political warfare." The epiphany that self-care is both compassionate and political affirms notions of care and lived experience promoted by Patricia Hill Collins in *Black Feminist*

Thought: Knowledge, Consciousness, and the Politics of Empowerment (1999). The link to therapeutic healing and writing is made even more explicit in Foluke Taylor's *Unruly Therapeutic: Black Feminist Writings and Practices in Living Room* (2023). Recovering histories of Black women academics' observations about self-preservation has been an immensely practical way for me to embody mental health.

Black feminist writing is a generational practice. Well-known scholars that have informed my thinking include Anna Julia Cooper, Audre Lorde, Toni Cade Bambara, bell hooks, Beverly Guy-Sheftall, Barbara Smith, Patricia Hill Collins, and Rosalyn Terborg-Penn. But my writing is also grounded by lesser-known historical writers such as Sadie Iola Daniel and Hallie Quinn Brown (early chroniclers of Black women scholar-activists), educators like Eva Dykes, Georgiana Simpson, and Sadie Tanner Mossell Alexander (the first three to earn a PhD), and the hundreds of women who penned memoirs or autobiographies that I've collected over the years. Consequently, my work subscribes to a very broad definition of Black feminism, generally including writers who self-identify as such but also referencing those whose work demonstrates feminist ethics of justice, equity, or care.[1]

Black feminist writing is a compassionate practice. It is also a mindful practice where we understand care and emotional work has been a location of exploitation and abuse. Lorde centers self-care as a political necessity because our energy has been extracted to our detriment. Generations of writers offer the gift of context so we can develop discernment of when to give and when to withhold compassion for our own safety and well-being.

Black women are not a monolith and scholarly writing by academics runs the gamut between conservative, liberal, progressive, and radical. Conservative feminism is an oxymoron, and liberal Black feminism does not sufficiently challenge capitalism, colonialism, or what Moya Bailey and Trudy have called misogynoir. Also, I acknowledge that historical feminists must be studied in the context of their era so there is no one uniform way to categorize Black feminism. Like Roxanne Gay in *Bad Feminist*, I often feel that I "fail" as a Black feminist because I am not radical enough—but, like Gay, I make no apologies for my position and would rather be a bad feminist than not a feminist at all. I believe that ideas and individuals can be radical, but institutions cannot (with few exceptions). Accordingly, I mainly engage progressive and radical feminists in my work, but I understand there is no one way to write as a Black feminist.[2]

Black Feminist Writing:
Definitions, Values, and Traditions

> Black feminist-womanist life writing, as regular and common practice, lies at the heart of Black women's health history.
>
> —Stephanie Y. Evans, *Black Women's Yoga History*

I define Black feminism as a liberatory practice. Liberation is a radical project because Black feminism seeks to fundamentally uproot, overturn, or disrupt behaviors and systems that harm Black women and others. Higher education, by definition, is largely a middle-class environment. Liberal, middle-class Black feminism is neither the epitome nor the goal of Black feminism; it is merely the arena where I happen to work and I don't take my experience or perspective to be representational or aspirational. Black feminism in academic space is only one locale.

Black feminism is transnational, meaning it is a global phenomenon that transcends geographic or political boundaries. While my own work is US centered, I recognize that Black feminism operates very differently in Africa, Latin America, and the Caribbean. Black feminist writers like Chimamanda Adichie, Christen A. Smith, and Yomaira C. Figueroa-Vasquez exemplify drastic contrasts within the community of those who identify as Black feminists. Further, radical writers like Sylvia Wynter or Africana writers like Clenora Hudson-Weems show the complex relationship of traditions like decolonial theory that reject feminism altogether. There are also feminist and womanist positions that have a clear agenda to exclude queer or trans women. There are, in effect, many Black feminisms—plural. What they have in common is a commitment to liberation. Black feminists worldwide are committed to change and transformation, as Wangari Maathai wrote, in order to improve the quality of life. Higher education is one critical site where that work happens.[3]

I *am* a Black feminist writing and I *do* Black feminist writing. The phrase "Black feminist writing" functions as both noun and verb. Black feminist writing names a body of scholarship that affirms the humanity of Black women and insists on equality for all marginalized groups. It includes both Black feminist writers and the works they have produced that lay the foundation of what is commonly known as Black feminist thought. Black feminist writing is also an action. It fights against ignorance and violence and aims to "build a better world." It is both advocacy (in the spirit of educator Anna Julia Cooper) and activism (in the spirit of educator Mary McLeod Bethune).

I am a Black feminist writing—I write as part of a Black feminist tradition. Despite the portrayal by some that scholarly writing is painful, boring, out of touch, or useless, I have experienced the opposite. My worldview centers levity and light. Formally, I identify myself as a Black feminist-womanist. There are several strands of womanism, and I am especially influenced by Layli Maparyan's epistemology outlined in *The Womanist Idea*. She posits "Luxocricy, rule by light—a magnetic force that draws us to operate from impulses of positivity and peace." Black feminism is the bedrock of my career, but I engage womanist life-writing traditions as my ontological paradigm. The result is an abundance of creative, intellectual expression that some, relying on the language of the academy, mistake for "productivity."[4]

Black feminist writing is both deconstructive and constructive. It is a liberatory practice—a multigenerational movement of willful expression. As an academic project, Black feminist writing—and *Black Feminist Writing*—is ultimately less about what work has already been produced and more about how readers and authors will take this work, validate or critique it, and incorporate it into their own to create something new that can be used for liberation in a new world with new challenges. It is not enough—or possible even—to create new scholarship without reference to the old. Nor is it enough to sit on the heels of old research as it stands.[5]

As a practice, Black feminist writing is not a mere commodity, method, or standpoint that can be reduced to an essentialized identity—Black womanhood. It is a radical and progressive ethos grounded in Black women's historical narratives that, collectively, shows how to navigate and create healthy and thriving lives despite interpersonal, cultural, or structural violence. This ethos engenders the courage to change oppressive conditions and clear a path for effective communication. Black feminist writing must, by definition, support actions of radical scholars who take positions that center Black women's experiences across the globe, affirm queer and transgender lives, demand antimilitarism, and call for an end to all war, including the everyday war of capitalism.

Black feminist writing is not confined to formal university spaces. It is an organized but decentralized political culture rooted in Black women's liberation movements. These movements point the way for collective self-care and have long used writing and publishing to express, exercise, and expand universal human rights. This book draws inspiration and guidance from scholar-activist groups such as the Combahee River Collective while situating their work in a long history of Black feminist writing. I spend considerable time in chapter 4 defining this long history.[6]

In her edited collection *Telling Histories: Black Women Historians in the Ivory Tower,* Deborah Gray White writes how she wanted the book to serve "as a sort of 'how-to' survival manual for those who are currently struggling against entrenched historical methods, historiographies, and faculties." White is one of a multitude of Black women academics who write books, in part, as a mentoring tool. This work continues the tradition of academic mentoring by Black women writers who, for several generations past, have written as a means of connecting to and instructing future scholars.[7]

African Feminist Values: Survival (Mental Health) and Self-Reliance (Collective Care)

> Perhaps the two most dominant values in the African feminist theory, which can be traced through a time perspective into the New World, are developing survival strategies and encouraging self-reliance through female networks.
>
> —Dr. Rosalyn Terborg-Penn (1997)[8]

The voice of Dr. Rosalyn Terborg-Penn, cofounder of the Association of Black Women Historians (ABWH), rings especially clear as a guide to research and writing. Dr. Terborg-Penn coedited *Women in Africa and the African Diaspora*, a book that names and applies two African values: self-care and collective care. Terborg-Penn and her coeditor, Andrea Rushing, insist that care of the self and care of the community can coexist. One can prioritize the self and also practice collective self-determination. African women's *both/and* complicates the duality of the pervasive binary of *either/or.* We can prioritize our own needs *as well as* contribute to the needs of a community—in African feminist thought, one does not necessarily rule out the other.

A foundational tenant of African philosophy states, "I am because we are"—a profoundly different idea compared to the Cartesian "I think therefore I am." My roots as an academic are necessarily grounded in the relationship I have to scholars who have come before me. I attribute any "flourishing" or productivity I have enjoyed as a writer over the past two decades to the fact that I have dedicated my career to "bringing the gifts that my ancestors gave." *I am* a published author because *they are* (my ancestors) otherworldly thinkers. Compassion is a Black feminist value that is at the center of what Angela Davis calls collective self-care.

This book draws on these values by encouraging you to 1) prioritize self-care while—and even by—creating a writing practice and 2) develop a communal writing strategy for completing book manuscripts, whether single authored or edited volumes. Communal writing means citing Black women writers and scholars of color who have come before and also writing collaboratively with contemporary scholars. I will address the importance of mental health and communal writing in greater depth in the next two sections. Here I share some of the writers and books that have shaped this section and give context to our individual and collective work of survival.

It is hard to survive as a writer in these academic streets. In compilations like *Presumed Incompetent: The Intersections of Race and Class for Women in Academia* and *Written/Unwritten: Diversity and the Hidden Truths of Tenure*, scholars have documented the inequities in professional review for minoritized authors. Peer mentoring and writing in community can alleviate some stressors. While it is important to learn the formatting norms of your particular disciplinary area (English, history, psychology, anthropology, philosophy, etc.), it is helpful to learn from other disciplines that inform Black Women's Studies. This may cause a bit of frustration, but keep in mind each genre of writing has conventions that you are responsible for learning if you want to be in conversation with others. Though I was trained primarily as a historian, my degree in Black Studies and Women's Studies mean that I have basic introduction to other disciplinary approaches. Black Women's Studies is an interdiscipline—that fact alone is part of the reason why it intimidates others in the academy. BWST is a truth-telling tradition in educational environments filled with people who prefer to tell lies and be lied to. Lies are more easily told and affirmed in disciplinary silos. While gaining competence in several fields is a challenge, your writing will benefit from doing so. Self-reliance in network means that you can lean on peers and editors but, equally as important, you can learn from advice of writers who have come before you.

Care Traditions: Regeneration and Cultivating Your Academic Family Tree

> Like the Tree that looks at God all day and lifts its leafy arms to pray . . . Here was activity, planned and purposeful, strenuous but joyous, not hunger-driven animal action to appease wants, rather spirit-driven by the inner spur and need for life—the more abundant life.
>
> —Dr. Anna Julia Cooper, "The Early Years in Washington" (1951)[9]

While many scholars talk about the value of *generative* discussion, it seems to me that regeneration is a more useful concept to understand Black women's historical legacy and activist work and how to write yourself in both historical and disciplinary context. The inspiration that shapes much of my work is derived from Dr. Cooper's notion of regeneration. In "Womanhood: A Vital Element in the Regeneration and Progress of a Race," published in Cooper's book of essays *A Voice from the South, by a Black Woman of the South* (1892), she argues that those who wish to advance society must look back for wisdom (retrospection), look inward for strength (introspection), and look forward for hope and faith (prospection). Cooper's conceptualization of regeneration places us in a continuum with both our ancestors and our descendants.

Writing in the Black feminist tradition involves cultivating what I call an academic family tree, which includes intellectual ancestors, formal mentors, authors you cite, colleagues, and students. I employ a tree as a metaphor instead of a pyramid or ladder, the more typical professional analogies, because it's nonhierarchical. Communal well-being requires collective investment. While there are roots, a trunk, branches, leaves, fruit, and other parts, the health of one part of the tree impacts the entire tree and a healthy tree requires attention to all parts. Compassion is the sunlight that fosters growth of all living beings. Certainly, foremothers like Cooper, a lifelong scholar-activist, recognized the value of creating a healthy educational ecology.

In an essay written at the age of ninety-three, Cooper reflects on the scholarly community she shared in Washington, DC, with like-minded adult learners. By her recollection, educational "growth" means "activity that is planned, purposeful, strenuous, joyous, spirit-driven, inner spurred, and toward abundant life." From citing the ancestors and self-reflection to thinking collectively with current scholars and newer students, writing a book should position you within an intellectual community.

In her reminiscences, Cooper intimates that education is about "the inner spur" and a collective desire to create a "more abundant life." For her, writing does not simply "appease wants" or animal hungers, like being motivated by ego, fame, or economic prosperity. I have been fortunate to be productive, and I use this productivity to fulfill my desire to connect to timeless ideas and knowledge while helping others live an abundant life. For me, abundance is beyond material comfort (though that plays a part in having the leisure time to learn), but this work is about an abundance of purpose and joy. I add "practice" to Cooper's gifts of planning, purpose, and progressive peace. Dr. Cooper's gift of an abundant life is one of quality and longevity. Her legacy is a gift that assures us one's ideas can endure and be a source of timeless inspiration. The writing life should be about life as much as about writing.[10]

Workspaces are not family spaces, yet they are relational. Though we should not confuse colleagues with family members (there may be a few exceptions to this), we are working in relation, so recognizing intellectual relationships is essential. When close ties form, they resemble a professional genealogy. I believe education can be one mitigating factor for the creation of a sustainable social, economic, and political national/global ecology. Of course, education is not the only tactic, and there is no guarantee that instruction—for children or for adults—will equate to freedom. But those who are committed to justice can recognize the role that progressive and radical adult education plays in transforming our world. Building a close-knit set of relationships with thinkers, ideas, and schools of thought helps expand space in academe.

In Black feminist writing, three inextricable themes emerge: celebration, courage, and care. By writing books we learn from and celebrate our foremothers, create knowledge and care for our intellectual selves, and display courage to navigate through the demands of academic publishing in order to teach others. Our writing is regenerative, meaning we preserve the past, chronicle the present, and guide future writers.

Black feminist writing is a celebratory practice. Joy is a Black feminist value. I join a multitude of fiction writers, artists, and activists who celebrate the work of collective, coalitional, and constructive rebellion. Poet Toi Derricotte claimed, "joy is resistance." I agree and I consider writing a joyous act. Black feminist writing intrinsically builds on ideas offered by prior generations. While we must apply a critical lens, our writing works towards justice and recognizes work done by those who have come before. Regardless of the agenda of universities and presses, Black feminists think and write to advance our own agendas.[11]

Black feminist writing is a courageous practice. Maya Angelou's beloved poem "Still I Rise" encourages Black women writers (whom she identifies as her daughters) to claim our power and reject the expectation of walking with "bowed head and lowered eyes." Instead, Angelou encourages us to walk—haughtily—into our rightful role as writers. Not only does Angelou recover others' history in texts such as *Singin' and Swingin' and Gettin' Merry like Christmas* or *All God's Children Need Traveling Shoes* but she also charges us to write ourselves into history.[12]

Black feminist writing is a caring practice. Taking time to read and engage Black women's ideas is a way to care for ourselves because we learn and teach necessary perspectives and survival skills. Reading the work of our foremothers and peers is also a way we can honor people who have struggled to make the world a better place for us. As sociologist Patricia Hill Collins makes clear in her ethics of caring three central elements should be central to our practice: expression, emotion, and empathy. At its best, scholarship is a way to care for ourselves by deeply investing in celebrating our intellectual genealogy. Our ultimate responsibility, then, is to pass on these lessons.

Below are brief samples of how I connect the work of ancestors, lessons from my own journey, and recommendations for future writers. Together, these views of writing—retrospection, introspection, and prospections—show you ways to cultivate mindfulness, compassion, mental health, and collective well-being in historical context. These sections (learn, create, and teach) are the core of the chapters in this book.

LEARN (The Gift):
Celebrating Black Women's Historical Wellness

This is a call to celebrate the inherent value of all Black people.[13]

—Charlene Caruthers, *Unapologetic*

Black feminist writing celebrates a distinct intellectual lineage. Black women's writing is a case study of persistence. Black women's experiences offer higher education a unique locale from which to define work-life balance (or lack thereof) and to chart a course for institutional change. In addition to caring for the self and collective, historical wellness includes reclaiming ancestral work as an act of intellectual care.

Claudia Tate's revelatory collection *Black Women Writers at Work* has been recently followed up by Courtney Thorsson's recovery effort, *The Sisterhood: How a Network of Black Women Writers Changed American Culture*. Both books expose the well-documented challenges writers face. Tate provides first-person reflection of writing itself and Thorsson gives the historical context. Thorsson surveyed two years of agendas and meeting minutes from gatherings led by June Jordan, which included Alice Walker, Toni Morrison, Ntozake Shange, Vertamae Smart-Grosvenor, and others. Thorsson's account offers insight about the ascendancy of some figures but, more importantly, the literary history shows the power of Black women writing in community.

Tate's collection, originally published in 1983, interviews writers at the height of ascendancy and overlaps with efforts from others including *Black Women Writers, 1950–1980: A Critical Evaluation* by Mari Evans and *Flat-Footed Truths: Telling Black Women's Lives* by Patricia Bell-Scott and Juanita Johnson-Bailey. Tate focuses specifically on the writing process and provides a deep dive into fundamentals of Black feminist practice. *Black Women Writers at Work* is required reading. Tate's interviews unpack the multitude of variables writers must manage, including time to write, professional development resources, audience, selecting topics, positioning subjects, style, career longevity, politics, activism, frequency of output, control of publishing decisions, plagiarism, industry politics, prizes and bestseller lists, market trends, technology, motivation, evolution and growth, editing processes, critics and reviews, routines, collaboration, competition, identity development, habit formation, sacrifice, compensation, elitism, impact, and many other considerations. For Black women writers and other authors marginalized in academic spaces, maintaining our time and attention is a constant struggle.

In *How We Do It: Black Writers on Craft, Practice, and Skill* (2023), the beautifully curated collection by Pulitzer Prize–winning poet Jericho Brown affirms that genres often overlap (blurring lines of fiction and academic writing). The anthology also demonstrates the prominence of life writing (memoir and autobiography) as an anchor of the Black literary tradition. As Brown's collection shows, lifelong writers do exist and they flower most furiously in community.

Black feminist authors have insisted on giving equal weight to writing as to feminism—writing well is a reflection of both self-care (craft) and collective care (peer review). I acknowledge the truism shared by poet Rita Dove: race or poverty are no excuses for poor writing. If you have issues with verb tense, subject-verb agreement, punctuation, vocabulary, or other weakness, you must take action to improve. In graduate school, I took time with sentence structure workbooks and taught writing in an Upward Bound program, which helped me identify and rectify basic issues in student papers . . . and in my own. Your writing does not have to be perfect—you must write in your own voice—but you shouldn't necessarily write like you speak. Your writing must demonstrate competence at basic language skills and a commitment to endless revision. Ideally, your work will have what Daniel Black calls *rhythm*. If you can't offer prose as fine and refined as Dr. Black's (most of us cannot), at the very least, you must edit enough so the reader does not trip over your words and lose your message.[14]

Academic books are my focus here for the very simple reason that they're what I have always written. This focus does not diminish the fact that scholarly books in BWST have always been rooted in principles and found audiences that go far beyond the academy. We shouldn't undervalue the role scholarly books play in shaping fields in humanities and social sciences, but the larger goal of Black feminist publishing is to produce work that defines and expands universal human rights.

I theorize Black women's intellectual history and the act of writing as a practice. Some imagine writing as an art, a craft, a skill, or a science. I experience writing as a practice, habit, and way of life. Like those who practice medicine, religion, yoga, an instrument, or a sport, I practice scholarly writing. As a practitioner, I hope to improve my writing even as I seek to support others in their practice. When I call this book a "practical guide," I mean *practical* quite literally. My objective is to move *you* along in the work of writing and publishing scholarly books, but also to do so in a way that nurtures your mental health and enhances your collaborative environment. As generations of writers demonstrate, to write and publish scholarly books in a sustainable way requires a commitment to practice. You must *practice* practice.

For some, one academic book will be enough to last a lifetime. Others will branch out into creative writing. Regardless of your writing journey, writing in the Black feminist tradition means that when you produce an academic book, you are not publishing in isolation and therefore should not write in isolation. For me, writing has been a process by which I personally flourish and also foster belonging for my colleagues and students. As a Black woman in the ivory tower, that is no small feat. The African feminist values of survival and collective self-reliance explain why, how, and with whom we write for health and well-being.

Writing can service community agendas but does not have to come at the expense of one's mental health. Writing well requires a playful, experimental approach to finding your flow. Several tips Dove offered in *How We Do It* shifted my self-editing habits forever. First, she railed against "orthodoxy," meaning she emphasized the need to resist one-size-fits-all approaches and to make room for "magic." Second, her experimentation with writing at different times of day is aspirational. Find your own way. This is a guide, not a mandate. But however you develop your writing practice, your work should be informed by the historical wellness traditions of Black women writers.[15]

The healing traditions of Black women—particularly the enduring practices of prayer and spiritual engagement, yoga, music (listening, singing, or dancing), exercise, and meditation—continue in popularity into the twenty-first century, but they also have identifiable roots in writing, as far back as the early nineteenth century. Historical wellness, the theoretical framework I have developed over time, focuses on the behavioral aspects of healing self to sustain mental health regardless of time, location, or circumstance. These self-healing practices have worked to improve individual and communal quality of life despite the personal, social, or structural violence that operate to thwart optimal health. This idea is grounded in Black women's intellectual history and narratives of women like Harriet Tubman and Rosa Parks, who both lived into their nineties.

Beyond the academy, narratives of long-living women, like Tubman (90+), Sadie and Bessie Delany (109 and 104), Marian Anderson (96), Ida Keeling (106), and Dona Irvin (the mother of the historian Nell Irvin Painter—Dona lived to 92!), show historical wellness is an act of mental, physical, and spiritual resistance. I call this tradition of Black women's self-care and collective care *historical wellness*. I define historical wellness as a necessary practice of self-care to survive generations of violence and oppression. Celebrating historical wellness offers a pathway to care for your own academic mental health.[16]

CREATE (The Lesson):
The Courage to Care for Your Academic Mental Health

Courage is your greatest achievement, for you, without it, can practice no other virtue with consistency.

—Maya Angelou, *Letter to My Daughter* (2008)[17]

Writing has been a fundamental practice that undergirds my mental wellness. Conversely, meditation, yoga, exercise, and other holistic practices have stabilized my writing—and stabilized me so that I can write. Meditation in particular is my key to ensuring that my writing practice is also a wellness practice. I write to breathe. I write to heal. I write to discover and explore. I write to recover what is forgotten, discarded, or purposefully erased. I write to learn. I write in the hopes that people will read, meditate on this work, and be changed. I write to create conditions in which academic wellness is not a remote possibility but a norm.

Frustrated by several personal and professional challenges, I began to study mental health in early 2013. When faced with personal loss from health issues and increasing stress from a challenging career, I did what I have routinely done in the past two decades: query Black women's memoirs to find solutions to the problems I faced or questions I needed answered. In 2014, I published two articles on inner peace: "Healing Traditions in Black Women's Writing: Resources for Poetry Therapy" in *Journal of Poetry Therapy* and "Inner Lions: Definitions of Peace in Black Women's Memoirs, a Strength-Based Model for Mental Health" in the *Peace Studies Journal*. My inquiries seeped into discussions with two colleagues, psychologist Dr. Kanika Bell and media scholar Dr. Nsenga Burton, both of whom I spoke with to learn more about the relationship of intellectual history to mental health and contemporary stressors in the popular context. Those discussions spawned a fruitful collaboration that nurtured work in our respective areas and resulted in a coedited book, *Black Women's Mental Health: Balancing Strength and Vulnerability* (2017).

Even if one thrives in community, at some point writing requires solitude. In the midst of bending my written work toward wellness, I enrolled in several meditation training courses. There I learned several means of meditation, each of which can help to create more relaxing conditions for writing. These include being present in the moment, expressing gratitude, learning purposeful struggle and resilience, and creating communities of kindness without judgement. These techniques are informed by Jon Kabat-Zinn's Mindfulness-Based Stress Reduction (MBSR, developed in 1979 at University of Massachusetts Medical School). Being present, in the moment, on purpose, with no judgement are techniques that are useful for anyone voyaging into the academic multiverse. Compassion is another strategy for enjoying the writing ride. Compassion-Based Cognitive Therapy (CBCT), created by Lobsang Tenzin Negi in 2004 at the Emory University Medical School, helps meditation practitioners to reenvision how to relate to ourselves and others. Both MBSR and CBCT grew out of medical schools (University of Massachusetts and Emory respectively) but include interdisciplinary explorations of how cognitive and spiritual techniques can be mastered for physical and social benefit.

Meditation, compassion, and other stress-reduction strategies can be uniquely helpful for those who are historically disadvantaged, who are first-generation scholars, who have survived or are surviving violence, or whose scholarship challenges dominant narratives.[18] Their goal—and the goal of this book—is not just to plug you back into a broken system. I envision *Black Feminist Writing* as a universal practice and "system behavior" that is collectively owned and not something that can be wielded by those in power.

Certainly, bell hooks writes about Black women's academic survival from a personal perspective. *Wounds of Passion* reveals innerworkings of "elite" learning environments, the travails of teaching in all-white spaces, and trials of the writing life. The essay "women who write too much" in *Remembered Rapture* holds special significance as my productivity is aligned with writers hooks names, including Pat Parker, Toni Cade Bambara, and Audre Lorde. My focus on wellness is mindfully designed to counteract the trend of early deaths these writers experienced. Transgressive writers persevere and through their paper trails encourage us to do the same. Wellness is my transgression. Wellness is my resistance. Regardless of if I live a long life, I am determined to live well.

Philosopher Olúfẹ́mi O. Táíwò calls the tendency of systems to absorb resistance movements *elite capture*. I hope to contribute to a culture of "practices of information gathering, accountability, redistribution of resources, power, and construction" that Táíwò recommends. Generally, the goal of clear writing is to show don't tell. This maxim is useful but here I defy that advice because not everyone has access to even the most basic writing guidelines made available through well-funded retreats, college preparatory programs, or top-tier writing tutors. I don't want to be pedantic, elementary, or insist that there is one structure. Yet, my extensive explanations throughout this book are for the benefit of those not yet initiated as well as for those who have to unlearn writing in ways that serve colonial agendas.[19]

Sometimes working on a book may feel like an act of desperation. One might use the Greek myth of Sisyphus to characterize the task of providing progressive education to college students in the twenty-first century (endlessly pushing a boulder up a hill only for it to roll back down). But

I believe that would be cynical. Yes, scholars in race and gender studies bear the load of researching, writing, and teaching against the grain. And academic freedom remains in question amid ongoing challenges to radical approaches such as intersectionality and critical race theory. Yet, the radical resistance to regressive mandates and oppressive policies is not at all futile. Writing changes the world. As seen in life narratives by self-emancipated authors Frederick Douglass and Harriet Jacobs, writing against the grain is a vital democratic act.

I have experienced writing as *creative* in ways similar to traditions of jazz music: my practice of writing is improvisational and interactive. I also posit Black feminist writing as *resistance* because, for Black women, writing has historically been used as a tool for liberation—both individual and communal.

All education is self-education. While there are some elements of "how to" write in this book, I emphasize resources as much as methods because there is no one magic approach to writing and one book will not hold all the answers you seek. *You* have to find the courage to develop a practice that works for you—it is easier to identify practices when you expose yourself to various types of information. If you have to make your own way in academe and build networks from the ground up, self-learning is the most valuable habit to embrace. Mentors and sponsors are important. But not every person will have someone to attentively train them, arrange introductions with publishers, provide letters of recommendation for writing fellowships, and shepherd them through the publication process. Favor isn't fair and first-generation students are at a career-long disadvantage.

The citations I present in this book far exceed the usual amount in writing guides. This is deliberate. I purposefully highlight a multitude of diverse source types, including some references to my prior work and other published writing resources, as an instructional tactic. Here, you will also find references to digital projects, community agencies, archives, wellness programs, and other resources that might help you ease your mind so you can shape your project in more creative and impactful ways.

Historical Black women, all of whom were first-generation college students, could only thrive by building communities. Today's first-generation scholars must learn that individualism and elitism will only get you so far. Those who endear themselves to tyrants and empire will only be crushed by disappointment when they realize they will only be used for fodder. But the good news is that you get to build your extended academic family tree in ways that help you to move beyond nepotism and foster complex professional relationships that last but are not bound by unconditional allegiance, quid pro quo, or mob mentality.

This is not a style guide. It's a guide about developing a practice. Your practice may not look exactly like mine BUT my hope is that this book will help you establish practical strategies and access resources that enable you to flourish, to find success on your own terms even as you need to adapt to different institutional and disciplinary expectations.

This distinction between offering resources (which I do in abundance) and proposing a singular, universal, fail-safe writing method (which I do not offer) is important because I do not assume I am a model writer or that my "everyday" approach will work for everyone. I have my style and habits that generally meet professional standards. But there are so many relevant examples of academic writing that widely differ from each other. You might be, as I am, influenced by the school you attend, whom you have studied with, workshops you attend, and disciplinary norms. There is no one way to write well or that guarantees results. Instead, I offer this book as a resource guide for you to access relevant information to increase your odds of professional success on your own terms.

I write with temerity. While many use the word *audacity*, I choose to say I am *temeritous* because there must be, on some level, a commitment to reckless abandon to write about Black women. So many have advised me that this work is foolish. Black women's studies is not viable, professional, or sustainable, they said. And yet I have managed—and dared—to write about Black women for a living. Some people may not like my level of productivity and that's ok. Some may not like my writing, and that's ok. Some may not like me, personally, and that's ok too. My work is a tribute to courageous women and this work seems to encourage my students. Knowledge of my intellectual tradition is all the affirmation I need but, honestly, maintaining the courage to write can still cause mental stress and strain.

Mental health matters and, for Black women, it mostly matters to us. Historical policy decisions from health care to housing show that Black women cannot depend on other demographics to take action to protect our mental health or material conditions. In *The Suffering Will Not Be Televised: African American Women and Sentimental Political Storytelling*, Rebecca Wanzo makes several points about affect and change.[20] She traces the use of Black women's victimhood in various cultural spaces and concludes that while sentimentality is inadequate to impact political justice, emotion can be a powerful tool for rallying resource for necessary social change. Moral suasion is one of the "master's tools" of which Audre Lorde spoke that will not dismantle houses built on misogynoir. That said, paying attention to our own emotional, mental, and ethical conditions are essential steps to generating enough energy to free ourselves. When writing becomes a tool of mental health rather than mental duress, we can begin to change institutional oppressions without sacrificing ourselves in the process. When we have the courage to prioritize our own mental health, we can also have energy to care for others.[21]

It is imperative to do more with writing than advance one's individual career—publishing books can be a means to expand justice in practical ways. This is why I argue that one central tenant of Black feminist publishing should involve collaborating with community organizations to produce work that is defined by and deemed useful by those outside of the academy. Academic writing also means that, while celebrity culture may dominate in other spaces, scholars—even public intellectuals—are not above critique and accountability.

TEACH (The Work): Cultivating Collective Care

> Black women's memoirs reveal a tradition of inner peace (mental, physical, and spiritual self-definition) serving as a pathway to outer peace (social, political, and economic resistance).
>
> —Stephanie Y. Evans, *Black Women's Yoga History*

Black feminist writing affirms inner peace, but writers cannot function in isolation. Ours is a communal practice. As a first-generation scholar who attended state schools, I had to establish my own professional networks, which spanned many institutions, professional organizations, and community agencies. Though I have regularly attended conferences and served in associations, my community building did not stop there. Nurturing an intellectual family tree should defy disciplinary boundaries and include those who constantly challenge you to revisit and improve your research. Anything less than critical peer review (albeit from a caring circle) results in poor-quality scholarship, but we cannot assume that only those at the top of the prestige hierarchy have the most valuable perspective.

My professional network includes a mix of colleagues from community college, Historically Black Colleges and Universities (HBCUs), state university, and Ivy League institutions. Community is messy and subjective research inevitably will be incomplete without acknowledging and working through substantive differences, debates, and disagreements within a diverse demographic. Additionally, no matter how meticulously you craft your subjectivity statement in published research, peer review is not limited to the academy. The academy is part of vast ecosystem that includes thinkers and workers in your city, state, region, nation, and international circles.[22]

Writing communally is not simply about citing work and manipulating it to your own ends—it requires vetting with contemporary scholars to offer critique and validation in a process where you must defend your work and justify your methods while seriously contending with established ideas. Exchanges that happen at professional conferences are often contentious, but there is a palpable collective investment in exploring ideas and building a community around that commitment to exploration. This network should be one way to shape your work, not stifle it. Being a scholar means you are familiar with the field but does not mean you are unconditionally beholden to others. That said, scholarship that is not connected to past publications is simply incomplete.[23]

Scholarly writing and academic publishing are two separate things. Both are arduous but viewing them as a continuum can make a difference in your enjoyment of either. Part of the reason I have published so many books is because I began to understand the writing process, anticipate the publishing process, and to hone my approach to both in tandem. Working at writing and working on publishing as a holistic practice has increased my enjoyment and efficacy in both areas. Writing is my practice of thinking. Publishing is my way of effectively communicating my thoughts.

Academese is a unique genre that does not always lend itself to intrinsic satisfaction, not least because of the requirement of anonymous peer review. Self-fulfillment operates very differently in research—whether poring over an archive, closely reading a passage, or interviewing community members. Yet envisioned correctly, peer review before and after publication can become an effective means of coalition building on and off campus. While demands of the job may prevent close-knit writing circles like one depicted in *The Sisterhood*, we must all work to develop writing community in some way.

At its best, publishing puts you in close contact with several editors and reviewers. I am talking about many kinds of peer review—informal workshopping, formal preparation of your manuscript for submission, anonymous review handled by an editor, and reaching readers in higher education. Though professional relationships vary widely, selecting a press and choosing to work with an acquisitions editor is an opportunity to work over a long period of time with someone who has professed an interest in helping you produce the most complete, sound, and clean book possible. After publication, critics may challenge your style and critique your interpretation. But faculty reviewers are also called to verify facts, question methods, and ensure new writing includes due consideration of existing scholarship. While celebration of historical writers is an act of care, truth-telling and critical assessments are requirements as well. Publishers are charged with securing credible reviewers and identifying markets for your work. Accordingly, scholarly writing and academic publishing are internally and externally conjoined. Though you may write for and by yourself, academic publishing is fundamentally a communal practice.

Publishing can also be a long activity. Consider the long, slow, drawn-out process of academic publishing as a blessing in disguise. If you are contributing quality scholarship that will endure the test of time, it stands to reason that your work will take time to produce and will not be subject to the ebb and flow of the news cycle in order to determine relevance. Quality writing is always timely. Full transparency, it has taken me to this point to really appreciate this truism. I remain impatient to see my work in print and still succumb to the impulse to ascribe an arbitrary publishing deadline. Realistically, I'm still working on patience. There is a fine line between pushing deadlines and completing work. There is also a fine line between wanting to work for a perfect document and knowing when a work is complete enough to let it go.

While we certainly have a responsibility to engage a wide variety of scholars—even those whom we dislike—our work and worth are not dependent on status quo scholarship. Said another way, like Maya Angelou, we can rise above others' perceptions of us, write our life story on our own terms, acknowledge those with whom we disagree, affirm those who have come before, and pen cautionary tales or love letters to future generations in hopes they can continue the fight for human rights on and beyond campus. Writing for our individual and collective growth is our contribution to growing a mighty forest of knowledge.[24]

A Note on "Audience"

> The larger questions are here too: why and for whom do I write? What is the writer's responsibility to one's work, to others, to society?
>
> —Tillie Olson (2023)[25]

Black Feminist Writing primarily focuses on Black women writers. As widely evidenced in research and documented in articles like "Killing Us Softly: Chronic Stress and the Health of Black Women" (2018), Black women experience a disproportionate number of systemic stressors, which is why this academic demographic is my primary audience. I work in close community with a legion of Black women scholars across the country and around the world—I write for them, first and foremost.[26]

My broader imagined audience includes academic researchers in areas that center race and gender studies. This includes authors in the humanities and social sciences, which are vital to higher education. These audiences include scholars who are invested in publishing books in order to advance freedom for all. Cutting-edge interdisciplines, specifically Black Women's Studies, often validate experiences that are largely ignored or scandalized in established academic and public spaces.

Fields like life and physical science, technology, engineering, and math (STEM) are indebted to cultural studies because science is neither understood nor applied in a vacuum—science is social. Though scholars in disciplines like history, literature, philosophy, art and theatre, film, cultural studies, anthropology, sociology, political science, and religious studies will more than likely find this guide relevant, scholarly writing also has a bearing on areas like STEM, given the subjectivity involved in asking questions, social implications of funding decisions, and public nature of those disciplines when applied.

The need to support Black women's academic writing is global. After spending one month surveying women's dissertations at the East Africa library at the University of Dar es Salaam in Tanzania, I published an article titled "Gender and Research in the African Academy: 'Moving Against the Grain' in the Global Ivory Tower" (2008). This article shared findings about African scholarship in gender studies across the African continent, identified trends in interdisciplinary research, and traced women's challenges to equal access in youth and adult education. Around the world, higher education remains a contested place of meaning making, where marginalized communities write, as one African scholar shared, "against the grain." Thus, our charge to care for Black women intellectuals is a global one. Globally, publishers like Sage, Taylor & Francis, Springer, and Oxford University Press are among the largest outlets for scholarship. It is the charge of those publishers to commit to substantively diversifying their leadership and evolve their engagement with Black women scholars in the African diaspora.

Perhaps this book might be taught in a feminist research methods course, an English life-writing seminar, continuing education courses, or Black intellectual history class. Certainly, it can be used for workshops that might range from two or three hours to a full week or several months of writing. The outline is meant to be flexible so you can use what is most relevant for you to complete your book project.

In addition to Africana and feminist authors, this book will be relevant to a multitude of secondary audiences. I present information useful to all faculty authors, undergraduates considering graduate school, or graduate students working on a thesis or dissertation, as well as their advisors and chairs, university writing center mentors, freelance developmental editors, and writing coaches. In addition, nonfiction literary agents and university press or academic trade publishers might suggest this guide to scholars submitting manuscripts for consideration or to help authors finalize manuscripts that have been placed under contract.

I also have higher education administrators (defined broadly) in mind as a distinct audience for this book. I have held unit leadership positions at three distinct institutions. Each of these experiences has informed me of how changes must be made across the profession, regardless of institution type. Leaders of foundations, nonprofits, academic journals, and other university adjacent organizations can also benefit from this refresher.

Given my experience as a department chair, I provide writing strategies (presented as tasks and discussions) that do not require a lot of time. For those chairs, directors, deans, provosts, vice presidents, and presidents who desire to share their expertise, this guide can help you to clear your calendar, and your mind, and write despite the demands of executive service. For administrators, everyday incremental writing not only helps you produce your own research, it also reminds you of the need to have empathy and offer support for researchers of all experience levels on your campus. Administrators can be reminded of their role as part of the intellectual community by remaining active in their writing practice. Otherwise, they will be subsumed in the business model of education that pits "laborers" against "managers," which is a failing model for education on any level.

Beyond the academy, I envision this book supporting online education, including college curriculum in prisons, where many colleagues have made significant inroads. Over the years, I have developed partnerships with several schools, programs, and organizations, including with organizations like youthSpark, No More Martyrs, Center for Black Women's Wellness, Black Women's Mental Health Institute, Black Women's Health

Imperative, and Social Justice Café for Girls. These partners are part of my primary audience and have had an indelible impact on my writing.

Intellectual care is not worship. Self-care is not selfish. Communal care is neither charity nor transaction. Táíwò rightly cautions against the corrupting nature of deference. We do not have to agree with everything our ancestors did and, equally important, we must identify and call out abuse wherever it exists. Failure to do so can be seen in the "circle the wagons" mentality that some Black women have exhibited to protect serial abusers in higher education settings. Celebration, courage, and care simply means we recognize we would not have the privileges we enjoy were it not for the sacrifices of others, that we are capable of feeling empathy, and we are committed to exercising compassion for ourselves and others.

Expecting rigor is an act of care. As Black feminist scholarly writers, collective care should not be an optional practice but should be recognized as a core part of research ethics.

Like Erykah Badu in her breakout hit "Appletree," I acknowledge the life-giving fruit that trees offer—especially academic family trees. Further, I recognize that a tree is part of a collective environment, part of a thriving ecology. My use of academic family tree allows for diversity: your work can be a willow tree, an apple tree, or an oak. Trees exist in the company of various flora and fauna and together can form an orchard or a forest.

Badu sings, "my soul flies free like a willow tree, doo wee, doo wee, doo wee." Find what makes your soul fly free and write about that. Black feminist writing can be an act of death-defying freedom. We need new worlds, new futures, but without studying predecessors, it is impossible to state whether something is new or not. By deepening your connection to other thinkers, you can increase your motivation and efficacy. Regenerative writing is an act of liberation—a way to let your soul fly free and to create conditions for universal equality.

Reflection Questions

Question 4: Personal Practice. How would you characterize your writing voice? Do you identify as a feminist or womanist?

What personal experiences have impacted your research focus? What are you afraid of?

Question 5: Professional Practice. What are the writing requirements of your job? How does your job get in the way of writing? What scholars most impact your writing? Who are you agreeing with and disagreeing with?

Question 6: Publishing Practice. Why did you decide to write your book? What questions do you have about publishing? What makes you most excited or nervous about the publishing process?

Question 7: Public Practice. Who is part of your academic family tree? Who do you work with in your community? Do you have a writing group or accountability partners? Who is your scholarship intended to help besides yourself?

Question 8: Political Practice. In what ways does your work affirm extant scholarship in BWST? How might your book disrupt norms of traditional discipline(s)? How do you learn, create, and teach BWST?

Practical Tasks

- Attend or plan a virtual or in-person writing retreat.

- Name your big idea (theory). Decide on a working title, data set, method, argument, and chapter organization. Give your rationale for chapter organization.

- Identify your publishing goal. Start developing your routine. Set aside a bit of time every day for one week to write (or read or edit). Change to a different schedule the following week. See which works best and go with that as the centerpiece of your plan. Do not create a schedule at the expense of your health and well-being. Find a balance between regularity and exhaustion.

- Create a playlist of main themes in your research. Name inspirational artists (in music, poetry, literature, etc.) that connect with the main messages you want to convey.

- Cite three comparative books that most impact your project. Contact one author to let them know their impact on your work.
- Discuss project goals, tasks, and timelines with a colleague or mentor.
- Share the concept of an academic family tree with a next-generation scholar.

3

Voice

Personal Practice

Black feminist writing is a private practice. Intimate even. There is a common adage by Black elders: education is the one thing people can't take away from you. Reading and writing become yours only by your own action. Accordingly, literacy is a personal practice. Finding your voice will mean exploring resilience strategies to gauge what works for you. Often, confidence is an issue for new faculty—especially those of us who are first generation scholars, have disabilities or are learning diverse, or for whom English is second (or third or fourth) language. Not everyone grew up with faculty as family or with an understanding of how to navigate the academy. Fortunately, there is a long tradition of writers who embraced self-education and those writers serve as guides on how to find your voice through literacy.

In her dissertation titled "Great Influence on My Mind: African American Literacy and Slave Rebellion in the Antebellum South," historian La'Neice Littleton explains the relationship of literacy to social power and points out that most rebellions were led by Black people who learned to read and write.[1] In this same vein, Frederick Douglass quipped that reading made one unfit to be a slave and Patricia Hill Collins intimated that mastering literacy was tantamount to mastering oneself. Collins wrote, "Under slavery it was illegal to teach African Americans to read and write. Mastering these skills was an expression of political activism not because education allowed slaves to become better slaves but because it offered skills essential in challenging the very tenants of slavery itself."[2] Verily, writing is a freedom practice and when Black women place ourselves at the center of study—when Black feminists write about Black feminism—it amplifies our power to declare we are free, regardless of what others claim. Paying attention to your literacy can be a means to secure your liberty. Freedom is not a guarantee anywhere—even in self-proclaimed democratic countries. But not paying attention to your intellectual growth will almost guarantee your enslavement to someone else.[3]

By committing to a practice of writing, I have established my own aesthetic that reflects my identity as a Black woman optimist, humanist, global traveler, die-hard academic, and former youth writer. My voice is deeply affective, which is no surprise given my position as a survivor of several types of violence. I value my own insight but do not think I'm right about everything. My experience is only the start of a much longer process of exploration to understand why I have experienced what I have and how that relates (or fails to relate) to others' experiences.

I am a subjective writer. While I ensure my assessments consider alternative possibilities and synthesize an array of perspectives, I do not shy away from centering myself, my experiences, my values, and my critical insight. With all the hype and worry about artificial intelligence, I embrace the idea of musical geniuses De La Soul—"me, myself, and I"—all the more. AI can neither cite sources, accurately synthesize information, nor speak from lived experience.

Stress and Your Personal Practice: The Imperative to Resist Academic Anxiety

> Our ancestors fought for us to be literate, educated, self-sustaining people who have a future.
>
> —Sonia Sanchez, *Black Women Writers at Work* (1983)

Sonia Sanchez is recognized as a founding pioneer in the modern field of Black Women's Studies. In 1968, she taught a course that is considered to be one of the first Black studies class at a predominantly white institution (PWI). While historically Black colleges and universities (HBCUs) have regularly centered the study of Black people and women, Sanchez broke new ground in mainstream higher education. In 1968, at San Francisco State University, she taught a course in Black literature and, in 1969, taught "The Black Woman," a course she also taught at University of Massachusetts, Amherst, in 1975. That syllabus is featured in the book *All the Women Are White, All the Blacks Are Men, but Some of Us Are Brave.*

Professor Sanchez and a cohort of educators who added similar courses in the 1970s and 1980s ushered in a new field of study. A celebrated poet and longtime distinguished faculty member at Temple University, Professor Sanchez identified the struggle for human rights as central to Black studies, in general, and the study of Black women, in particular. In her book *Peace Is a Haiku Song*, she writes "peace is a human right."[4] Fighting for peace in higher education is a fight to normalize human rights values. Black women in higher education have a long tradition of pursuing peace as a foil to the normalization of personal, structural, and institutional violence. Black women have studied critical race and gender to celebrate our lives and to advance human rights for ourselves and others. Our struggle is based on personal experiences of trying to declutter our minds and manage stress-inducing environments.

Authors of the Combahee River Collective statement observed, "Black feminists often talk about their feelings of craziness before becoming conscious of the concepts of sexual politics, patriarchal rule, and, most importantly, feminism, the political analysis and practice that women use to struggle against our oppression. The psychological toll of being a Black woman, and the difficulties this presents in reaching political consciousness and doing political work, can never be underestimated. There is a low value placed upon Black women's psyches in this society, which is both racist and sexist. We are dispossessed psychologically and on every other level, and yet we feel the necessity to struggle to change the conditions of all Black women."[5]

The United States has a higher stress level in this historical moment than in the past few decades. In the real-life world of power and domination serialized in the HBO series *Succession* (about the death-dealing politics of wealthy robber barons turned media moguls), voices of dissent are silenced at all costs. The founding of the United States of America was drenched in blood, and the turn of the twenty-first century did little to swing the pendulum toward justice. From guns, weaponized technology, "new" ways to enforce the unjust death penalty, and subsidized global violence to manipulative media and a marketplace of political influence, the present moment gives ample reason for those with less power, based on historical racial, economic, and gendered access to resources, to feel stressed. Abatement of these high stress levels does not seem likely in the near future.

Several times while completing this book I feared I might die of a heart attack. I feared, perhaps, that my demise would completely undermine my claim about writing and health. Other times I felt like I would keel over from excitement about being almost done. Sometimes I have felt sick while writing about wellness. I had the same feeling when I was completing my dissertation. The same feeling when I completed my first book. I catastrophize when I write—assuming horrible things will happen, regardless of lack of any actual evidence. But I know they might. For Black people, queer people, and women, one traffic stop or one interaction with a disgruntled stranger or relation may end our lives.

I'm a Black woman, so horrible things might actually happen any minute. One never knows. I started studying stress not because I didn't have any, but because I have suffered from anxiety since I was a child. While writing about wellness has helped me manage my stress, it has not prevented me from experiencing stress. Over time, writing has begun to calm me down more than stress me out. Progress.

Discussions about mental health and self-care rose dramatically among academic and civic communities in the aftermath of an increasingly stressful political environment. These exponentially rising political stressors emerged after the 2016 US presidential election, when a barrage of hate was unleashed throughout the nation. The thin veneer was stripped away and the ever-present underbelly of hatred was again exposed. The 2017 report *Stress in America: The State of Our Nation*, by the American Psychological Association (APA), showed Americans worried about the future of the nation (sixty-three percent), money (sixty-two percent), and work (sixty-one percent). Areas of anxiety included issues of health care, the economy, trust in government, and hate crimes.

The highest percentage of respondents in the *Stress Report* agreed on the need for mental relief: "Despite the divisiveness in many areas, most Americans (eighty-seven percent) can agree on at least one thing: a desire for people to take a deep breath and calm down." Stress around these issues increased exponentially after the 2016 election, intensified in 2020 with a global pandemic, and exploded in national unrest with the necessary push for social justice by movements like Black Lives Matter, which called for an abolition of structural violence and equitable value of labor. The treasonous attack on the United States Capitol building—the January 6, 2021, insurgency that attempted to overturn democracy—pushed the nation's frayed nerves and tenuous systems to the brink. Assaults on K-12 and higher education have been a key part of the attempts to undermine democratic freedoms. The freedom to learn remains as precarious as freedom of speech and academic freedom to teach without coercion or backlash. And every four years, a new election cycle ensures more dread and confusion.[6]

And yet somehow we're supposed to write amid all this chaos. Sometimes being real about mental health needs can free your mind to write. Regardless of your academic discipline, paying attention to what your mind does during the writing process can provide clues to how you might improve the way you research, edit, and publish. Do you breeze through writing but stall during editing or vice versa? Do writing groups work best when conceptualizing, writing, or editing? Do you enjoy writing in silence or with music? Do the people around you support your writing, resent you, or mock you for it (or all three)?

It is difficult not to feel selfish when prioritizing your own needs. As an academic author, we too often buy into the "publish or perish" narrative and forget that we have the option of writing for ourselves and our communities, not simply writing for promotion. Name your motivation(s) for writing a book. Define what health, happiness, and joy mean to you. When it comes to writing practice, determine what sustainable joy feels like for you.

One of the main impediments to writing is finding time. Educators are rarely allowed time to think, let alone research and write. Teaching classes—especially for those who are not on the tenure track—can be overwhelming. Personal challenges to time management include family responsibilities, personal illness, and social responsibilities. The more you can align your teaching and your research with your personal interests and higher purpose, the easier it will be to get excited about writing. The disproportionate level of institutional service performed by women and faculty of color is well documented. Though it is easy to get overwhelmed, making use of your workspace for writing can become a habit. Talk about your research at every opportunity and use any on-campus resources (especially libraries) not only to progress your research but also to escape into silent spaces.

When I was department chair, I made use of either a private writing room or the quiet floor in the library. Quiet floors or law libraries are ideal. Coffee shops are vibrant public spaces, but noise or unscheduled encounters (even pleasant ones) can be distracting. Block out time on your calendar and protect that time at all costs. To find out the best writing schedule for you, I recommend Wendy Laura Belcher's classic book, *Writing*

Your Journal Article in 12 Weeks: A Guide to Academic Publishing Success. There are excellent exercises there that help you determine how long to write or what time of day to write, as well as sort out your hesitations in order to be more productive.

I recommend the first thing that you do when creating a writing schedule is set aside time to rest. This can be a five- to ten-minute meditation or a fifteen-minute nap. As you begin to block out time to write, know that your mind cannot focus if you are exhausted. It may seem counterintuitive, but you need to rest well if you want to write well. One way to create more time is to limit your screen time. Whether TV, computer, or phone, broadcast news, entertainment, and social media are preventable drains on your time and energy. Stop doom scrolling. Put your phone across the room—do not keep it in arm's reach. When you are on the computer, locate resources that help you understand the publishing process a bit better. For example, the University of California Press has a webinar series titled "Demystifying Book Publishing for First-Gen Scholars." This is the type of screen time that will help you commit to your writing practice by addressing the fears that might be keep you from raising your voice to full power. You can also find alternatives, like audiobooks, which can help you "read" during commutes or other times when you don't have capacity to hold a book.[7]

In his book *Why Zebras Don't Get Ulcers: A Guide to Stress, Stress-Related Diseases, and Coping* (1994), Robert Sapolsky identifies five strategies to cope with stress that produce measurable results: exercising, meditating, gathering information (to increase one's sense of control), practicing religion and spirituality, and developing a network of social support.[8] Rather than providing a strict regimen for adopting these strategies, Sapolsky underscores the importance of experimenting:

> But don't get crazed, holding off on doing something until you figure out the perfect approach for you. On a certain level, it doesn't matter what management technique you use (beyond it not being abusive to those around you). . . . Don't save your stress management for the weekend, or for when you're on hold on the phone for thirty seconds. Take the time out to do it almost daily. And if you manage that, change has become important enough to you that you're already a lot of the way there—maybe not really 80 percent, but at least a great start.[9]

As you begin to understand the behavioral, physiological, and historical aspects of mental health, it is helpful to process information in a way that creates a personalized map for you to follow. In short, I found that my deep dive into stress-management research helped me fine-tune my everyday approach to writing. Reflect on information that has been helpful, find out what works for you and make a plan to move forward based on that information. Writing can be a part of your exploration process—a way you identify what habits produce the best results for your emotional stability and satisfaction. Write in a way that feels right. *Right* may not be easy or comfortable but experiment to find a good fit to maintain a daily (or at least regular) practice.

Resources like Therapy for Black Girls or Innopsych, which provide a directory of therapists, are starting points to consider or share with others who express need. Identify counseling services and follow up as often as needed. As with all subjects, delving into the history of a topic can also inform your understanding. For me, taking time to consider the intellectual history of mental health research enabled me to locate how best to combat deficient models for understanding myself as an academic. Early African American women pioneers of mental health research, including psychologists Ruth Howard Beckham (PhD, University of Minnesota, 1934) and Mamie Phipps Clark (PhD, Columbia University, 1943), made critical interventions in psychology, particularly child psychology, by operating from strength-based assessments of Black children and analyzing the impact of racism in American society. Clark, for example, developed mental health intervention programs to understand self-esteem development in terms of power and strengthen self-consciousness. Along with her husband Kenneth, she developed the famous doll test to identify internalized racism in Black children that became a cornerstone of the 1954 *Brown v. Board of Education* desegregation case.

You might consider embracing creativity and incorporating mental health, wellness, and joy into your professional queries. Later in this chapter, I will share how I have begun to explore yoga, wine, and tea as experiential study, creative outlets, and areas of scholarly research. These studies have given me time to ease my mind, but also guided my pedagogy and administrative leadership style in a way that supported and sustained me. Writing helped me balance teaching, campus service, and community building in ways I could not have done without it. Writers like Maya Angelou have been pivotal in my drive to write historical wellness.

LEARN: Maya Angelou's Guide to Mental Health

> Books about life lessons show readers how to foster what Maparyan calls "vibrant health." Many contemporary Black women, particularly survivors of violence, struggle with mental health and wellness; studying these narratives can offer useful resources of how those who have come before have effectively dealt with social injustice and still kept presence of mind to record their voice for the benefit of others.
>
> —Stephanie Y. Evans, "Letters to Our Daughters" (2021)

Black women's writing is a wellspring of information that can benefit all of humanity. I often say "memoirs are mentors." As Maya Angelou conveys, Black women have written life stories to teach their "daughters" critical lessons, particularly lessons pertaining to rights, justice, and peace.

Angelou was born Marguerite Annie Johnson in 1928 in St. Louis and raised in Arkansas before journeying to California and globe-trotting to dozens of countries. To recount her life and travels, she penned a series of memoirs that made her an international icon and an impactful speaker. Angelou published several types of books, including cookbooks, children's books, poetry, speeches, and essays, in addition to recording a calypso album. However, memoir was her primary genre, and she wrote seven full-length works in addition to the autobiographical pieces included in other genres. Of her thirty-six published works, most are best sellers, and Angelou's arc of productivity in recording the phases of her life, up to her final work, *Mom & Me & Mom* (2013), is unmatched in the genre.

In *Letter to My Daughter*, Angelou makes explicit her intention to gather recollections in a way that guides future generations. In a summary of how to deal with life, she writes, "You may not control all of the events that happen to you, but you can decide not to be reduced by them." Her narratives reveal that she was raped at the age of eight by a boyfriend of her mother, was manipulated into hustling as a sex worker for a short time (at one point managing other women), and lived in the entertainment industry in ways that some might find unsavory, at best. Yet, she wrote herself with clarity, fairness, and dignity—in ways that sought not to diminish anyone else's humanity or set herself apart from those, like sex workers, not deemed respectable. Angelou taught us how to find home in the self. Her writing created a paradigm for self-awareness and self-acceptance and was a healing journey to sustainable optimal mental

wide range of learning environments, and although I was often treated as exotic because of my travels, I do not consider myself special. I was simply a curious Black girlchild with not enough places to satiate my desire for more information. I hungered for information about myself, my history, and my culture.

After traveling overseas, I attended junior high and high school in Arizona. Notorious for limiting the curriculum with bills like HB 2281 (passed in 2010 and overturned in 2022), which outlawed ethnic studies and Mexican American history, Arizona's education provided no books about Black girlhood or womanhood in ways that centered health, wellness, or belonging. With the exception of whitewashed thumbnail sketches for Black History Month, Black women's lives were not part of my formal education. No major books by Black authors were a part of my K-12 curriculum, and I was not assigned a book by a Black woman author until my second year of college at the age of twenty-six. Since reading Anna Julia Cooper's essay "On the Higher Education of Women," the first essay I encountered where I recognized myself, I have paid attention to the learning life of Black women. And, over time, my library of books about Black women has grown.

I graduated high school in 1987, then moved from Tucson, Arizona, to Las Vegas, Nevada, to Ventura, California. I moved to New Mexico to begin college after the Northridge earthquake of January 17, 1994. I worked as a waitress in restaurants and comedy clubs then moved into hotel management. The earthquake helped me make up my mind to finally return to school and pursue my writing passion.

In 1994, the year I began college at the age of twenty-five, I developed a stomach ulcer, overcome by the stress of entering college and trying to adjust to that major transition. Initially, I had difficulty processing a new normal that would require not only intellectual development but emotional growth as well. That same year, I self-published a collection of poetry titled *What Lies Inside?* In addition to some fun and funny pieces, the poems were a laundry list of rhyming lamentations, my attempt to make sense of the violence and abuse I had experienced as a Black girl and young woman.

Black Women's Studies saved my life. I started at St. John's College, home of the "Great Books" curriculum of "dead White men." While I certainly enjoyed reading Plato, Herodotus, Thucydides, and Homer, as well as doing Euclidean math, I hungered for evidence of Black women's intellectual existence. I wanted to not be seen as weird, special, exceptional, or not Black enough. When I cultivated my interdisciplinary studies humanities curriculum at California State University, Long Beach (CSULB), the courses validated and challenged me intellectually. Studying race, gender, and humanities also improved my quality of life by helping me to understand the cultural and institutional social systems that were largely responsible for the violence I had experienced as a young Black girl. Black Women's Studies gave me the tools to change those systems of domination and oppression by transforming the academy from within.[13]

The first academic work that I saw in print was my 1997 California State University, Long Beach, Ronald E. McNair Scholars Program research paper, which was published in a university profile. The paper "How Solid Is the Rock?: Gauging the Historical Accuracy of *Schoolhouse Rock*," was the culmination of a six-week summer research program named for astronaut Ronald McNair. My assessment (in hindsight, developed out of anger as much as analysis), compared the ten episodes from the history and government series of *Schoolhouse Rock* to events listed in Howard Zinn's *People's History of the United States*.

My tone in that first research paper was one of indignation—disbelief that I could not find myself adequately represented in history. Also, too, I was disturbed that what I had once celebrated as a child, *Schoolhouse Rock*, was inadequate because it reified established narratives—and set it to music. By comparing that series to *People's History*, I began to find me, deep down, submerged "in the interstices of history." The *People's History* was supplemented two decades later with *A Black Women's History of the United States*. An answered prayer.

The conclusion of my paper explained that a cherished mainstay of my childhood only reinforced oppressive messages, which amounted to indoctrination more than education. The following summer, my 1998 McNair project compared text from the United Nations Universal Declaration of Human Rights with the United States Bill of Rights. I concluded that activists should focus more on the global document than simply settle for domestic civil rights. My insights have been validated by those invested in global solutions, such as Carol Anderson's brilliant *Eyes off the Prize: The United Nations and the African American Struggle for Human Rights* (2003). Since my college graduation in 1999, I have continued to investigate human rights and historical accuracy in Black women's writing.

Black women's writing tradition gifts authors with the ability to ground ourselves in a historical exploration that affirms and centers our own humanity. No one is compelled to affirm a history that marginalizes or dismisses the reality or perspectives of our ancestors. And, unlike the indoctrination of "conservative" politicians that push a single-narrative nationalism, progressive education demands that we square our perspectives with those of other communities as well. As bell hooks offers with her extensive body of work, we must continually transgress, commit to love, share the values of feminism with the world and, at the same time, move ourselves from margin to center.

Once I began to study Black women's history, I enjoyed a greater sense of agency by understanding ways others had found theirs. As a student and teacher of Black women's intellectual history, the connection of memoirs to mental health became a natural transition. Professionally, reading narratives by elders helped me to reach increasingly challenging career goals as a scholar, writer, and higher education administrator. Memoirs have helped me to deal with the fickleness of academics wherever challenges like overwork, double standards, extraordinary scrutiny, inequality, and exclusion exist. Personally, reading elder memoirs taught me how to love myself in a world that seemed to hate me. Reading and writing about Black women's wellness from ancient times to the present has eased my sense of anxiety and allowed me to feel deep fulfillment.

In the thirty years that have passed since I first entered college and began writing formal research papers, my interests have converged around the topics of history and healing. An essential part of my personal growth has come from understanding the context in which I am educated. For example, in 1994, the same year I started college, a collection of Black women scholars gathered at MIT for the conference "Black Women in the Academy: Defending Our Name, 1894–1994." This conference was convened to protest the appointment of Clarence Thomas to the Supreme Court despite Anita Hill's testimony of his sexual harassment. When I learned about this conference, I began to make the connection between my personal experience with sexual violence and the broader socio-political environments that made my abuse not only inevitable but also invisible. Studying Black women's lives was a means to improve my emotional health, but the intellectual pursuit was also emotionally difficult.

Two decades after my initial ulcer, I suffered a traumatic personal setback in 2013 when I had a miscarriage that toppled over what remaining balance I had at a high-stress job. A few years later, the losses of my mother and father (within six weeks of each other) served to remind me that mental health is a lifelong journey, not a definite destination. It was then that I began to expand my exploration of Africana mindfulness and connect my experiences not only with the past but also with identifiable lessons useful for future generations. I realize the impossibility of my own journey and although I may never be able to write the details of my pain, I am blessed enough to have the opportunity to chronicle my healing.

Reading the women who have come before me has saved me from despair, guilt, shame, and unnecessary self-sacrifice. In my writing and meditation workshops, held over the past several years at academic conferences, faculty retreats, student wellness sessions, and community-based staff trainings, I have offered stress-management tools to students, faculty, and staff who are overworked, underpaid, and burnt out. This is a tiny but necessary intervention for those struggling with their day-to-day. It is a common sentiment that self-care is imperative, especially for those engaged in social justice work.

Like three out of five Black women worldwide, I am a survivor of sexual violence. When I moved out of my mother's house at the age of sixteen, she gifted me a pearl-handled .22 revolver and a set of baby blue silk sheets. She was trying to provide me with the tools to survive a wild world. The tools she provided me, one to deal with violence and one to deal with sex, spoke volumes about the tumultuous world she experienced as a Black woman. She was not wrong about the need to be prepared to combat sexual violence . . . I had learned that lesson several times by that point. But I would need other tools to survive beyond those that would only equip me to either fight or fuck for a living. I needed to find tools to equip me for freedom. Later, I would recognize the other tools my mother gifted me, like the commitment to dance and exercise and the fierce declaration of boundaries. But as a newly self-emancipated youth, I was in a desperate battle to simply survive.

As a Black woman, the daily triggers of sexual violence in the news and on social media feeds are sometimes overwhelming. But the generations of Black women's voices in my head keep me balanced and enable me to raise my voice. Learning about the impact of mental health on physical health, and vice versa, has improved my ability to manage stress and share ways others can do the same.

Black women who are survivors of violence experience power in various ways. Sexual assault survivors have documented their journeys out of powerlessness ever since Harriet Jacobs detailed the horrors of sexual assault during her enslavement in her 1861 autobiography, *Incidents in the Life of a Slave Girl*. Many survivors have refashioned power by firing up their pens to define their experiences, collectively address the need to heal, and increase activism for Black women's rights as human rights.

Life writing is a radical act of self-care; by penning stories of struggle and growth, Africana authors have resisted invisibility, dehumanization, and injustice. On the whole, Black women's memoirs are a compelling dataset that connects voices through time and space. This particularly can be seen in the narratives of twentieth-century elders who lived into their nineties and beyond. Centenarian and nonagenarian narratives clearly depict a connective generational quality connecting past, present, and future generations. Black women's memoirs reveal a tradition of inner peace (mental, physical, and spiritual self-definition) serving as a pathway to outer peace (social, political, and economic resistance). The journey to self-worth involves several strategies, beginning with steps toward self-definition and self-determination to improve one's sense of self and expand our sense of agency.

My journey from seeing writing as a challenge to viewing it as a pathway to liberation was long and arduous. After settling my ulcer (and even after I found my stride and claimed my role in the profession), I encountered plenty of rejection and discouraging reviews that stressed me out and almost knocked me out. My love for writing was not enough to guarantee a successful academic career—but I did gather stress-management skills along the way to help focus my energy to make the publishing process bearable and, eventually, predictable, and even pleasurable. Writing requires becoming comfortable with imperfection, rejection, and failure. Writing requires becoming comfortable with sitting with yourself.

Sometimes, being present with yourself is uncomfortable. This is especially true when you are working under duress and barely hanging on. For women and queer scholars of color, we are expected to serve others in our marginalized communities, a process made even more stressful because we are also fighting generational oppression. These roles often require shouldering disproportionate responsibilities as caretakers, enforcers, peacemakers, breadwinners, and other roles antithetical to the free time, energy, and headspace necessary for writing. Sometimes our energies are needed just to survive and make a living.

TEACH: Find Your Voice through Everyday M.E.N.T.A.L. Health

My commitment to the work of everyday writing (and writing every day) as a wellness practice shines most brightly in my book *Black Women's*

Yoga History. There I identified Black feminist and womanist articulations of common practices such as breathing and creating sister circles, then connected them to Black women's common use of yoga and meditation. I placed feminist-womanist authors of *Black Feminist Thought* (Patricia Hill Collins), *The Womanist Idea* (Layli Maparyan), and *Words of Fire* (Beverly Guy-Sheftall) in conversation with health activist Byllye Avery. These authors not only wrote about mental health, but their writing also demonstrated the commonality of and consistency among Black women's wellness practices. Consistency for me has been crucial. Having grown up in chaos, developing routines for living was a basic necessity. I have derived intellectual and emotional strength from knowing that every day the sun rises and every day, in some small way, I will write. In this way, writing has become a practice of healing.[14]

Influenced by the stress research in Sapolsky's work as well as by Dr. Kanika Bell's research on Black women in *Black Women's Mental Health*, I characterize my wellness practice with the acronym M.E.N.T.A.L., representing the six most effective stress-management strategies that I have used in my career as an academic and especially as an academic administrator. Chairs, deans, and other administrators in particular must try to keep a clear head in order to write amid constant disarray for which they are held directly responsible.

Over the years, I have discovered M.E.N.T.A.L. health through various practices: Meditation, exercise, networking, trust in God, advocating for what I need, and lifelong learning. Mindfulness practices like meditation and yoga have helped me understand that both writing and publishing are practices. With continued practice, the publishing process has not become easy, but it has become easier. Experiment. Sit and think a little bit every day with the strategies shared below.

> MEDITATE—Sit still. Take at least five minutes each morning and each evening to breathe. Don't reflect, think, or plan . . . just breathe. Declutter your mind. Consciously release thoughts that no longer serve you and allow them to leave. Breathe slowly enough to feel your heart beat.
>
> EXERCISE—Move. Sitting as an academic Chair for a dozen years made my body stiff. That is one of the reasons I incorporated the study of yoga into my research. Do what you love to keep your body moving and release the pressure in your head.

NETWORK—Ask for and provide social support. As a writer, I seek out and create collaborative and community-based projects. Even as an experienced chair, I found myself sinking so I reached out to others to create the Chair at the Table Network, a peer mentoring group of Black women academics in the US and Canada. This group empowered me to move forward in solidarity and joy. Keep your social support system of family, friends, and *framily* (especially academic sisters) close—you need them, and they need you.

TRUST—Have faith. If you are a praying person, pray. Talk to God, if so inclined. However you express spirituality, embrace it as central to developing and maintaining your whole being.

ADVOCATE—Ask for what you want and push for what you need. One of the main responsibilities of the privileges we enjoy as academics is to advocate for resources and amplify those whose voices are not generally heard. You may not be able to control the outcomes and decisions around your campus or in your field, but you can at least identify the changes that can be made where possible and support those working for those changes.

LEARN—Study your job. Study higher education. Study the world. Nourish your brain and feed your soul. Academia can be a soul-sucking place—find a library, a tea garden, a skating rink, or some other creative space in your life where you can take time to continuously prune, cultivate, and grow your *self*. Making time to unplug, read new books, and study old books will make all the difference to your wellness practice—and your writing practice. Reading new books like *How We Do It* and perusing classics like *Strunk and White* will help you hone your craft and find your voice.

Years before formally entering college, I completed a one-hundred-hour training in hypnotherapy. This formal investigation into the physiology of attitude provided a foundation of mental strengthening techniques that continues to serve me well. I pay attention to my mind in ways that have enabled me to focus for long periods of time, and also to fully rest, relax, and recover from extended writing binges. Like musicians who use circular breathing (Dizzy Gillespie and Lalah Hathaway come to mind), training my mind has resulted in an ability to think, write, relax, and repeat without irrevocably exhausting myself.

Lifelong learning is central to expanding your mind. Over the years, I have taken classes in hypnotherapy, cardio kickboxing, qigong, yoga, meditation, Feng shui, wine tasting, and tea tasting. I am a firm believer in adult and elder education and whether you are interested in gardening, oceanography, or outer space, find a way to reconnect to the joy of learning.

Some days I set the timer for five minutes or fifteen minutes to meditate. Some days I spend an extra few minutes in the bed, bathroom, or car to focus on slowing my heart rate. For exercise, I enjoy stretching and yoga, but in recent years have benefited from the Peloton bike as a way to increase my heart rate, steady my breath, and sweat out stress. When I write, I try to get up each hour and stretch, fix a cup of tea, squeeze in a load of laundry (which I loathe), or take a short walk around the kitchen. During the pandemic, I got a standing desk and that helped alleviate stiffness in my hips from sitting in front of the computer all day.

Taking the time to understand the physiological characteristics of stress has been an essential part of my stress management. Once you clarify your mental health practices, incorporating the lessons learned into your intellectual and professional process can increase your productivity and also satisfy your emotional need to write in ways that ease anxiety.

Developing a writing network can be tricky. While there are many examples of successful groups (for example several groups of Black women historians have sustained a long-term practice of sister-writers), there are also many instances where writing groups actually impede progress. Before committing to a professional writing group, make sure everyone is on the same page about roles, expectations, duration of the group, and explicit writing outcomes. While I have not participated in formal writing groups *per se*, my coedited projects have served as a motivation to complete books and a means to keep my spirits up while doing so. I also remember that networks of family, framily (close friends), and sister-friends are essential to my spiritual development . . . and I understand that they are not always *only* interested in what I'm writing.

Advocating for yourself and others is at the root of Black feminist writing. I've spent countless hours serving students, colleagues, and community members in ways that create an easier path for them. Doing so has also empowered me to identify when I need support and to ask for it outright. One example of advocating for myself was tendering my resignation from the chair position when I felt it was negatively impacting my health. Both at Clark Atlanta and Georgia State, not only did I insist on protecting small pockets of time to write, but writing about mental health also helped me recognize when it was time for me to pass the baton to the next department head. The Chair at the Table Network meetings and discussions helped me learn what were "normal" administrative roadblocks and which behaviors were diminishing my wellness. The network helped me create a habit of asking for what I wanted and demanding what I needed. Witnessing others gracefully master the art of saying "no" helped me to learn to do so as well so I have energy to focus on what is important to me.

Finding your scholarly voice means being willing to follow your mind as it wanders. Again, the creative, improvisational way of thinking can replace the pressure to "produce" publications and replace it with curiosity and wonder that makes writing a form of exploration and adventure.

After examining mental health history, I expanded my exploration of wellness studies and turned to the library of Black women's life writing with new questions. Two of the inquiries that I pursued were about Black women's wine history and Black women's tea history. Though different, each topic expanded my understanding of mental health and healing traditions. And the research—learning about tea and wine history—was exceptionally fun. The excerpts below offer clear examples of the limitless possibilities you can create in your personal practice. Finding your voice means claiming your ability to chart your own research agenda and explore topics, no matter how far from the mainstream they seem.

"Mother Vines" and "Take No Tea for the Fever," two journal articles that are the mustard seeds of current book projects, examine the rich history of Black women's diverse global wine tastes and tea culture. Over 250 Black women's memoirs mention wine and reveal a deeply rooted tradition of enjoyment absent from discussions in the mainstream wine world. In this project, based on a series of lectures, I explore Black women's international winemaking, drinking, and sharing, unpacking these themes in my article for *Phylon* journal (2022).

My voice amplifies a chorus of Black women's historical narratives. I have found satisfaction in creating and surveying a large dataset of memoirs. This method of mass content analysis shows both nuances of how individual express health strategies and also points to larger traditions across the African diaspora. A survey approach to narratives allowed me to identify unique experiences in Black women's wine culture that would later inform how I approached a similar query into tea traditions and wellness in memoirs.

The study of wine led me to the study of tea. Over time, your work might begin to develop a specific pattern. This does not have to be prescriptive but can be an opportunity to dig deeper into parts of a subject only mentioned at a surface level in other works. Though I diverted through wine to get to tea, fortuitously, tea returned me to my study of yoga. In Annie Lee's art that graces the cover of *Black Women's Yoga History*, the woman featured in the painting is meditating or praying, and a cup of tea sits on the table next to her.

As my work on healing traditions progressed, it has occurred to me that I continue to ask questions about how to locate and use tools for health and wellness. The study of memoirs and the analysis of yoga and tea answer questions about Black women's humanity and healing that I sought decades ago when I entered college. The excerpt below shares basic ideas of my research on tea and wellness.

The full-length monograph about tea will take me several years to complete, as I am still in the research phase and have plans to travel in the upcoming years. In the meantime, I published a scholarly article (also in the *Phylon* journal, as a follow-up to the wine study). I also worked with an artist and a sociologist to self-publish an illustrated book, *Africana Tea: A Global History of Tea and Black Women's Health* (Balboa, 2023). The excerpts show the flexibility of writing wellness and the creative possibilities available when you expand the idea of what "scholarship" can do.

"Mother Vines: A History of Black Women and Wine" (*Phylon* Journal, 2022)

Black women's wine stories expand worldwide appreciation for this ancient beverage and unearth deeper roots of the relationship between race, class, gender, and drinking. Memoirs show that palm, plum, banana, blackberry, orange, muscadine, and honey wine are as present in Black women's lives as champagne, cognac, or cabernet, and their tastes also include sangria, sake, and slivovitz. Memoirs are narrative "mother vines" that guide readers through Black women's complex tasting experiences, spanning four centuries, forty wine types, thirty countries, and fifteen states in the US.

In Mother Vines, Evans samples twelve narratives, including the communion diary of Ursula de Jesús, a seventeenth-century Afro-Peruvian holy woman; chef Edna Lewis's recipes for blackberry and plum wine; singer Natalie Cole's warnings about addiction; centenarian athlete Ida Keeling's daily shot of Hennessey or port wine as a secret to longevity; and Grace Jones's devotion to French red, white, and champagne.

This history expands the cultural conception of drinking and renders Black women oenophiles (wine lovers) visible—in the past and today. This study also lays groundwork for future social science and humanities research.[15]

"'Take No Tea for the Fever': Tea in Black Women's Mental Health History and Traditions of Self-Care as Resistance" (Phylon Journal, 2023)

Africana Tea: A Global History of Tea and Black Women's Health (Balboa, 2024)

Memoirs in *Africana Tea* introduce over 100 types of tea, tasted in over 40 countries and 30 states in the US. This book is a visual representation, inspired by W. E. B. Du Bois's "data infographics," of an extensive set of narratives. This study represents a mosaic of sources. Some Black women's narratives include references to enjoying tea in the Asian tradition. Educator Dr. Anna Julia Cooper was introduced to oolong in a weekly community gathering in Washington, DC; author Alice Walker learned to manage caffeine in Chinese green tea; and Jan Willis visited chai stalls in India as she trained in the Buddhist tradition. From hibiscus in Egypt and Jamaica to black tea in Kenya, sassafras or orange pekoe iced tea in the US South, and aromatic herbal teas of California, Black women's wellness is steeped in tea history.

Inspired by Byllye Avery and the National Black Women's Health Project, *Africana Tea* advances a discussion of holistic history. Specifically, I build on my research about stress management strategies in *Yoga History* to define Black women's tea history and six types of health: physical, mental, spiritual, social, economic, and political. The goal of the project is *not* to make health claims about tea but rather to document how Black women's tea stories and socialization can inform our collective self-care strategies.

As a follow up to the two journal articles, I have published an illustrated tea table book. *Africana Tea* is a creative project that catalogs 320 narratives about Black women's diverse experiences with tea as a tool for health, healing, and wellness. *Africana Tea* reveals the roots of Black women's international tea culture. This book traces historical, geographic, and educational traditions of collective care and offers a tea tasting journal for self-care.

∽

A research topic that at first seems farfetched, obscure, or ridiculous may delight you, especially when you build a community with others. As you begin to solidify your publishing plans, ideas may arise that seem tangential. Make note and store these snippets in a place that will allow you to return to them later. Some pages that end up on the cutting-room floor may be the missing puzzle piece to a picture that holds great joy for you years down the road. That said, feel free to privilege the topics that bring you joy or healing now if only a little bit—especially if you are doing work that describes in detail the pain of oppression, genocide, or hatred. While tea may seem like a simplistic topic, memoirs deepen understanding of historical issues like colonialism, labor and plantation politics, fertility control and reproductive rights, political organizing, social justice movements, and other areas of interest beyond frivolity.

I sometimes lie to myself and pretend I'm not afraid of being laughed out of conference rooms because I write about tea and inner peace. But if that happens, it just means I need to find other rooms. Embrace your weird creative self and convert the laughter of others into fuel for your resolve to write your way—regardless.

You need to feed your spirit to keep doing difficult work. Even the work that seems pleasing and easy on the surface will require mindful checking in with your spirit to fully realize the potential of your book project. Even more so, research topics like enslavement and other pervasive oppressions will require diligence to periodically relieve pressure from exposure to generational trauma and intense suffering. The requirement for balance can be seen in the growth of studies about joy that are matching the focus on trauma.

Make Time to Think: Create Space to Listen to Yourself

Time is often identified as a common stressor for academics whose job it is to produce but whose profession seems to make that production impossible. The internet is a time thief. One does not *find* time to write—one has to *make* time. Given my longtime administrative service, I have most often had to write in small snatches of time between meetings, course preparation, grading papers, and during downtime while preparing for other tasks. I have had to snatch time between personal illness, family caretaking, political threat, and global crises. I make time to write because I value my profession as a writer, and I honor my commitment to the craft of writing. For me, writing is resistance. Through writing, I rebel against the forces that conspire to keep me silent, that try to keep me too busy to critique policies (or people), or that demand all of my energy so that I cannot effectively organize against oppressive systems.

Time management is essential. Stephen Covey, author of the longtime best seller *Seven Habits of Highly Effective People*, describes "big rocks" as an impactful organizational concept of time management. The exercise asks participants to place large rocks, pebbles, sand, and water into a jar. Fitting everything into one space depends on the order. Unless the items are placed in the jar from large (rocks) to small (water), they will not all fit. The exercise, oft repeated at leadership trainings and business retreats, makes plain the need to assess the scale of different tasks in order to fit them all into your life.

In writing and publishing, you must name important tasks and complete them first, then get to minutia. I prioritize large tasks, like creating or editing a proposal draft, reading (or rereading) a source that is central to my argument, or addressing issues raised in reader reports. Once each task of a phase of writing or publication is completed, I then tackle smaller, celebratory tasks like arranging a book talk or conference panel. Don't put the cart before the horse—if you don't map your priorities, you might unnecessarily stress yourself out by working on small things before it is time. Map out a sense of all tasks ahead of you, then make a plan according to your personal style and professional goals. Of course, processes are not always linear, so you have to multitask, especially if juggling multiple projects at once, but make small items wait.

Writing is an opportunity to share a message with your peers, to shape your academic discipline, and to contribute to the knowledge bases of future and other worlds. As an author, you must decide on the tone and language most appropriate for the message you want to convey. Make purposeful decisions about word choice and style of prose because they can impact how your message is received and by whom. Take time to consider the meaning of your title, subtitle, chapter headings, and other ways to underscore the big picture you want to share. Humane academic scholarship requires that writers consider and express their positionality. Though there is a range of ways you can offer reflexivity statements and acknowledge your position, it is not advisable to pretend your work is free of bias or subjectivity.

Consider the goals for your book and anticipate how the book might carry your message to audiences you did not initially imagine. Use artwork, music, and other creative sources to help sharpen your message. For example, deciding on cover art to recommend to the press can sharpen your ideas of what you want to convey in writing. Even if that image does not end up on the actual book cover, art used for visual presentation can help you clarify and more fully communicate the meaning of your message.

When you are making choices about your personal style, think of yourself as a singer or musician. Jazz, hip-hop, country, and rock and roll all have different norms. Your voice can be a blend of genres, but you should be mindful of the sound of your writing voice so you can demonstrate the most range while maintaining consistency for your readers. Regardless of your chosen genre, it will take time to tune and refine your sound. Once you have found your voice, don't be afraid to experiment with different genres to learn how you might sound in alternate arenas or with unfamiliar audiences.

I'll pause here to offer one small practical piece of advice that might spare you unimaginable frustration: save your written work early and often—and save often in multiple places. Specifically, save several versions of old drafts in a folder. You may choose to delete something that you want to recover later. Surely, you have heard about (or experienced) a nightmare scenario of losing a whole manuscript due to a technical glitch, theft, fire, or leaving your most recent copy in a hotel, coffee shop, or airport. To avoid the crisis of writing loss, save your work every few minutes and after every section of writing or editing, save a copy of the updated document to the cloud. Do NOT write in the cloud but save drafts to your cloud account after each hour or so (I use Dropbox). At the end of each day or so, email yourself a copy of the updated document so you have two backup locations of the full draft. If you email yourself a copy—double-check the email address before sending (yes, every time) so you don't share your manuscript with a random person. Normalizing this habit of cataloging your work means that even if something happens and you lose a part of your updates, you won't lose a significant amount of work.

Understand that you will experience numerous stressors along the way, but your ability to identify any negative feelings about writing will work to your advantage as you make your way along the path to publication. Finding your voice will mean facing your fears and challenging the prevailing normalization of stress in the academy. It will not be easy because much of the culture of higher education operates to silence or mute voices that are unconventional and loud or that illuminate the merits of changing the status quo.

First things must come first—especially rest, reflection, and listening to your inner voice—or else not everything will fit in the space and time allotted. When properly prioritized, you can fit most tasks into your jar. Make the things you care about most "big rocks" and you will get them done. Build in a ten-minute nap, extra-long shower, short walk, or cup of tea before writing and the jar will expand to accommodate what you deem to be essential.

Maxi Priest released "Wild World" in 1987, the year I graduated high school. It was one of my favorite songs from that year because I had survived the first year on my own in the wild world. Academe is wild. Sometimes savage. Sometimes the wild west. Sometimes people be wildin' out. I connected to the soothing lyrics of Maxi Priest and, fortunately, new artists have emerged to carry the torch of self-care in their songs, such as Mayah Dyson, a Berklee College of Music graduate who began as a backup singer for India Arie. Dyson's EP *Evolution* is steeped in the ethos of wellness. In her song "Elevation," she sings that she does not want to elevate others at her own expense because "I know what's best for me." Dyson's title track projects a message of balance that has been embraced by a new generation of professional women who are not willing to sacrifice their soul for fame or "success." The cost of stress is too high and the payout—more stress—is simply not worth it.

Reflection Questions

Question 9: What was your earliest piece of academic writing? How did it impact your research trajectory? What song or poem best characterizes messages conveyed in your writing?

Question 10: How would you describe the tone of your voice? What is your message? What lies have you told yourself during the writing process?

Question 11: How do you practice mindfulness and compassion? How do you declutter your mind? What are your barriers to mindful work? How will you manage your time to get more rest (even a little bit)? Can you manage your space to ensure at least five minutes a day to sit with yourself?

Practical Tasks

- Name two sources of your stress and name a longtime wellness practice. Create a five-minute daily practice to address stress and sustain it for one week. Cite a source that takes your mindfulness practice to the next level.

- Arrange your writing to preserve it for posterity. Consider keeping a journal and, perhaps, writing a memoir.

- Organize a writing calendar. List regular activities and block out "focus time" (FT)—at least one hour every day for six days per week. Increase the amount of time and schedule around that time. Focus for at least one hour per day: fifteen minutes breathing and forty-five minutes writing. "Pay yourself first."

- Discuss your questions with a mentor or colleague.

- Share answers to questions with a next-generation scholar. Share your mindfulness practice with a friend or family member.

4

Argument

Professional Practice

Black feminist writing is a referential practice. Feminist knowledge is only recognizable in the aggregate—it is a collective meaning making project. Understanding higher education history, intellectual history, and disciplinary evolution are necessary first steps before you can claim to make an intervention. As you present the argument for your book, you must demonstrate how your professional contributions advance the field, challenge problematic traditions, resist pervasive habits (like egotism, underdevelopment, or plagiarism). You must make a convincing argument for how your work can nurture the growth of new areas of study. Academic writing must cite existing research in addition to adding your original perspective.

Literature reviews are not perfunctory. To argue that you are contributing to your academic discipline or to the broader knowledge base on a topic, you have to demonstrate that you are familiar with existing publications, theories, methods, and arguments. That said, you must do more than offer a summary of what others have written. In addition to developing your own style and voice, you must make a unique argument. The question your research answers should be relevant and compelling. Your thesis statement for a scholarly book should be clear and identifiable. There is a reason why peer review is an essential element of academic writing: anyone can offer an opinion, but only those in your field are best equipped to assess your contribution.

What is your main point? What is your big idea? What are you saying that others have not said before? As you can see, my main idea for this manuscript is "academic writing is a practice." Many other writers in various genres have acknowledged this. However, I ground the work of writing in Black feminist wellness practices to perceptibly expand current offerings. Further, I have presented several factors to develop this idea into a unique, multilayered approach, which then makes the thesis worthy of a full manuscript. Specifically, I combine a survey of popular writing guides, map dimensions of scholarly writing, demystify publishing, incorporate my own contributions, and demonstrate relevance to my fields and profession to generate new knowledge for my particular audience.

The question of writing for a specific audience is up for debate; while focusing on an imagined community is fine, you also have to anticipate a broader readership and address a universal group beyond your demographic, geographic location, and era. Said succinctly, your main point must relate to academic disciplines and, if Black feminist writing is central, the argument must move beyond higher education contexts and relevance.

Inventory the approaches others have taken on your topic. Then, make clear what concept, theory, data set, or method you are adding to what is already known. You could easily self-publish a book, so choosing to write an academic book should be a conscious choice, not a default activity—especially if you are fortunate enough to obtain a tenure track position. Don't solely write for tenure, write to expand your profession and improve pedagogy. Convey to your reader exactly what intervention you are making and use theory not to obscure your ideas but to explain them. In plain prose, define your substantive contribution.

My first year at St. John's College, we learned Euclidian math. The step-by-step unfolding of *Elements* problem number I. 47 "if-then" propositions that proved the Pythagorean theorem helped me better understand how to logically organize my ideas and present them in a progression toward a recognizable conclusion. Once I have the outline of minute details of my project, then I scale down to the main points and add my own special sauce to transform the practical into magical. I often explain to my students that the forty-seven steps of Euclid's proposition are like the dissertation: you have to show every step of your work. The book project is like a simplified version of the Pythagorean theorem, which reflects, simply, $a^2 + b^2 = c^2$. In the book, you strip away or condense much of the explanatory statements or citations that are required in the dissertation and give your straightforward assessment for a readership beyond your doctoral department. Before you write a book in a discipline, you have to demonstrate you've studied the discipline. Once you have shown you have the fundamentals and have been assessed by a qualified panel, you can let loose and have much more fun with the book than you did with the dissertation.

Ideally, your professional contribution will present a convincing argument, new method to gather or analyze information, useful theory, relevant means to solve a problem, or will expand the scope of interesting topics. Do not mistake writing about a topic for engaging the literature in a field. As Moya Bailey points out in *Misogynoir Transformed*, writing about Black women does not necessarily mean that you are writing in the tradition of Black feminist studies.

The comprehensive BWST history below moves readers beyond the three or four venerated scholars who are repeatedly cited. This list also challenges those who want to essentialize, romanticize, or make all Black women subjects of hero worship. Not only does quality scholarship identify the shortcomings of "uplift" traditions, but we must also parse through how each author should be identified as progressive or conservative (or mixture of both) in her respective era. We must be clear that Black feminist writing requires, at least, a progressive ethos and radical commitments; this is not always a neat way to evaluate what that means. While Condoleezza Rice is clearly identified as conservative and aligned with regressive politics, we must also interrogate the actions of beloved figures like Eartha Kitt and Tina Turner both who traveled to South Africa during apartheid with "honorary White" status. Two stellar biographies—one of Mary Seacole (by Helen Rappaport) and one of Merze Tate (by Barbara D. Savage) beautifully demonstrate how to interpret the historical record of a life in ways that acknowledge what we might consider shortcomings of character, bad decision making, or anti-feminist behavior.

As a scholar, there is a distinct probability that the way you interpret something will be wrong, incomplete, or lacking nuance. Proceed anyway knowing this will be true. Case in point, I am aware my work is limited to Anglophone narratives, painfully provincial, rooted in notions of professionalism (often the death knell of creativity or critical thought), narrowly focused on Black women, and progressive but not radical. Though I gesture toward diaspora, my efforts to date are woefully inadequate and my focus on the US limits the range of much of my work. Charisse Burden-Stelly's work on Sylvia Wynter is an example of how to write about the US in ways that genuinely tap into diasporic thought. Keeanga-Yamahtta Taylor's writing constantly calls out the shortsightedness of assuming ideological alliance based on identity. Tiffany King's work is gorgeously written, artistic, nonlinear, and fluidly moves between disciplinary, demographic, and geographic boundaries. With a deep appreciation for their scholarship, I write about Black women anyway, acknowledging my limitations but also knowing my comprehensive contributions are sound. I write and work for justice in my own way. My way is to synthesize various sources and contextualize them by framing the big picture in a way that advances Black women's studies.

Reading contemporary theorists, Black feminist scholarship in multiple disciplines, and keeping up to date with new scholarship will help you avoid some pitfalls of shallow writing, but unless you dive into intellectual history, you are almost certain to present work that can't survive in the deep end of the pool of public scrutiny.

I pause here to acknowledge what Jennifer Nash calls "the politics of reading" and "the politics of care" in *Black Feminism Reimagined: After Intersectionality* (2018). Nash rescues Black feminist scholars from what she names "intersectionality wars" and recenters Black feminism. Instead of glomming on to one theory or one set of thinkers, presenting your case as a reflection of the kaleidoscope of Black thinkers will position you to say something more informed, complex, and unique. It is essential that we become intimately familiar with foundational work of a wide swath of Black women writers. I resist the simplistic idea of creating a cannon. The timeline below traces the vast ground we must begin to collectively cultivate if we are to truly see the forest and not just one or two trees.[1]

This Is No Small Cannon:
An Intellectual History of Black Women's Studies

> African American women have been passionate about education and consummate institution builders for over a century both here and elsewhere. Despite racist and sexist treatment in a variety of institutional contexts, they have continued to struggle for equal access, fair treatment, and images of themselves within the academy.
>
> —Beverly Guy-Sheftall, *Words of Fire* (1995)[2]

It is easy to fetishize wellness and deify Black women writers. Each of our "sheros" has flaws and artists are only human. Our favorites, like ourselves, are flawed. Although reference is a mandate, deference and reification should not be the goals of producing scholarship.

Individual people or big ideas are not enough to create conditions of change, transformation, or justice. Yet, as Sheftall makes clear, Black women have been constructing parallel and alternative educational institutions in the United States for centuries. Collectively, we solve problems and offer solutions. This chronology I created for an online resource called the *Black Women's Studies (BWST) Booklist* presents an opportunity to understand the complex tensions within a large community of Black feminists and Black women who may not identify as such. As seen below in a truncated timeline, Black women's scholar-activist narrative, literary, and creative traditions have a long, rich, and dynamic history.

1773	Phillis Wheatly, *Poems on Various Subjects, Religious and Moral*
1830s	Colored Convention Movement
1850	Lucy Stanton Sessions, LD, Oberlin College (Ladies Course)
1857	Mary Seacole, *The Wonderful Adventures of Mrs. Seacole in Many Lands*
1859	Frances E. W. Harper, "Two Offers" short story
1862	Mary Jane Patterson, BA, Oberlin College (Gentleman's Course)
1869	Fanny Jackson Coppin, Principal of Institute for Colored Youth
1873	Bennett College
1881	Spelman College
1887–88	Anna Julia Cooper and Mary Church Terrell, MA degrees
1896	National Association of Colored Women's Clubs
1908	Alpha Kappa Alpha Sorority
1913	Delta Sigma Theta Sorority
1915	Association for the Study of African American Life and History
1920	Zeta Phi Beta Sorority
1921	First three PhDs (Eva Dykes, Georgiana Simpson, Sadie Tanner Alexander)
1922	Sigma Gamma Rho Sorority
1925	Anna Julia Cooper, PhD, Sorbonne University

1931	Sadie Iola Daniel, Women Builders (Extended 2nd Edition, 1970)
1935	National Council for Negro Women; Merze Tate, Oxford University, B. Litt
1937	College Language Association
1944	Pauli Murray, Howard University Law School Degree
1950	Gwendolyn Brooks Pulitzer Prize, Annie Allen; Merze Tate, Fulbright to India
1954	Constance Baker Motley, *Brown v. Board of Education*
1957	Dr. Willa Player, Bennett College President
1957	Septima Clark, Citizenship Schools at Highlander
1960	Student Non-Violent Coordinating Committee
1965	Toni Cade Bambara begins to teach at CUNY, joined by June Jordan and Audre Lorde among others
1968	National Association of Black Social Workers; National Council for Black Studies Conference
1969	African American Women's Clergy Association
1973	National Black Feminist Organization
1974	Combahee River Collective
1975	National Council for Black Studies
1977	National Women's Conference; National Women's Studies Association; The Sisterhood writing group
1978	Association of Black Women in Higher Education
1979	Association of Black Women Historians
1981	Beverly Guy-Sheftall founded Women's Research and Resource Center, Spelman College
1982	Akasha Gloria Hull, Patricia Bell-Scott, Barbara Smith, editors, *All the Women Are White, All the Blacks Are Men, but Some of Us Are Brave: Black Women's Studies*
1982	Africana Women's Studies Program, Clark Atlanta University
1984	*Sage: A Scholarly Journal on Black Women*
1987	Dr. Johnnetta Betsch Cole, Spelman College President
1988	Temple University Africology PhD program
1991	African Women's Action for Revolutionary Exchange
1994	"Black Women in the Academy: Defending Our Name, 1894–1994," conference held at MIT

1996	University of Massachusetts—Amherst PhD program
1997	*Meridians: Feminism, Race, and Transnationalism Journal,* Smith College
2000	The Association for the Study of the Worldwide African Diaspora
2004	Africana Women's Studies Program, Bennett College
2010	Crunk Feminist Collective
2012	*Palimpsest: A Journal on Women, Gender, and the Black International*
2014	African American Intellectual History Society
2015	Black Feminist Think Tank
2016	#CiteASista; Irma McClaurin Black Feminist Archive at University of Massachusetts, Amherst
2017	#CiteBlackWomen
2018	Black Women's Studies Association
2018	Fiftieth anniversaries of Black Studies and Women's Studies[3]

It is easy to claim that you are Black feminist writer. But intellectual wellness requires historically informed rigor. We cannot be dependent on others to set the agenda for the study of Black history or Black women's lives. Black feminist academic writing must consider the totality of educational attainment, leadership, publishing, and inclusive community development beyond the low standards often set by colleagues.

The years 2018 and 2019 marked the fiftieth anniversaries for several Black studies departments in the United States. Similarly, many of the above institutions and organizations are gearing up for fiftieth-anniversary celebrations, and in the next few decades, commemorations will continue to allow scholars to reflect on professional gains and come to terms with losses. Black Women's Studies began as a formal academic discipline in the 1970s, at the intersection of these two academic movements, Black studies (BST) and women's studies (WST).

As students integrated into campus spaces, Black students also demanded integration into the curriculum. When Black women scholars began to earn graduate degrees and enter the professoriate in the late 1970s and early 1980s, an explosion of Black women's scholarship emerged, enabling collectives to grow into associations and professional organizations of scholars committed to critical race and gender studies in both disciplinary and interdisciplinary ways.

In 2019, I created the *Black Women's Studies (BWST) Booklist* as an online resource. The *BWST Booklist* connects foundational texts of critical race and gender scholarship to newer publications. Beyond a "generative" project, the *BWST Booklist* identifies past, present, and forthcoming works to create a robust and *regenerative* discussion. In short, this comprehensive bibliography identifies long-term trends and places recent contributions in historical context. This approach enables more clarity in the formal study of Black women's theories, identities, academic disciplines, activist work, and geographic locations.[4]

The *BWST Booklist* follows several traditions of scholars who have defined and redefined this field of study with purposeful attention to geographies, disciplinary trends, and emergent themes in research. By collecting over 1,400 book publications and organizing them thematically, this comprehensive bibliography clarifies past, present, and forthcoming areas of research in a dynamic field. The *BWST Booklist* is useful as a guide for research citation and course instruction, as well as for advising undergraduates or graduate projects, theses, dissertations, and exams. For example, the five historical memoirs that I selected to pair with the themes in this work can be connected to a keyword search in the *BWST Booklist*.

At its core, Black Women's Studies is interdisciplinary. In the guide *Interdisciplinary Research: Process and Theory*, Allen Repko describes how to combine academic disciplines to answer large problems: "Interdisciplinary studies is a process of answering a question, solving a problem, or addressing a topic that is too broad or complex to be dealt with adequately by a single discipline, and draws on the disciplines with the goal of integrating their insights to construct a more comprehensive understanding." The value of interdisciplinary studies lies in the ability to draw upon the strengths of traditional academic disciplines to consider multidimensional aspects of a research question. For example, in the area of critical legal theory, Kimberlé Crenshaw draws on many aspects of Black women's history and literature to develop her interdisciplinary study of intersectionality in her much-cited article in the *Stanford Law Journal*.[5]

The *BWST Booklist* served as a library from which I chose a lion's share of the citations that appear throughout this book. The *BWST Booklist* fueled how I shaped this work and contextualized my arguments, offering a roadmap for scholars to facilitate more fruitful, deliberate, and informed discussions. Yet this is just one of many source types. *Toward an Intellectual History of Black Women* (2015), edited by Mia Bay, Farah Griffin, Martha

Jones, and Barbara Savage, has expanded discussions of race, gender, and ideas. Significantly, scholars continue to also underscore that intellectual history is not confined to academic institutions or formal publications.

Since the early BWST classes in the 1970s, there have been several continuities, changes, and expansions within the field. Notable examples of evolution include increased global and diasporic awareness in the curriculum and in a growing interest of international students. Also, queer and transgender studies have started to become as central to BWST departmental offerings as feminism—though not without some resistance. New directions include formalizing the study of intellectual history, inclusive of but beyond the "feminism" in Black feminist thought. Each of these areas of inquiry has plenty of room for expansion, but we cannot expand if we have not clearly identified the existing boundaries.

In 1981, Beverly Guy-Sheftall founded the Women's Research and Resource Center, and Spelman College named her as Anna Julia Cooper Professor of Women's Studies and English and head of the center. This institution began a tradition of holding benchmark gatherings where Black women scholar-activists could discuss a range of topics including arts, health, and politics. The next year, Akasha (Gloria T.) Hull, Patricia Bell Scott, and Barbara Smith published *All the Women Are White, All the Blacks Are Men, but Some of Us Are Brave: Black Women's Studies* (1982), the first comprehensive anthology of Black Women's Studies. *But Some of Us Are Brave* contained six main sections: feminism, racism, social science, health, literature, and a bibliography of history, poetry, novels, playwrights, composers, and material culture. Within this text, the authors explored the meaning of sisterhood, the Combahee River Collective statement, music, the Black church, racism, literary traditions, and how to research and teach about Black women.

The growing development of BWST since the 1980s has been another phase of inspiration. In the final section of *But Some of Us Are Brave*, the course content at several institutions reflects what is still the case: BWST courses can be found in Black studies, women's studies, and traditional academic departments. Classes in the 1970s and 1980s were held at institutions including San Jose State University (Bettina Aptheker, Women's Studies), Wellesley College (Marsha Darling, Black Studies), University of Maryland (Sharon Harley, Afro-American Studies), University of Massachusetts Amherst (Sonia Sanchez, Black Studies), University of Massachusetts Boston (Barbara Smith, Women's Studies; Alice Walker, Afro-American Studies), Morgan State University (Rosalyn Terborg-Penn,

History), University of California, Berkeley (Barbara Christian, Afro-American Studies/Women's Studies), and University of Delaware (Akasha Gloria T. Hull, English).

When womanist scholars began to gather in Atlanta to begin the first program in Africana Women's Studies in 1982—the same year *But Some of Us Are Brave* was published—they created four volumes of resources. Topics in *The Atlanta University Africana Women's Center* series (1985) include course syllabi, course bibliographies, cross-cultural bibliographies, and Africana women's studies in the United States. The African continental and diasporic focus in some areas of BWST can be traced to its origins, with political scientist Shelby Lewis, the founding director of Clark Atlanta University's Africana Women's Studies (AWS) program, who worked as a Fulbright scholar in Uganda. Patricia Hill Collins, who was mentored by the foundational feminist, spiritual, and legal scholar Pauli Murray while at Brandeis, crafted a sociological tome, *Black Feminist Thought*, that expanded on the sociological tradition founded by Du Bois at Atlanta University. Collins crafted a focus on intellectual history in ways that would shape multiple fields for generations.

Milestones of the 1990s and the early twentieth century include landmark gatherings like the 1994 conference at Massachusetts Institute of Technology (MIT), "Black Women in the Academy: Defending Our Name, 1894–1994," as well as the establishment of several academic journals dedicated to Africana women's research. University of Maryland established an undergraduate minor in Black Women's Studies and several research centers were founded to offer support and critical collections for concentrated research, from the Black Women Oral History Project at Harvard University's Radcliffe Institute to the Black Feminist Theory Project at Pembroke Center at Brown University, joining HBCUs like Howard University's Moorland Spingarn Research Center and the New York Public Library's Schomburg Center for Research in Black Culture.

In addition to *But Some of Us Are Brave* and *Soul Talk*, major works of Black Women's Studies include many books that are either anthologies or surveys of the broad swath of Black women writers. Benchmark books include *When and Where I Enter* by Paula Giddings and *Words of Fire* by Beverly Guy-Sheftall, but the BWST library is ever-expanding.

The Black Feminist Think Tank, founded by Sherie M. Randolph and Erica R. Edwards, along with support of Beverly Guy-Sheftall, provides an example of a contemporary collective that centers rigor and communal support. Randolph states the origin and goals of the project: "From March 20–21, 2015, hundreds gathered at the University of Michigan,

Ann Arbor, to examine black feminism as an intellectual and political practice and to chart a way forward. We assembled as the Black Feminist Think Tank with the express purpose of examining how black feminism and women of color feminism have deepened our understanding of the multiple systems of stratification in the United States and abroad." Among the symposia, writing retreats and other "mischief," Randolph suggests the group is working on a book project. Their ever-expanding circle of collaboration reflects the tradition of intellectual organizing at the roots of BWST as well as the critical published work like Randolph's *Florynce "Flo" Kennedy: The Life of a Black Feminist Radical* (2018) and Edwards's *The Other Side of Terror: Black women and the Culture of U.S. Empire* (2021) that constitutes the *Black Women's Studies Booklist*.[6]

Today, formal training for Black studies and women's studies degrees, minors, and certificates has bolstered graduate and especially undergraduate course development. A cursory search for online syllabi reveals courses at institutions like Brandeis, Gonzaga, North Carolina State, and Purdue. Yet, there are gaping holes in certain departments, where few classes are offered and too few BWST-trained faculty are hired. Given the constant attacks on the field, this will remain a challenge. Further, there is no discernible parity of content in course offerings; some classes incorporate foundational journal articles from *Signs*, *Black Scholar*, and *NWSA Journal*, but some do not. Some include LGBTQIA+ reading, some do not. Most assign *Black Feminist Thought* as required reading, yet too few syllabi mention womanism at all. While there should be no effort to create an immovable "canon" for Black Women's Studies, the curricular choices made must be done with a deliberate acknowledgment of the texts and contexts of the field and with a mindful acknowledgment of how a range of departments operate. Since the 1980s and 1990s, several degree programs signal the continued growth and institutionalization of the field despite efforts to stifle this important area of study.

In my first faculty appointment as assistant professor, I published a book—my tenure book—to reshape the field that had shaped me. In *Black Women in the Ivory Tower*, I offered the first comprehensive investigation of Black women's educational and intellectual history. The chronology earlier in this chapter demonstrates how I understood myself as a small part of a much bigger picture. Still, that book remains "a benchmark," as Professor Darlene Clark Hine herself intimated at the "Black Women in the Ivory Tower: Research and Praxis" conference at Rutgers University in 2009. Our attention to BWST must necessarily be placed in larger academic and disciplinary contexts as well.[7]

BLACK WOMEN IN THE IVORY TOWER: FOUNDATIONS
OF AN INTERDISCIPLINE

While the undergraduate degree was a product of England, the doctorate was German by design. In 1810, Johann Fichte established the first doctoral program at the University of Berlin. The University of Gottingen awarded the first Doctor of Philosophy in 1817 to Edward Everett. Yale awarded the first three American PhDs in 1861, and the first African American man to earn the doctorate, Patrick Healy, did so abroad in Louvain, Belgium, in 1865. Edward Bouchet was the first African American male to earn a doctorate stateside, from Yale in 1876, and, in 1877, Boston University awarded the degree to Helen Magill White. The first American White woman to earn the doctorate abroad, Rowena Mann, did so in 1904, from the University of Jena. Learning this trajectory helped me to understand my own place in the timeline. It also helped me complete my PhD with more confidence than I had when I started.[8] One of the most effective ways I reduced my stress while writing my dissertation was to study the history of Black women doctoral scholars. I learned what a dissertation was from an insider's perspective. The first three black women to earn doctoral degrees all did so in 1921. Their fields varied—English philology, German, and economics—but their findings all exemplified the complex negotiations of their identities as both Black women and scholars. Early Black women doctoral candidates injected their cultural mores into disciplinary epistemology and contributed sophisticated, practical knowledge.

Before 1954, the majority of women pursuing doctorates (what Anna Julia Cooper called the "third step") did so in education. This is not surprising, but bolsters appreciation that we are beneficiaries of a long line of academic women who value education. Here is a list of degrees granted to Black women before national mandate for desegregation in 1954:

Education: 17
Languages: 12
Social science: 6
Psychology: 3
Biology: 3
Home economics: 2
Music education: 1
Library science: 1
Geology: 1

It is interesting, then, that none of the three scholars in 1921 earned their degrees in education. This was because the field of education was in its early stages of development: Harvard granted the nation's first PhD in education in 1920.

These first three Black women doctorates—Eva B. Dykes, Georgiana R. Simpson, and Sadie T. Mossell Alexander—wrote dissertations that varied greatly in discipline, length, content, and structure. Despite the multitude of challenges, there were over sixty doctoral degrees awarded to Black women between 1921 and 1954. Before *Brown v. Board of Education*, Black women earned their doctorates in English, dental surgery, education, psychology, nutrition, history, library science, zoology, anatomy, government and international relations, geology, theater, chemistry, mathematics, and musicology. These accomplishments were astounding considering the existing barriers for Black women scholars. Yet, the vast array of fields in which they distinguished themselves shows their wide range of interests, and their intellectual abilities traversed the academic map. Remembering intellectual ancestors means investigating and citing these and other historical scholars to better situate your work.[9]

It is also important to place professional university publishing in historical context. Within institutions, departmental specializations created professional organizations, which then established stylized guidelines for publication. The American Philological Association, founded in 1869, was the first such modern organization, followed by others like the Modern Language Association (1883), the American Historical Association (1884), and the American Economic Association (1885). Each disciplinary faction sought to "prove" its academic worth when placed against other fields, but all fields subscribed to the myth of Black inferiority. Racists in the humanities claimed superiority based on dichotomies of "civilization" and "primitiveness," concluding that African Americans were not cultured enough to understand, interpret, or produce great art. The incorporation of statistical and other quantitative methods used "science" to make race calculable and to make claims of white supremacy numerically and "logically." While "publish or perish" became the measure of academic worth, the ability to publish was strictly regulated by what the insiders of these racist, sexist, and classist organizations deemed worthy to print. Medical historian Deirdre Cooper Owens clearly shows the deadly detriment to Black women in fields like gynecology and the murder-for-profit organization that higher education institutions often prop up.[10]

African American women educators in the nineteenth and twentieth centuries produced valuable ideas about education, but because they were barred from the upper echelons of higher education, membership in professional societies, and publishing houses, their ideas were not widely utilized. Even when mainstream academics acknowledged Black women's ideas as interesting, their work failed the "rigor" test of objectivity, and they were seen mainly as "teachers," which was considered less valuable than "researchers." As Black feminist writers, the old stereotypes remain; use lessons from past scholars to remove barriers to completing your work.

One of the earliest publishing interventions by Black women was *Women Builders* by Sadie Iola Daniel. Originally published in 1931 with support from Dr. Carter G. Woodson and the Association for the Study of Negro Life and History, it featured seven biographies: Lucy Craft Laney, Maggie Lena Walker, Janie Porter Barrett, Nannie Hellen Burroughs, Charlotte Hawkins Brown, Jane Edna Hunter, and Mary McCleod Bethune. Expanded in a second edition as a project funded by a 1969 grant from the Alpha Kappa Alpha Sorority, the expanded 1970 edition included five additional biographies: Fanny Muriel Jackson Coppin, Mary Louise Baldwin, Harriet Ross Tubman, Ida B. Wells-Barnett, and Hallie Quinn Brown.

Despite an extensive archive to the contrary, women have often been characterized as non-intellectual beings simply by virtue of sex or gender. In their 1973 book *Complaints and Disorders: The Sexual Politics of Sickness*, Barbra Ehrenreich and Deirdre English dismantle historical pseudoscience by unpacking the racist and sexist terminology found in much of the research and publications that formed the foundations of the American medical field. Women were considered bodies without minds. The conflation of symptoms with dehumanizing diagnoses continues and is present in the victim-blaming language of survivors of all types of violence. Black women are often defined as the source of our own psychological problems, which compounds our pain. Purposefully, I choose to use *syndrome* instead of *disorder* when discussing mental health challenges to correct a shift in focus to the mainly environmental causes of trauma.[11]

Black Women's Studies is a vehicle for Black feminism and vice versa. Though feminism is a multigenerational, historical, and diverse movement it is often portrayed as anti-Black. Black feminism is community-centered and this guide builds on generations of research collectives advancing scholarship in this area. Black women's writing conveys accountability to groups beyond campus, while at the same time reflecting a commitment to transform campus spaces by celebrating Black cultural traditions. Academic writing can be a Black feminist practice.

The embodied identity that scholars of color bring to our work can sometimes serve as the calorimeter of academic freedom. Maintaining a writer's focus while navigating graduate school or a professional career as a faculty member is a uniquely stressful undertaking, regardless of identity. For scholars whose identities and research are historically and consistently under attack, stress management is a cornerstone of a healthy and sustainable publishing career.[12]

My focus on Black women in the academy provides a foil to those who like to pretend race and gender studies are new, useless, or not valid intellectual pursuits. Using your writing to challenge damaging norms in your discipline or profession is one way to sustain your motivation to keep writing despite complex barriers. Knowing that I can change and nurture minds has allowed my mind to change and grow. Active intellectual pursuit is a foundational pedagogical tenant in the tradition of progressive educators like Fanny Jackson Coppin.

LEARN: Fanny Jackson Coppin's Guide to the Ivory Tower

> I am always sorry to hear that such and such a person is going to school to be educated. This is a great mistake. If the person is to get the benefit of what we call education, he must educate himself, under the direction of the teacher. . . . Again, we want to lift education out of the slough of the passive voice. Little Mary goes to school to be educated, and her brother John goes to the high school for the same purpose. It is too often the case that the passive voice has the right of way, whereas in the very beginning we should call into active service all the faculties of mind and body.
>
> —Fanny Jackson Coppin (1913)

Argument is a critical element of active learning. Research preparation should not be reduced to a compulsory literature review or surface citation of popular texts. Engaging in the professional work of academic writing requires a serious consideration of the intellectual history of your field. Deep reading is active reading, moving beyond the texts that are generally assigned for graduate seminars or only celebrating mainstream authors.

Coppin's story helps readers appreciate active learning and the imperative to move beyond received instruction.

Fanny Jackson Coppin was born enslaved in the nation's capital to Lucy, who was also enslaved. It was rumored that Fanny's father was a white "senator from Carolina." Fanny's aunt Sarah purchased her niece's freedom at the age of thirteen or fourteen for $125. Fanny attended school in New Bedford, Massachusetts, and then in Newport, Rhode Island. At the time, the curriculum was segregated by gender. In 1860, Coppin began the "ladies' course" at Oberlin, and the following year she began the more rigorous "gentlemen's course." She graduated from Oberlin in August 1865, and she immediately began teaching at the Institute for Colored Youth (ICY) in Philadelphia. As a result of her excellence in teaching, Coppin was appointed by the Quaker Board of Managers to the position of principal, which she held from 1869 to 1902. In 1881, she married Levi Coppin, fifteen years her junior, and they were both involved in the African Methodist Episcopal (AME) Church. In 1902, the Coppins conducted missionary work in Cape Town, South Africa. Her life narrative and teaching manual *Reminiscences of School Life and Hints on Teaching* (1913) was published by her husband after her death.

Fanny Jackson Coppin documents her administration and pedagogy at ICY and includes travel diaries and biographical narratives of students. In this collection, she reveals the challenging aspects of her college years, but she also recalls her fruitful relationships in Oberlin and Philadelphia. *Reminiscences* melds genres: it is at once autobiography, memoir, textbook, and organizational history.

In the chapter "Methods of Instruction," Coppin writes: "I am always sorry to hear that such and such a person is going to school to be educated. This is a great mistake." Coppin clarifies that all education is self-education. Her philosophy of teaching predates both Carter G. Woodson's notion of "mis-education" (*Mis-Education of the Negro*,1933) and Paulo Freire's oft-cited treatise against the passive "banking method" of teaching (*Pedagogy of the Oppressed*, 1970).[13]

As a first-generation college student who attended state schools, I could not rely on inherited or intergenerational information about college education. But most of my professors were committed to my instruction, and programs like the Ronald E. McNair Scholars Program gave me enough guidance to take active learning and learning communities seriously. When I first read Coppin's story of a woman born enslaved who received exemplary education and left a legacy of instructional excellence,

I was inspired to do the same and recognized the debt I owed to previous generations of scholars who toiled under exponentially worse circumstances to make the way for me.

Sometimes, especially in elite spaces, you may be the only one or one of the few Black women or feminist scholars. In these cases, it is important to recognize scholars who have come before you as part of your mentoring network. There is a vast library of books, dissertations, theses, and journal articles by those from your community. Seek out the intellectual history of your community and let the collection of voices serve as a means to tune your voice. Historical dissertations are a way to learn about the evolution of thought in your field as well as to clearly state how you are diverging from established patterns. You might appreciate the new *tunes* you can create when you take the time to familiarize yourself with the catalog of *songs* sung before you arrived on the scene. But, like sampling music, when referencing someone else's catalog, formal recognition is required. Ancestors also remind us that one way to show gratitude is to increase access and opportunities for others.

According to Dr. Sood of *The Mayo Clinic Guide to Stress-Free Living*, gratitude is the first effective means of starting each day with a positive attitude. Remembering those who have walked the academic path before us, like Coppin, is a way to ensure that we are grounded in the profession and do not lose sight of the fact that we are not the first to struggle in these ivory tower streets. While we rightly celebrate the living legends and contemporary scholars who loom large in our universe, we cannot forget the bright stars like Coppin and the first generation of diverse college graduates in the United States and in the diaspora who shone brightly generations before our lifetime. We also cannot forget that she was committed to community education and institution building.

CREATE, 1999: Dissertating with Du Bois, or, How Does It Feel to Be a Problem?

The thinker must think for truth, not for fame.

—W. E. B. Du Bois, *The Souls of Black Folk* (1903)

In 1996, Professor Esther Terry established the PhD program in Afro-American studies at University of Massachusetts Amherst—the second approved doctoral degree in the country (after Temple University). Following Professor Terry, John H. Bracey Jr., dedicated his life and career to building and chairing the W. E. B. Du Bois Department of Afro-American Studies at the University of Massachusetts Amherst. Given the placements of doctoral graduates from this program, the Du Bois Department is one of the most impactful doctoral programs in the nation. One of the fundamental questions Dr. Du Bois posed in his groundbreaking work *The Souls of Black Folk* was "How does it feel to be a problem?"

Black Studies is a problem-solving field. One of the main issues Black Studies scholars address is dehumanization. As stated in chapter 1, too many scholars (whether from marginalized communities or not) internalize the idea that those who *have* problems (like suffering from mental health issues, surviving violence, coming from low-income backgrounds, or experiencing food or housing instability) *are* the problem. Black studies scholars and women's studies scholars can sometimes act as a conscience for academe—we detail the contours and contexts of social problems and do not assume oppressed people are the sole cause of our own oppression.

BWST is an examination of the human condition. The study of Black women is a study of human rights. I study Black women and human rights because, as a Black girl, many of my human rights were violated. I write about Black women because reading Black women gave me the tools to navigate a wild, wild world. Though not all Black women are survivors of interpersonal violence, our collective position in the world has disproportionately exposed us to human rights abuses. As an interdisciplinary program, Black Women's Studies exists for collective healing and problem-solving, not simply individual measures of success.

While writing my dissertation, I had to face learning in the relatively new fields of Black studies, women's studies, and Black Women's Studies. This meant battling self-doubt while also working to stave off critique that my area of study was not legitimate or scholarly. My dissertation was a research effort grounded in intellectual history and historical methods, yet it is not intended to be a historical monograph or strictly chronology. Rather, the dissertation was an exploration of African American women's memoirs, intended to inform current and future educational philosophies and pedagogical practices. I surveyed the writing of Frances (Fanny) Jackson Coppin (1837–1913), Anna Julia Cooper (1858–1964), Mary McLeod Bethune (1875–1955), and Septima Poinsette Clark (1898–1987) and made connections between these educators' intellectual development and their work for local, national, and international community empowerment.[14]

When I was dissertating, I was also lonely, searching for love and companionship that would not ultimately come for another decade. In Massachusetts, I tackled a monumental research topic—Black women's education history—and while I built on several generations of researchers and was the direct beneficiary of wisdom from scholars like Linda Perkins and Darlene Clark Hine, the amount of work it took to construct what eventually became my first book was ridiculous. Maddening even.

A dissertation is not a book. Although some graduate programs have students simulate a book project, revision is still required for publication. While finishing my dissertation, I became insecure and impatient, so much so that I graduated from the program in four years with a defensible dissertation, but it would take me another three years to revise the manuscript to make it comprehensive, complete, and polished enough for publication. A dissertation requires you to explain every aspect of your process, including literature review, rationale, data, methodology, and explain, in detail, to a panel of judges that you have mastered all aspects of a research process in your field. A book requires shredding the elementary aspects of your writing and stripping down your ideas to the main points that are easily consumed by a (more) general audience. There are no shortcuts to either process; completing the dissertation often takes the wind out of your sails. Completing an academic book project can be a way to reinflate your sails and chart your own course. But the book journey will still require detailed critical guidance.

Throughout my writing career, I have included personal reflections in my academic writing for two reasons: to reject those who try to gaslight me about the depth of the difficulty I have overcome and also to be transparent with others who are struggling through the writing process so they do not feel they are struggling alone. If I had the patience to dissertate one more year, the path to book publication would have been shorter. Even if you insist on charting your own course, understand that review will be a requirement for completing a book that stands the test of time.

No matter the personal affronts I've faced, reading about the history of Black women scholars helped me navigate barriers. When I gained a position of power, such readings empowered me to assist in removing barriers for those who entered spaces after me. These barriers included creating my tenure packet, dealing with student bias in evaluations and persevering through denial of needed resources for my research—including the denial of much-needed research leave. By including my own narrative,

I not only write myself into the historical record, but I also facilitate space for my students, and their students, to write their narratives well.

"Sharing our stories or consciousness-raising is an essential form of healing that dates back to the early days of the women's movement," says Byllye Avery, founder of the Black Women's Health Imperative. Inspired by Avery, the authors of *Health First!* write:

> We all have good times, and we all have problems. It's important to realize that the problems we struggle with are also the problems of many others. We are not the only ones. But there's a conspiracy of silence that often keeps us from grasping this truth and the power it can give us. . . . By exchanging experiences, problems, and solutions with one another, we come together to forge a common bond, share a common struggle, and get affirmation that we can do something to change our lives.[15]

Here, again, we understand the importance of Black studies work as a problem-solving effort. Women's spaces model the intimate role of exchange. In addition to the pressures of being a writer, being an academic adds additional complexities to the task of writing. Publishing academic books requires managing the challenges of conducting rigorous research, teaching and mentoring the next generation of scholars, and providing substantive service to campus, local, state, national, and international communities. These challenges exist in the context of managing one's personal life and operating within increasingly stressful national and international politics. And still we write.

Beyond disciplinary and professional context, I have found it helpful to better understand the learning process—specifically asking questions and problem solving—as ancient human pursuits. My questions about historical accuracy and Black women's role in epistemological world-making attracted me to the stories about the Queen of Sheba's wisdom. Research on Makeda has been included in several books about biblical references, as well as in historical and archeological accounts by James Pritchard, Ivan Van Sertima, Nicholas Clapp, and Jacob Lassner. In *Demonizing the Queen of Sheba: Boundaries of Gender and Culture in Postbiblical Judaism and Medieval Islam* (1993), Lassner traces the history of Makeda (sometimes known as Bilquis) and records how her diplomatic power became villainized as Jewish, Christian, and Islamic religious doctrine became more entrenched.[16] It is telling that, long before the marker of race became a stigma for Africans in America, there was a concerted effort to diminish and erase the histories of powerful women. Fortunately, works of scholarship like *Black Women in Antiquity* (1984) by Ivan Van Sertima have ensured continuity in the telling of Makeda's story, as well as support for recognizing the African foundations of the "dark and comely" Sheba.[17]

I am not alone in my fascination with a wise African head of state who traveled to Jerusalem to query the great King Solomon. Makeda's history predates iconic Black women leaders Harriet Tubman and Rosa Parks, but her legacy similarly extends around the globe. Several memoirs, works of fiction, and academic research projects all mention Makeda or the Queen of Sheba. Early in her entertainment career, Maya Angelou imagined herself as Cleopatra, the Queen of Sheba, and Scheherazade for feather-dance numbers. Angelou also penned poems for the picture book *Now Sheba Sings the Song* (1987). Pam Grier played a character named Sheba in one of her films. Randall Robinson wrote a novel about the Queen of Sheba reincarnated entitled *Makeda* (2011), and Nalo Hopkinson's main character in *Sister Mine* (2013) is also named Makeda. The premier African woman singer of our generation, Angelique Kidjo, recorded the *Queen of Sheba* album in 2022.[18]

In "Moving against the Grain in the Global Ivory Tower," I studied contemporary African women's dissertations. By including ancient African women's thought in the timeline of my work, I locate where women's ideas can be identified as solutions to social issues. Identifying Makeda as a philosopher (as much as Plato, Aristotle, or Socrates) makes sense to me because, as I began my journey as a professional researcher, I wanted to create a map for myself based on the educational philosophy of women who had come before.

In my dissertation and the conclusion of my first book, *Black Women in the Ivory Tower, 1850–1954: An Intellectual History* (*Ivory Tower*), I wrote, "[My goal] is to . . . demonstrate how Black women's experiences, ideas, and *practices* can inspire contemporary educators to transform the academy" (emphasis added). Although I center Black women, and scholars of color in general, my work comments on global humanistic questions that exist at the very foundation of higher education. This current book, one in a series of my higher education studies, is a loose reflection of basic philosophical explorations found in most scholarship. After all, the doctor of philosophy (PhD) usually involves academics pontificating on some aspects of ontology (being), epistemology (knowing), and axiology (doing). As a Black feminist writing, mental health and wellness is central to my educational philosophy.[19]

As I revised my dissertation to complete the *Black Women in the Ivory Tower* book project, I streamlined the work to highlight only two of the four women and clarified focus on intellectual history. I maintained the strategic subjectivity from the dissertation but placed that as a conclusion. The revision for the book project identified the historical challenges of educational attainment but foreground that Black women's educational philosophies centered on community engagement. By cleaning up the broad strokes of the dissertation, the "so what" of the book became much clearer: essentially, I argued that Black women's writing conveys a tradition that education must be applied, identifies the cultural identity and standpoint of the author, conveys a critical assessment of oppressive power structures, and carries a moral obligation to serve marginalized communities.

Though I did teach a couple of community service-learning classes in my first years as faculty, I later gravitated toward community-based research. Keeping with the major findings from the *Black Women in the Ivory Tower* book, I have written books as a way to partner with organizations like youthSpark, Oldways, Black Women's Health Imperative, and Black Women's Mental Health Institute. In addition to singled-authored monographs, publishing books with and for nonprofit agencies has given me a deep sense of fulfilment and purpose. Defining problems and solving them collectively has been engaging. Though the concept of "thought leader" has taken on a feel of public intellectual (that is often more public than intellectual), I see leaders like Coppin, Dr. Cooper, Dr. Bethune, and Clark on the same professional plane as Dr. Du Bois and they were all part of community-based networks as well.

TEACH: State Your Argument and Place Your Ideas in Context

This is the first single-authored Black feminist writing guide for academic publishing. As such, I propose an alternative to the stress-inducing process of scholarship. Given the increasing attendance of diverse and first-generation scholars, a more culturally appropriate approach to writing is needed.

When you write, formulate your argument in a way that addresses one question of significance. In other words, "Who cares?" Remember, you must demonstrate relevance to your colleagues but also make plain the interest of your argument beyond the academy. My focus on race and gender studies in general, and Black Women's Studies in particular, directly addresses contemporary policies that ban books in these areas. Your argument should be substantiated with relevant evidence, and, in your work, do not hesitate to make clear why you are the person to write your book. Trust yourself to make the right claim . . . then follow up with evidence to convince readers. While more theoretical or creative works will not make the "scholarly" framework visible, sound research will always have identifiable foundations that are discernable, even if just under the surface.

Show the reader how they gain knowledge or advantage from the research you provide. In my case, penning *Black Women in the Ivory Tower*, a comprehensive assessment of the first one hundred years of Black women in higher education, added context to contemporary experiences of alienation, marginalization, and resilience today's scholars experience. Further, as you have seen in this chapter, by illuminating Black women's intellectual history, I inform readers about how higher education is structured and offer suggestions about how not only to restructure the academy but also how to rearrange your relationship to toxic trends in higher education. Black women's educational philosophies constitute creative approaches to resist oppressive structures and point the way to more sustainable institutions.

As you unravel your argument, offer signposts for new terminology that you create or who you cite as relevant experts. For instance, Kimberlé Crenshaw's intersectionality and Moya Bailey's misogynoir are terms that are now well established in the humanities and social sciences. Much like Crenshaw and Bailey, my concept of historical wellness is beginning to inform popular conversations beyond the college classroom (for better and for worse).

Organize your argument into logical subsections. Use sections to break down separate components of your thinking, make plain the argument's significance for your discipline, and lay out the implications for other areas of scholarship. As a reasonable practice, your argument should make plain how your work sustains others. Scholarship can take many approaches: description; comparison and contrast; cause and effect; problem-solution; classification; argument; discussion; definition; and identification. Most authors combine several approaches. Even if you rearrange your final manuscript into more fluid fragments, do so with purpose. Even if your work is not linear or concretely structured (think of the various approaches to poetry), your work should have some sort of flow.

When I say you need to clarify your argument, I mean that you must situate your work in direct relation to other works in your discipline. I am not the first to study dehumanization, racism, sexism, oppression, and stress management. Distinctive ways that I demonstrate the value of ideas like historical wellness is to deconstruct the ivory tower, interrogate how knowledge has been institutionalized, and propose alternative epistemological structures.

It is crucial to understand Black women are not saviors. The historical record shows some individual Black women were petty, antagonistic, elitist, and regularly held any number of counterrevolutionary stances. Erica Edwards unpacks these nuances in *The Other Side of Terror*. Historical Black women, as is still the case, were capable of harm. Of course. However, as a group (given the proximity to children in private and public spaces), Black women educators were largely responsible for grassroots organizing that educated an entire post-slavery population of over four million people. Black women's educational philosophies and administrative histories can help those who seek to fundamentally reshape the academy in a more progressive mold. As you answer questions and complete tasks below, identify your argument and contribution to your discipline and how your work demonstrates a necessary ethic of study and reference to a broad body of extant scholarship.

Songstress Jill Scott encourages us to "Find a spot for us to spark conversation," explaining to listeners of "Long Walk" that we must listen to each other if we want a participatory and democratic learning environment. When I created a music video for *Black Women in the Ivory Tower*, Jill Scott's thoughtful poetics provided a fitting soundtrack. The trek toward justice is a never-ending one. There are many problems in education, politics, law, health, culture, and other social areas that must be addressed. Looking to scholars who have asked and answered questions for generations is the wisest place to begin our problem-solving mission.

Not all writers experience academia the same way. I have been fortunate enough to work with numerous research collectives that show nuances of intra-racial diversity (the differences between Black women scholars). I know well that Black women academics in a research circle may have some similarities, but our intellectual and experiential differences are as weighty as our likenesses. What we do have in common is the opportunity to bring our experiences to bear on changing the academy to embrace diverse intellectual traditions.

Tracing Black educational histories was a significant factor in my ability to endure administrative service for so long. When reading about racism and sexism, I learned my experiences weren't particular to me and were not only systemic but also historical. I also knew how to strategize to counteract them. It was imperative for me to dig into the history of scholarship, the history of universities, as well as the history of Black Women's Studies, to better understand the varying landscapes I faced. Knowing the history of higher education meant realizing that no one could tell me that I was an "outsider," that I did not belong, or that I was a problem to be solved. Academic writing is a way to remember that no one can tell you that either.

Reflection Questions

Question 12: When and where were your academic disciplines established? What have Black women written in dissertations about your topic?

Question 13: What are the foundations/evolutions of a major disciplinary theory? What interdisciplinary iterations have emerged over time?

Question 14: What is the problem (or question/idea) your research addresses? What argument are you contributing to advance your field? Whom do you cite as relevant comparison authors and why?

Practical Tasks

- Name three major figures in higher education history that have contributed impactful concepts. Identify three professional role models in your academic discipline and one outside of your discipline.
- Compare three academic disciplines. What are the advantages/drawbacks of their theories and methods?

- Cite foundational Black feminist research in your area (books and articles). Locate archives, newspapers, oral histories, and other resources related to your discipline.
- Discuss these chapter questions with a mentor or colleague.
- Share your chapter answers with a next-generation scholar.

5

Editing

Publishing Practice

Black feminist writing is a formal practice. Academic publishing requires a willingness to recognize contributions of others, invite critique, subdue your ego, accept guidance, and acknowledge shortcomings of your work. Part of my mission with this book is to point out how many tools you have at your disposal to tighten up your own writing. No one resource will have all the answers you need for organizing your book. More importantly, you cannot rely on other people to write your work—otherwise it is not your scholarship. Recent political trends use the charge of alleged plagiarism to attack the intellectual character of Black women. I will not dignify these orchestrated attacks here, other than to reiterate that they are fueled by hypocrisy, extraordinary scrutiny, abuse, and double standards. However, those charges of plagiarism do make it even more relevant that you write in ways that are transparent, ethical, organized, consistent, and formally vetted.

If I were to recommend any best practice, I would challenge you to do these three things: (1) read as widely as possible on your topic, (2) gather as many reading and writing guides as possible, and (3) subject yourself to as much peer mentoring and professional writing consultation as you can. These habits of self-education allow you to make informed decisions about how best to complete your project. You are in the driver's seat. While editors are in the passenger seat and writing partners or reviewers are in the back seat, only you are in charge of making your vehicle go. Don't rely on others to tell you where to go; gather information and map your own journey. Black feminist writing is neither performative nor intellectual submission. Publishing Black feminist books requires studying extant literature, contributing something fresh, and committing to endless revision to present your work in the best possible light.

Partnering with an Academic Press

As a Black feminist researcher, your methods of gathering and analyzing data should be transparent. Make your assumptions clear to the reader: Are you affirming womanism in your writing, or not? Radicalism? Anti-capitalism? Afropessimism? Afrofuturism? Intersectionality? What type of Black feminism are you asserting? If you are citing *Black Feminist Thought* or any other popular text, you must justify your use and detail why this is the most appropriate approach. With whom do you disagree and where do you diverge from those whom you recognize as models?

As you develop an outline for your book, correlate your theory, data, and methods. The content of your book can get muddled if there is not a discernible relationship between your language and style. That said, the structure you choose to present your ideas should not impede the flow of your prose nor overshadow the straightforward presentation of your message. Academic publishing at university presses provides a vast rainbow of possibilities. Though I focus on scholarly writing, it is a mistake to interpret scholarly as inaccessible, obscure, or unrelatable. One of the reasons I have maintained relationships with university presses and opted to only publish with this type of outlet (with the exception of two self-published creative projects) is that I appreciate the attention a full team of professionals pays to my manuscripts. The high bar set by academic publishers may seem like gatekeeping, and, in some instances, there are predatory, exploitative, and exclusionary organizations and staff. But that is the case in any industry. Still, it must be said that publishing with a university press has certain disadvantages, especially the length of time it can take to publish due to the many stages of the process: internal review, peer review, revising and resubmitting (most times), editorial board review, preproduction, copyediting, typesetting, and so on. Equally troubling, diversity in leadership at UPs is virtually nonexistent. Tokenism is rampant. Relationships that UPs have with authors must evolve.

I began editing the Black Women's Wellness series at SUNY Press because my own writing was heading in that direction and my editor,

Rebecca Colesworthy, actively encouraged me to expand my conversations by inviting others to write in the area of mental and holistic health. The series was conceived to invite interdisciplinary scholarship, and, to date, we have featured work in the disparate fields of history, English, psychology, public health, and political science. Beyond supporting the series, Rebecca repeatedly demonstrated an active care for my work. She gave feedback on several drafts of this present book and continues to advocate for me and all authors with whom she works. Evidence of her ethic of care can be seen in her publishing advice column for *The Chronicle of Higher Education*. She has been transparent, consistent, and patient even while insisting on standards for acceptance. She continues to hold me to standards (like submitting a book proposal for each project) and working together Rebecca and I often identify work that is not a good fit for the press or the series. Having received many rejection letters, I now understand that a "no" is not always about quality but often about fit for the objectives of the press or series. Ideally, nothing about a manuscript review should be personal (neither acceptance nor rejection) and nothing in the process should be taken personally.

Regardless of the type of publishing house you choose (university press, for-profit press, or independent press), I highly recommend that you read Laura Portwood-Stacer's *The Book Proposal Book: A Guide for Scholarly Authors*. This resource will save you so much time and effort while you figure out how you want to structure your book. Portwood-Stacer's step-by-step approach helps you to navigate the process of creating a discernable outline for your book project, reveals factors for choosing what press might be a good fit for your work, and unveils when and how to approach an editor.

As you decide on the press where you envision your work, think about your academic discipline, content, structure, and sources. Look at the website of the press to ensure it is a good fit and feel empowered to talk to editors, whether at a conference or just by reaching out via email. There are external factors and internal factors that might inform your decision-making process about the organization of your book. If you find a specific press appears frequently in your bibliography, that might be a good place to start when considering your options, as you are already engaging with the folks who are discussing the topics adjacent to your own.

Check to see if a particular press has a series that can help you think creatively about how to approach topics and develop your work in conversation with others publishing in that direction. When designing your outline, survey as many presses as possible to get a sense of the new books in your field. Your contribution may find a home at Pluto Press or Haymarket Books if you center progressive or radical foundations like Marxism or abolition, while U of North Carolina P or U of Illinois P might be a great fit for historical monographs or cultural studies. But lesser-known presses have much to offer if you look closely.

Wayne State UP has aggressively sought to build its catalog since Stephanie Williams was appointed. Williams is the first Black woman director of a university press in the country, and she is serious about supporting feminist work. In addition, there is the *Literary Conversations* series at U of Mississippi P with a stellar collection of Black women interviews, including Margaret Walker, Rita Dove, Gwendolyn Brooks, Gloria Naylor, Audre Lorde, Sonia Sanchez, and Toni Morrison. My relationships with SUNY Press, in addition to University of Florida and Wayne State University Presses as an author and as a reviewer with numerous more, has afforded me a comparative perspective and appreciation for not relying on large or popular presses as a default.

The most popular or well-known presses won't automatically be the best fit. Branch out, explore, and dig deep to locate a press that will invest in you as an active partner, regardless of how "reputable" they may be. That said if you have a more creative or nontraditional piece, explore smaller independent presses like Universal Write Publications (UWP) or The Feminist Press as well as global trade presses like Sage, Macmillan, Routledge, Harper Collins, and others. Also, check out innovative new spaces like the series *Black Lives in the Diaspora: Past / Present / Future*, a collaborative effort between Howard University and Columbia UP.

Before committing to a contract with any publisher, discuss your career goals with your mentors and your peer network to get feedback on how other folks might have fared at the press you are considering. You can also gauge how their work is received in the disciplinary spaces you want to join. Know that there are numerous people involved in the publishing process so, inevitably, you will encounter problems. Problems may include a late reader report or tracking down citations needed by a copy editor. As much as possible, shop around before signing a contract so you know what you are getting into. I will go into detail in the "tips" section later in this chapter. Most importantly, work with someone who values your work and has a clear communication style. If someone ghosts you, that is a sign . . . pay attention. But don't take a delayed answer for lack of interest. It is rare to receive a response in twenty-four hours, so breathe and check the Frequently Asked Questions (FAQ) page for clues about timeline to save yourself unnecessary stress. Know that if a press does not express interest in one month, you should move forward with those interested. Though editors are busy, they make time for what they deem priority. I have had one press express interest, but not in a timely manner, so I chose to work with someone else. Selection is a two-way street. No matter the response time for the initial inquiry, understand that publishing is not a fast process; if you are in a hurry, this is not the path for you.

As you prepare your book proposal, read books that are in the same vein as yours, especially those at a press you are considering. Read, read, read. Read books for structure as well as content. Consider how you want to organize your chapters in the book and what information will dictate the structure of each chapter. Determine how you will decide on the terms for your subheadings and measure the rationale for what data or information will guide the order in which you present your work. Play with the chapters and consider arranging details from specific to general (pyramid), general to specific ("V"), broad to narrow to broad (hourglass), or narrow-broad-narrow (diamond).

The chapters in *Black Women in the Ivory Tower* move from specific to general: from individual portraits to Black women's educational history, to Black educational history, to general education history, and, finally, to general American history. This structure can also be seen in *A Black Women's History of the United States* coedited by Daina Ramey Berry and Kali Gross.[1] Alternately, you might choose to create a layered, flowing structure for each chapter, as Farah Griffin does in her brilliant *Read until You Understand: The Profound Wisdom of Black Life and Literature*. Demonstrating a mastery of form and function, Griffin intersperses personal narrative with literary criticism to guides readers in and out of a reflective and evaluative consciousness. In this present book, each chapter is loosely structured around the parts of a tree: roots, trunk, and branches. It is fine to be creative, but it is good to be consistent. If you are focusing on a set of representative people, events, and figures, give a clear rationale for your criteria, data, and decision making.

For those not exposed to higher education at a young age, the expectations, systems, culture, protocol, and norms can be confusing. Fortunately, there are ample guides and resources to help the uninitiated navigate the lay of the land. *Skills for Scholars*, a series of books from Princeton UP, is specifically designed to help undergraduate students, graduate students,

inevitably (excruciatingly) slow and the road often rocky. The snail's pace of academic publishing is actually an advantage: when you haven't looked at a manuscript for three or six months, you see it with fresh eyes. Reviewing a draft, revision, and proof copy affords you time to not only ensure accuracy, but also to read the piece at different times to see what sticks out as enduring and what is only written for a moment. Tightening a work over the period of two years will inevitably produce a book that is more stable than one where you have only quickly reviewed in a short time span. Remember this: once it is in print, it will be there forever—you want to produce a work that lasts, so it will necessarily require much revision.

The nature of creating a scholarly monograph means that there will be dozens of rounds of editing. This means that you must make peace with the process of writing, editing, revising, and critical review. It is what it is. Before releasing a book to the public, you will most likely run through many steps, including a book draft, endless rounds of editing, and external review.

There are more than likely three types of editors that you will encounter in addition to the acquisition editor to whom you submit your work. You may choose to engage developmental editors (those who offer big picture support) and copy editors (those who ensure accuracy and identify errors) sometime before you submit your final manuscript to the press. The press will employ a proofreader for your manuscript (line editors who clean up the draft as it readies for printing) to prepare for publishing. Each step is an opportunity to clarity main points, fact check your claims, identify sources, and catch small typos. Given this level of review it is a horror show to find a typo after your book is published, but it does occasionally happen. I've found one in almost every book I've published . . . and in others' as well. Take note of major typos and, if egregious, perhaps they can be addressed in a reprint if not for the electronic version.

Amid the editing process, your work will also be submitted for internal and external review. Internal review may include an employee of the press or an editor who may be considering your work for a series. External reviewers are those who can offer an objective, informed, and (necessarily) critical assessment. You do not want someone who simply says "this is wonderful work!" External peer review is really a place to identify weak spots that, if let go, will result in humiliation or fights when the work is released to the public. Having a committed editor means they will not shield you from challenges and (sometimes) harsh suggestions for revision.

Learn to discern what is a fair question and what is intended cruelty. Not everything that hurts your feelings is actually inaccurate. Put down the reviewer report for a few days, then come back to it to separate what you will revise and what you won't. Your reply to the press requires that you address every question, it does not require that you comply with suggested edits. If you choose to not follow a recommended change, simply clarify your rationale and know you are prepared to deal with that question when it appears later after the book is released to the public.

A side note: when it comes to listing potential reviewers to submit to the press, beware of wolves in sheep's clothing. Sometimes sisters of the cap and gown are complicit in academic gatekeeping and personal vendettas. It is perfectly fine to identify people who should NOT receive your manuscript. This is an item to include on your list to bring up in your conversation with any potential editors.

Best case scenario, a Black feminist editor or someone intimately familiar with your field will shepherd your work. Given the paucity of Black women and queer folks in professional publishing, that will not likely be an option. Further, in reality, some self-identified Black feminists are not above sabotaging your work through erasure, plagiarism, or blocking your advancement or recognition. No matter. With discernment and perseverance, you can locate those who will support you despite those who will not. Ultimately, you must learn to be intellectually self-reliant. Do not rely on hook-ups—they will do a disservice to your reputation and quality of your work. It is fine to work with people you know, but let your scholarship (not your connections) be the thing that opens the door for you. As a scholar, you need to spend time exploring the deep recesses of your own mind and to develop an inner strength—to meditate and establish a conduit to your inner critic.

LEARN: Toni Morrison's Guide to Book Publishing

> It is in the interstices of recorded history that I frequently find the "nothing" or the "not enough" or the "indistinct" or "incomplete" or "discredited" or "buried" information important to me.
>
> —Toni Morrison, *The Source of Self-Regard* (2019)

Toni Morrison is one of the most recognizable names in literature. Daughter of the Midwest, she was born Chloe Anthony Wofford Morrison in

Ohio and grew to be an internationally decorated author. A graduate of Howard University and Cornell University, she worked as an editor for Random House, where she shepherded contributions by some of the most important Black novelists and public figures, including Chinua Achebe and Angela Davis. As an author, she crafted instant classics, including *Beloved*, *The Bluest Eye*, and *Sula*. She was awarded the Pulitzer Prize in 1987, the Nobel Prize in 1993, and the Presidential Medal of Freedom in 2012. Her work is fervently attacked by those hostile to critical history and culture, but it is also beloved by readers worldwide. Morrison's writing not only encourages thoughtfulness, it also demands it.

Mindfulness plays a part in Black women's narratives. Sometimes mindfulness is concentrated in the essence of Black women writers, as seen in narratives by Jan Willis. Willis is recognized as a religious leader and a leading intellectual on religious studies. She is professor emerita of religion at Wesleyan University and a visiting professor at Agnes Scott College in Decatur, Georgia. She studied Buddhism with Tibetan teachers for more than forty years and is the author of the memoir *Dreaming Me: Black, Baptist, and Buddhist: One Woman's Spiritual Journey* (2008). Willis's writing on inner peace is critical for appreciating the meditative value of practice and writing. As a professor of religion, as well as a practitioner, meditation permeates her work.[2]

Sometimes, however, mindfulness is more nuanced—perceptible but not recognized as a driving force. For example, in my interviews with Anna Julia Cooper's great nephews, they made note of how she wrote every morning in her sunroom, claiming space for an uninterrupted and meditative practice, even though she did not use the term *meditation*. Similarly, Toni Morrison's essays reveal that she also viewed writing as a form of meditation, as evidenced by the title of her final collection, *The Source of Self-Regard: Selected Essays, Speeches, and Meditations* (2019). Morrison was a contemplative writer, with a robust catalog of nonfiction and fiction, and to fully appreciate her work we have to take notice of how her practice of writing, editing, and publishing served as a form of self-care.

In the essay "On Beloved," Morrison considers an enslaved woman's notion of her own humanity and seeks to understand what, despite every message to the contrary, could warrant the enslaved woman's vigilant struggle against oppression and insistence on her own personhood. What, Morrison queries, is the source of her notion of self when everyone around her regards her as a beast? Morrison finds this source in motherhood and draws attention to the sparsity of representation of Black women and girls in the literary world:

> For example, in 1963, my first novel, *The Bluest Eye*, was a consequence of being overcome by the wholesale dismissal of a certain part of the population (to which I belonged) in history texts and literature. Of all the characters chosen for artistic examination, with empathy or contempt, vulnerable young black girls were profoundly absent. When they did appear, they were jokes or instances of pity—pity without understanding. No one it seemed missed their presence center stage and no one it seemed took them seriously except me. Now, I didn't blame literature for that. Writers write what they like and what interests them. And even African American writers (mostly men, but not all) made clear that, except as background, prepubescent black girls were unable to hold their interest or stimulate their curiosity. Nevertheless, writers' lack of curiosity was not the point. To me the enforced or chosen silence, the way history was written, controlled and shaped the national discourse.[3]

My first scholarly paper as an undergraduate was a query titled "How Solid Is the Rock?" and it was born from an unarticulated longing to see myself, a young Black woman, as a central historical figure. I've since reread that first research paper, and, while the text, tone, and depth of analysis are not tremendously sophisticated, the message erupts from the same geyser as Morrison's observation about the glaring absence of Black girl personhood in literature and history.

Writing can be a source of mental freedom. And an uncolonized mind is a powerful thing. In her thoughts on *Beloved*, Morrison observes, "Through that door [of the not-yet written] is a kind of freedom that can frighten governments, sustain others, and rid whole nations of confusion. More important, however, is that the writer who steps through that door with the language of his or her own intellect and imagination enters uncolonized territory, which she can claim as rightfully her own—for a while at least."[4] Morrison's work should encourage you to put yourself at the center of your analysis. This does not mean that your writing will be easy—quite the contrary. Morrison was an exacting editor, on her own work as well as that of others. She is a model for how to take the writing process seriously and to commit to longevity in developing a writing

reminders of male prejudice against women and white prejudice against blacks." In 2007, the reviewer tried to isolate me and my assessment of the past and present academy, indicating that I was but *one* voice and chastised the university press for not editing out the unpleasant, unfortunate, and *sad* experiences had by some Black women (note the passive voice). The implication was that my work did not meet the usual standard of merit. Typical regressive gatekeeping at its finest.

Thinking about the state of the academy and the ongoing struggle for *progressive* change in higher education, I'm learning so much from a growing number of books by, for, and about Black women (especially queer, non-binary, and trans Black women), with various feminist and womanist agendas. *Any* success that I've had in the academy is built on the foundation of Black women's intellectual guidance, specifically from the historical figures who revealed the intellectual and emotional violence of academia. Given my study, I was aware the reviewer's attacks were routine, and charges of low standards—especially for Black women scholarship—is a tradition all its own.

I concluded my Twitter reflection by insisting that, while there are no safe spaces, there are a multitude of tools left by those who came before. Further, I encouraged folks who were struggling to finish a thesis, dissertation, book, article, or any "peer reviewed" academic piece to *keep going*.

As chapter 4 emphasizes, when managing professional stress, reading past scholarship in race and gender studies can serve as a self-professed guide to help you move through and beyond the intellectual abuse and gaslighting. I am glad there is record of such a hurtful and inappropriate review of my work—from a feminist reviewer, no less. I would eventually become more involved in NWSA, the professional organization led by luminaries like Professor Guy-Sheftall, Bonnie Thornton Dill, Barbara Ransby, and Karsonya "Kaye" Wise Whitehead, who actively work to expand inclusivity in ways not available to me then. That said, Black women must also be inclusive, especially given exclusion of transgender and queer women from some mainstream discussions. The library of BWST has been useful reading material and serves as a reminder of the ongoing struggle for intellectual inclusion beyond symbolic measures.[7]

I value the amount of control I do have with my university press partners. I would have total control with self-publishing or with some trade presses (and reap much more financial gain), but my work would not be nearly as clean, complete, or compelling without a whole team of people with whom to partner in the process. As I mentioned above, the workload of production is too much for authors to take on alone and the lone scholar is not a desirable model.

Some graduate students I have encountered at conferences confide their negative experiences when encountering some senior faculty. Though I won't always make myself available, I try to be as kind as possible because I will never forget the senior scholars who were indifferent, cruel, or dismissive when I first approached them. I try to model the faculty like Sheila Flemming, Sonia Sanchez, and Beverly Guy-Sheftall, who are gracious and supportive of younger scholars even as they fiercely correct us and require our commitment to self-improvement. Some conference settings have devolved into a mean girl fight club where entry to certain circles is only granted to those who are sponsored or those willing to kill someone else in order to be admitted. This is not the way. For young scholars, refrain from seeking to affiliate yourself with a named scholar as a way to get authenticated. Only your own writing will put you—and keep you—in conversations with people you admire.

While peer review has certain drawbacks, at its best it affords the opportunity to receive anonymous or invited review from someone likely a member of your intended audience. Anonymous review requires you to respond to critique on merit while invited review affords an audience with respected colleagues and mentors. Though I have heard of some cases where anonymity was betrayed or peer reviewers conspired to hold a book back from release, most times the process takes place with people of good faith.

Peer review is the lifeblood of scholarly publication, but sometimes that review process is harmful. In a review of my first book, my heart was broken by a senior faculty member who took issue with the subjective nature of my historical assessment. Furthermore, I was dismayed to be dismissed for acknowledging the oppressive history of United States practices of colonialism and empire. Many senior scholars seem to want to make you question your own sanity. When others review your work, critique is essential. The need to overcome reactionary responses to critique requires the ability to dissociate ego from intellect and determine what is valid assessment and what is biased or baseless nit-picking.

II. Promotion to Full Professor

My productivity has been an effort to maintain my professional autonomy and mobility. Given the politics of academic promotion I have encountered, working to create a portfolio that is my own (and not owned by the institution where I am employed) has been a necessary strategy. Publishing books has been a way to maintain relative ownership of my labor.

In 2014, when I applied for promotion to full professor at my former institution, it was a devastating process. At my first institution, I earned tenure outright, and even though the environment had several deadly legacies with which to contend, I was evaluated on my record. At CAU, even though my first-level review swung unanimously in my favor, a group of senior male colleagues on a dean's subcommittee voted unanimously against my promotion. It was made clear in the letter that the vote was not based on my research record (which they admitted was exemplary) but on a vague and invisible bar that I had not done "enough" for the university. At that point, I led three academic units and carried a 3/3 teaching load. By the time of my review I had also conceived, planned, organized, and hosted the multi-year W. E. B. Du Bois Legacy Project—a year-long seminar, international conference, bust dedication, graduate course, and relaunch of the *Phylon* journal.

A vague paragraph of a "no" vote wafted into my inbox from the committee chair. I wrote a brief response to the dean and let the process play out. The burden of proof was theirs, not mine. I had heard this happened to a stellar male colleague as well, so it was more a reflection of the committee than on my portfolio. In the end, I prevailed, and my promotion was affirmed at the dean, provost, president, and board levels, of course. But the lesson of sexism in Black spaces was as cautionary as the lessons I had learned at UF about racism in White spaces. My publishing record has enabled me to choose when and where to contribute my work, and when I chose to stay or leave, I could do so on my own terms.

Academic writing can sometimes translate into professional freedom—a ticket to move places of employment at will, if needed, a ticket to state your terms and conditions at an institution if you wish to stay, or a passport to other lands beyond academe. But those who do not regularly publish may want to punish those who do in order to assert dominance. Choice: that is what academic productivity might offer. But nothing is guaranteed for scholars pushed to the edges of their disciplines. There are many choices to make as you complete and submit your manuscript. As you find your voice, clarify your argument, and organize your book to contribute to an academic catalog, you may find yourself shedding feelings of powerlessness.

Peer review and academic freedom remain under attack. Patricia Hill Collins explicitly states that "peer review" in Black women's intellectual tradition includes a broader range of assessment than a small number of professional academic "experts" in a tiny discipline. Though Black women do develop and contribute to university-level specializations, Black women outside of the ivory tower, like blues singers, service workers, family members, and community elders are also recognized as knowledge brokers. Writing in community should be interpreted in the broadest sense possible, which is often deemed counter to reification and trafficking of elite status.[8]

By embracing the practice of writing as communal care—even when writing a single-authored manuscript—authors can enjoy a more rigorous process and sometimes a more accurate and celebrated final product. That is not to say that communal writing will be easy or result in consensus. To the contrary—broadening the scope of voices that influence scholarship creates a deeper sense of the fissures between values, assumptions, positions, and conclusions. But collaborative writing also can create a deeper appreciation for learning and sharing valuable information about one's research topic.

The editor with whom I've worked with the longest, Rebecca Colesworthy, has tirelessly demonstrated her commitment to supporting, uplifting, and critiquing my work. Her advocacy for authors—whether at her press or not—is one reason I have continued to enjoy working with her. In fact, she is the one who encouraged me to establish a series and she also spent considerable time reviewing this present manuscript to make sure it was as clear as possible. In her publishing advice column featured in *The Chronicle of Higher Education*, she is adamant that accurate editorial advice can only truly be given by saying "it depends." There is no one-size-fits-all approach to book publishing and she spends time bridging the gap between authors and editors by debunking myths. Her column offers perspectives such as how to approach editors and transforming of dissertations. Her earnestness and generosity of spirit are matched by her eagle eye and frank communication style—qualities to look for when considering a publishing partner.[9]

TEACH: Dr. E's Ten Tips for Publishing

Below are my specific tips to help guide your publishing practice and enable you to better anticipate potential potholes in the road. Learning more about the process and controlling the few choices you do have can

on the university or trade press, so develop a network and ask at least three trusted colleagues to share some details about rights and royalty rates. Do not hesitate to ask many questions and have an in-depth discussion (or two) with your acquisitions editor before signing. That said, be aware that university press editors are laborers and are usually spread thin, so if you are demanding, panicky, or prone to call or email someone fifty times, research publishing contracts first then take time to create a list to organize your thoughts before reaching out. Ask about the cover, artwork, production timelines, and ask whether the cloth (hardcover), paperback, electronic, or audio version will be simultaneously or subsequently released. Before the contract is signed, ask whether a certain number of copies must be sold before royalties begin. Consider the price point you want your book to be sold at and whether this will reach your target audience. Each type of press has its own merits and drawbacks. Find out what works for you and go with that. Consult guides in this book to glean valuable information before talking with editors. Again, *The Book Proposal Book* is a good start.

5. **Prepare for Peer Review by Front-Loading Critical Self-Review**. Anonymous peer review is a blessing and a curse. It can be an assurance that someone will be quality checking your work before it is viewed by the public. It is an opportunity to save you from high-profile embarrassment due to glaring omissions or inaccuracies. At its best, peer review is a defense of your work to critical but supportive audiences. Unfortunately, some reviewers are biased, petty, self-interested, and cruel. Not everything in a review will be helpful, but you must consider everything in the peer review. One way to handle the initial shock of the very detailed reader report is to learn to closely edit your own work. Be honest with yourself about your writing weaknesses and work on them. I'm wordy. So I do a targeted review of my work to eliminate wordiness (obviously I still need to work on this). Another way to edit is to scan your work for structure. Shrink the pages on screen to a two-page

view, then review the layout of each chapter, heading, and paragraph (first and last sentences) to check for flow and transitions. Here, you can identify irrelevant pieces to cut if they do not advance your argument. Review your work several times using the targeted review approach—scan the entire document to identify and correct one type of error, then repeat with a second type of error. This way, when you get the reader reports that point out flaws, you can more easily identify and correct them without holding on to your hurt feelings. Your response to the press is your opportunity to demonstrate that you have taken the reviewers' reports seriously . . . even if you choose not to follow all advice to the letter. A good relationship with your editor can also allow an opportunity to identify the folks who should not serve as reviewers. However, the relationship with your editor should always ensure the ethical anonymity of those involved in the process. There are occasions where semi-anonymous reviews are warranted, but, otherwise, respect the need for two, if not three, masked scholarly assessments (some say "blind review," I choose less ableist language of masked or anonymous review). Your serious response to a reader report is a reasonable ask in return for a press's investment in publication. That said, there are horrible practices where presses fail to maintain best practices (see the Cascade Books *Bad and Boujee* example in chapter 6) or where they have not acted in the best interest of authors. Quality peer review can help to keep the project on track, identify issues before publication, and stave off unnecessary public scrutiny. Prepare yourself for the process by reviewing your own work with clear-eyed assessment. Consider having the manuscript professionally reviewed several times by qualified colleagues and professionally edited before submitting to the press. Even though this book was written as a "trade" book, the SUNY acquisitions editor facilitated review by anonymous peers. I also took the step to work with a developmental editor in addition to my regular copyediting routine. Each of these engagements helped calm my mind. Perhaps when this book appears, it won't be perfect, but it will have been vetted.[10]

6. **Manage Anxiety and Control Impatience**. Toni Cade Bambara took a year to write *The Salt Eaters*. Zora Neale Hurston finished *Their Eyes Were Watching God* in seven weeks. It took Margaret Walker thirty years to publish *Jubilee*. Each is a masterpiece. Academic writing is quite a different genre than fiction, but these novelists exemplify the research necessary to produce work that will stand the test of time. Writing will happen at your own pace. Publishing timelines will happen at the pace of the press, so you might ask your acquisition editor the average or expected production time after you submit the final draft. The process of publishing an academic book (from submission to release) can take about two years, but it is sometimes longer. The peer review process alone can stall a project: while a reasonable time may be four to six months, if a reviewer is running late (which happened universally during the global COVID-19 pandemic, for example), the review time might even take six to nine months. If those who agree to review do not come through by the deadline, finding a replacement review may add additional time. Presses have catalog seasons (usually spring and fall), wherein they prepare a whole series of books along with yours. Press editors and production staff take on the task of locating reviewers, finalizing covers and promotional copy, loading information to websites, and collating release newsletters, in addition to other tasks. Those tasks will happen on the press's schedule and not yours. Anticipate that each step of the process can take months, if not years. Do not hesitate to get clarity and confirmation, in writing, about your timeline and process. Be clear and up front if you are operating on a specific deadline to meet your professional goals. Establish patterns of open communication directly with your editor—communication should be a part of the criteria for choosing your press. You want to make sure there are no unanticipated delays, and you don't want to fall through the cracks. However, if you have confirmation that your book will be in the spring or fall catalog, do something else while you are waiting for the process to unfold. While you do want to maintain regular

and frequent communication with your editor and production team, know that no number of emails or phone calls will rush the process. The advantage of working with the right press is that there is a whole team of people working on your project. The disadvantage is that the team is also working on a dozen or more other projects for the same catalog season as well. Get updates about delays in writing.

7. **Strategically Schedule Presenting Work in Public**. Given the length of time it takes to publish a book, it is helpful to publish one or two articles beforehand as a place marker for your ideas and as a source for others to cite. Unfortunately, many folks don't think citation is important, and, inevitably, your work might be stolen and plagiarized. In some ways, you cannot control where your ideas travel when you share them. Social media is a perfect example. However, the assumption is that scholarly writing has some accountability to identify sources, so don't hesitate to present at conferences or give talks on podcasts. This is one reason I stress the importance of unique data sets—it makes it more difficult for others to copy your research when it is so clearly your defined area. Ideally, your work should be so well researched and unique that, even if others try to copy your scholarship, they cannot truly reproduce it. It helps to build a professional community who will help hold folks accountable if your work is plagiarized. But do not turn into the idea police. Sometimes people have similar ideas at the same time. Do your work and leave others alone.

8. **Place Professional Journal Reviews in Context**. My first monograph, *Black Women in the Ivory Tower*, was reviewed in twenty-two journals. As a collection, they offer a range of foci and perspectives that reflect the interests of their readerships. As described in the section above, "Reviewer Bias," one journal reviewer chose the path of personal bias, and that review is now a perennial shining example in my classes of how each person is accountable for what they write, long after it is published. You will have people who wish you would have written a different book. As

Reflection Questions

Question 15: Why do you want to publish an academic book? How do you imagine this current project in the big picture of your career and holistic research agenda?

Question 16: What are the key steps in the academic book publishing process that you are most excited about? Which key steps intimidate you most?

Question 17: Which top five books do you cite as relevant comparison texts? What presses published them? What top three publishers appear most often in your manuscript bibliography?

Practical Tasks

- Read at least three additional "how to publish" guides (see bibliography for options).

- Create a project calendar and timeline. Be realistic about expectations. Gift yourself the grace of flexibility then move forward with diligence. Create a draft proposal outline.

- Using a publishing guide (definitely consider *The Book Proposal Book*), draft an interest inquiry letter for two presses. Evaluate what rationale you offer for each press about why your work is a good fit for their catalog.

- Discuss chapter questions with a mentor or colleague.

- Share your chapter answers with a next-generation scholar.

6

Community

Public Practice

Black feminist writing is a relational practice. This means there will inevitably be conflict, and sometimes your work with other writers might even turn volatile. Sometimes you will encounter those who would rather be celebrities than colleagues. Some writers desire followers, not active readers. But community building can also be a calming, sustaining, and energizing part of your writing work. In this chapter, I provide resources and case studies that emphasize the benefits of learning from Black women's intellectual history in community. Peer review and citation show the promises and perils of scholarly exchange. It is also imperative to engage a diverse range of sources in one's public practice, to both gather and disseminate information beyond campus.

The academic publishing world talks a lot about "audience" but too rarely considers the need to connect the source of one's information with the spaces where one intends to disperse published research. Creating an intellectual community involves citing historical references in addition to cutting-edge research, vetting your ideas with mentors and peers, and sharing research with younger scholars. Most importantly, include at early stages of discussion those outside of academia who might most deeply critique your manuscript as well as those who might actually benefit from your publications. It is not enough for you to claim your work will be beneficial—work with actual people who can tell you if your work is helpful or not. In her 2009 American Sociological Association presidential address, Patricia Hill Collins unpacked the politics and possibility of community. After unveiling the limitations of assumed community, she points to Ida B. Wells as an example of how to center social justice and build collective capacity for change.

For full-time faculty, book publication often centers around tenure. For non-tenure-track faculty, publishing is hardly discussed and rarely rewarded. For administrators, publishing is often sacrificed for the common good. The pressure of book publishing can seem insurmountable, regardless of one's rank or role, but collaborating around a particular issue can advance professional development and publication. Creating a culture of peer mentoring is one aspect of the collaborative style of leadership that exemplifies the best of Black women's leadership models.

Peer mentoring is an essential component of professional development. An example of this can be seen with the edited volume *Dear Department Chair: Letters from Black Women to the Next Generation of Academic Leaders*.[1] This coedited book emerged from Chair at the Table Network, a research collective established in spring 2018 as a peer-mentoring network. When I reached out to my partner Tracy Sharpley-Whiting, at the suggestion of Rhonda Williams, she graciously levied her considerable reputation and resources to build a network for the purpose of mentoring administrators. Members of the informal network are current and former Black women department chairs at colleges and universities across the US and Canada. This research collective considers Black women's perspectives of academic leadership, particularly in light of the recent fiftieth anniversary of the establishment of Black studies and women's studies.

Several issues have been discussed during the Chair at the Table gatherings. For example, the mentoring workshop held on January 8, 2021, addressed a series of questions on several themes, which we grouped into four categories: administration, leadership, DEI, and working with people. Discussions at this mentoring session included "how to" recommendations, including entering administration, managing time, negotiating diversity initiatives and challenges to institutional equity, as well as managing staff, supporting students, and mentoring faculty. These discussions evolved into a special edition of *Palimpsest Journal* and then the *Dear Department Chair* book.

Maintaining a writing routine while serving as an administrator offered unique challenges, but using writing as a tool to create community in various ways was helpful for me and for my chair colleagues. Eventually, the Chair at the Table network partnered with the Women in Higher Education Network (WHEN), an organization based in England, to exchange information and expand support. In 2019, WHEN partnered with several institutions to launch an initiative called 100 Black Women Professors Now (100BWPN), calling attention to the fact that out of 23,000 UK professors, only thirty-five were Black women. With attention brought by the initiative, numbers have risen to sixty-one, and the *Dear Department Chair* book is a conversation starter about how to expand opportunity for Black women scholars in both the US and the UK. Dr. Sharpley-Whiting is hosting ongoing conversations at Vanderbilt University to expand opportunity for those committed to serving their peers.

Gathering and disseminating information should be a means to connect. Toward this end, I created music videos for *Black Women in the Ivory Tower* and a related book chapter in the edited book *Black Men in the Ivory Tower*.[2] The videos allowed me to pack in a large amount of information about educational history into a short time span. As a visual learner, I found that compiling the pictures of scholars helped me to place scholars in their eras and track the evolution of how Black scholars have presented ourselves over time. The video also helped place scholars in relation to organizations and institutions. This helped viewers to see relationships like the impact of Oberlin College, the prevalence of Phi Beta Kappa Honor Society members, or the fact that the first four Black women who earned their PhD in 1921 and 1925 were members of a sorority.

I create videos, maps, bibliographies, and other types of resource pages as a commitment to digital humanities. The web pages that accompany each book project stand as timely resources for understanding a snippet of higher education history and social justice education advocacy. The web pages also have allowed me to share information with schools, churches, and other spaces beyond academe.

Beyond creating materials *for* community, much of the writing I have done has been in partnership with other scholars and we have written in community with several non-government organizations. These include Black Women's Health Imperative (Washington, DC), Center for Black Women's Wellness (Atlanta, GA), youthSpark (Atlanta, GA), No More Martyrs and Black Women's Mental Health Institute (Birmingham, AL), Social Justice Café for Girls (Atlanta, GA). As examples of public scholarship, I published *Purple Sparks* with youthSpark, *OASIS: Oldways Africana Soup in Stories* with Oldways, and *Africana Tea* with Black Women's Mental Health Institute.

Creative and community publications are usually very different than academic manuscripts. It is to be expected that your work will not be accepted in some circles; however, you must do all you can to ensure you have followed protocols or you open yourself up to challenges to the validity of your work based on fundamental inaccuracies or flawed ethical approaches.

#CiteASista, #CiteBlackWomen, and the Black Women's Studies Association

BWST is a vital part of social change. As I complete this book, my social media timelines are literally brimming with news of violence against Black women. I write with a keen awareness that my agenda is not only to change the narratives but also to change the policies, practices, cultures, and social systems that oppress Black women. The ideas I present in this book resonate with work like the Black Feminist Think Tank (founded in 2015) curated by Sherie Randolph and Erica Edwards and the more recent Black Feminist Summer Institute hosted by Jennifer Nash at Duke University. The gifts that I share below are reflected in the collectives like those and Sisters of the Academy featured later in this chapter.

Building community through citation is a part of the writing practice that most feeds your academic family tree. Communities of Black women, both within and outside of the academy, have been engaged in discussions for decades before the proliferation of campaigns celebrating Black women on social media and within popular culture. Some of these include Beverly Bond's youth empowerment organization and television award show *Black Girls Rock!* (2006); CaShawn Thompson's viral hashtag #BlackGirlsAreMagic, which is frequently shortened to #BlackGirlMagic (2013); Yaba Blay's #PrettyPeriod (2013) and #ProfessionalBlackGirl (2016); and Glory Edim's #WellReadBlackGirl (2015). Activist initiatives include #SayHerName and #BlackGirlsMatter, which was coined by Kimberlé Crenshaw's African American Policy Forum in 2015 and the #MeToo Movement founded by Tarana Burke. Significantly, three initiatives—#CiteASista, #CiteBlackWomen, and the Black Women's Studies Association (BWSA)—have formalized the sentiments of earlier campaigns by creating spaces in higher education dedicated to the advancement of critical race and gender research.

Brittany Williams and Joan Collier, then doctoral students in College Student Affairs Administration at the University of Georgia, convened the first #CiteASista chat on Twitter in July of 2016.[3] Their initial chat was inspired by the "#BlackGirlsMatter: Public Scholarship Engaging with the Race and Gender Interaction in Schools" panel at the American Educational Research Association (AERA) conference earlier that year. Since then, founders have defined #CiteASista as "a Black Feminist digital project that centers the experience, knowledge, and literature of Black women (cis and trans*) within and beyond the academy through digital programming (topical monthly Twitter chats), written content by contributors on the CiteASista.com website, national conference presentations, online group-chat spaces for Black women, and in-person engagements. Central to #CiteASista's praxis is the inclusion of Black women whose voices and knowledge have not been valued within the academy (e.g., sex workers, differently educated family members, etc.)." Williams and Collier have created a team of contributors and provide resources on their website for those who are new to graduate school and higher education.

In 2017, Christen A. Smith, a Black feminist anthropologist (associate professor of Anthropology and African and African Diaspora Studies at the University of Texas at Austin) created #CiteBlackWomen, which she described as "a campaign to push people to engage in a radical praxis of citation that acknowledges and honors Black women's transnational intellectual production." What began as a community-based T-shirt campaign to offer financial support for the Winnie Mandela School in Salvador, Bahia, expanded to include a collective of scholars advancing a discussion through conference presentations (featuring A. Lynn Bolles, Keisha-Khan Y. Perry, Erica Lorraine Williams, Ashanté M. Reese), social media campaigns, and a podcast that tackles questions of purposeful community building, Black feminist archival work, spirituality, and anti-imperialism. Smith writes, "As Black women, we are often overlooked, sidelined and undervalued. Although we are intellectually prolific, we are rarely the ones that make up the canon. Recognizing this, Cite Black Women engages with social media, aesthetic representation (our T-shirts) and public dialogue to push people to critically rethink the politics of race gender and knowledge production." Building on the demands of Black women for more visibility and formal acknowledgement of their epistemic contributions, #CiteBlackWomen mobilizes a multigenerational and culturally diverse scholarly collective.

In September 2018, African American studies scholars Nneka Dennie and Jacinta Saffold founded the Black Women's Studies Association (BWSA) as a professional organization connecting scholars from disparate disciplines. BWSA is the only association specifically designed to foment multidisciplinary engagement with the research and praxis of Black Women's Studies. Like the founders of #CiteASista and #CiteBlackWomen, Dennie and Saffold are interested in sharing resources about Black women's intellectual and professional production—and they are invested in creating a professional community that maximizes existing online and conference spaces to encourage those who work in the field of Black Women's Studies.

The first BWSA gathering was held in Atlanta, GA, in 2018, during the annual meetings for the National Women's Studies Association (NWSA) and American Studies Association (ASA), signaling a successful effort to operationalize its mission statement: "This organization is for scholars at all stages of their careers, whether they be undergraduate students, graduate students, independent scholars, adjunct professors, postdoctoral fellows, professors, and scholars with alternative academic careers. The BWSA is an interdisciplinary and multidisciplinary organization that welcomes various methodological approaches to studying black women's experiences, histories, politics, literature, and more."[4] As BWSA's genesis demonstrates, established academic conferences offer strategic opportunities to embody communities cultivated online, and BWST scholars have used these spaces to convene in person and been commended within these spaces for their work centering Black women. Notably, BWSA hosts weekly writing accountability sessions online, dubbed Word Count Wednesday.

#CiteBlackWomen featured prominently at multiple academic meetings in the fall of 2018, including the NWSA, which livestreamed Christen Smith's #CiteBlackWomen panel, and the Association for the Study of African American Life and History (ASALH), where an entire panel of scholars, led by historians Martha Jones and Natanya Duncan, sported #CiteBlackWomen T-shirts. In December 2018, Dennie and Saffold expanded their discussion of visibility, recognition, and sources for Black Women's Studies research on a panel titled "Archives Ain't Big Enough: Stretching Repositories to Fit Black Women" at the fortieth anniversary gathering for ABWH.

These three initiatives emerged in the context of other new developments that push the frontiers of Black studies scholarship, most notably the founding of the African American Intellectual History Society (AAIHS) by Christopher Cameron, Keisha Blain, Ashley Farmer, Brandon Byrd, and Jessica Johnson in 2014. AAIHS has expanded to include a popular blog but has also established an independent annual conference. These new collaborations enhance the growth of established organizations such as ASALH (1915), NCBS (1975), NWSA (1977), and the Association for the Study of the Worldwide African Diaspora (ASWAD, 2000), in addition to disciplinary-based Black women's caucus groups.

Professional academic organizations dedicated to the advancement of critical race and gender studies build upon the tradition of generations of collegiate Black women organizers whose work fueled the Black women's club and sorority movements of the early twentieth century. As with those earlier movements, questions of access, class, liberal uplift, radical activism, respectability, and town-gown relations are inherent in the growth of twenty-first-century professional organizations. With so much new growth, it is essential to consider available and forthcoming scholarship within the proper context of five decades' worth of cornerstone book contributions. As BWST is a relatively young field, it is imperative not only to note new contributions in Black studies and women's studies but also to thoroughly clock discussions happening within more established academic disciplines.[5]

Beyond writing for a specific group and cultivating partnerships with public organizations, one way to build community is to publish edited volumes. Coauthoring and coediting book projects require a commitment to serving more than your own interests and can be a means to initiate and sustain relationships with like-minded people beyond your institution, location, or discipline.

The more you have your work reviewed by groups you are writing about, the more you will be able to gauge the level of possible blowback that may come when your book is released. Creating mutually beneficial partnerships does not guarantee certain publics will accept or validate your work. But sustained engagement might at least help you identify fault lines in your research and how people—in real time—might react. The very unfortunate tale of *Bad and Boujee* is instructive.

Critical Peer Review: The Cautionary Tale of *Bad and Boujee*

Publishing an academic book and being granted tenure does not mean that your research is ethical. The last chapter of *The Black Academic's Guide to Winning Tenure* is titled "Succeeding with Integrity." Ethical research is not an abstract idea. Though public writing may often escape repercussions, academia is not always so kind. Plagiarism is a serious offense, which is why citation is so important. The extent to which Black scholars are charged with plagiarism and White scholars are guilty of plagiarism is a case study in academic hypocrisy.

#CiteASista and #CiteBlackWomen have become central to discussion about intellectual politics in the publishing world. These two movements insist on recognizing the contributions of marginalized scholars and serve as reminders about the use of citation as a measure to distinguish quality scholarly writing from public work that has no obligation to cite sources and often tolerates plagiarism as a matter of course.

In the humanities and social sciences, books are generally required for tenure and promotion. Reports in *The Chronicle of Higher Education* and *Inside Higher Ed* indicate Black women professors are scarce, disproportionately critiqued on teaching evaluations, and overall marginalized in the publishing field. Additional reports in industry magazines like *Publisher's Weekly* demonstrate how a lack of diversity among academic press editorial staff is a problem. Another one of those problems is the lack of diversity in leadership positions, which can sometimes translate to a lack of representation in print or even misrepresentation. There are many structural issues created by a lack of diversity.

One recurring theme in academic guides (though not covered widely enough) is the ethics of professional writing and publishing. Certainly, I have heard many horror stories of presses, editors, and reviewers skirting the lines of ethical behavior. Some don't merely skirt ethics; they have a whole closet full of secrets, lies, and unprofessional behavior. Yet, for authors, the acts of research, writing, and peer review are often mishandled or misunderstood as well. Peer review and rigorous citation are essential practices for academic publishing. Scholars who agree to review manuscripts must insist on broad and robust citations—not simply to get their own citation score up or to reify their favorite superstars but also to ensure scholars are accountable to a broad readership.

Though trade presses publish books with academic origins, even trade presses must pay attention to quality at all levels. One recent example of a trade press publishing something that a university press might not shines a searing spotlight on the dangers of subverting the peer review process or falling for the ruse of pseudo-academic writing that does not withstand professional scrutiny. I would call the *Bad and Boujee* fiasco a painful lesson in the politics of peer review, a reminder to choose your press wisely, and a classic case of "Knuck if You Buck."

Dr. Jennifer Buck, an assistant professor of practical theology at Azusa Pacific University, published her book *Bad and Boujee* with Cascade Books on February 17, 2022. The book was based on research Buck did with young Black women. Though the young women in the study were compensated (with funds Buck secured from a prestigious grant), the book reviewer who provided the back cover blurb was a White male colleague from her own university.[6]

The book description and promotional blurb are below:

Abstract

This book engages with the overlap of black experience, hip-hop music, ethics, and feminism to focus on a subsection known as "trap feminism" and construct a Trap Feminist Theology. Interacting with concepts of moral agency, resistance, and imagination, Trap Feminist Theology seeks to build an intersectional theology emphasizing women's agency in their bodies and sexuality while also remaining faithful to the "trap" context from which they are socially located. Such a project will redefine the "trap" context from one of marginalization to one of joy and flourishing within black feminist theology. This theology overlaps with black ethics in subversive empowerment that forms a new normative ethic and family system within a subset of the black community. Trap feminism emerges out of trap culture, where the black woman is creating a space outside of the barriers of poverty harnessing autonomy, employment, and agency to allow for a reinvention of self-identity while remaining faithful to social location.

Promotional Blurb

"Jennifer Buck has produced a deeply important and relevant work that gives voice to communities that are continuously marginalized and excluded from theological discourse. In the process, Buck contextualizes herself openly and honestly while seeking to elevate the voices and experiences of Black women. This creative and powerful look at the intersectional and theological reality of 'Trap Queens' and their social location(s) is a relevant theological exploration that will be important for years to come."—Justin Marc Smith, Azusa Pacific University

The book title was taken from a 2016 song of the same title, by the trap group Migos from Georgia. Another song from an Atlanta-based rap group might be used to tell the story of this publishing fiasco: Crime Mob's song "Knuck if You Buck," an anthem for those who invite an adversary to fight. The fact that the book was pulled by the publisher indicates the author and editors did not do their due diligence to get the book vetted before its public release. By appropriating culture and not seriously engaging critique before release, they invited a fight they were ill-prepared to endure. The book purported to center ethics, but that falsehood was also exposed upon publication.

Dr. Buck's book was released to withering critique, especially from Black women scholars. The press that released the book issued a public statement on Twitter explaining the rationale for pulling the publication:

Publisher Statement (on Twitter)

> Our statement regarding the publication of "Bad and Boujee" by Jennifer M. Buck:
>
> In February, Wipf and Stock Publishers released "Bad and Boujee: Toward a Trap Feminist Theology" by Jennifer M. Buck. Recently, a strong backlash to the project emerged on various social media platforms. We quickly realized that critics of the book—and critics of Wipf and Stock for publishing it—have serious and valid criticisms. We have pulled the book from circulation and continue to receive and process critical feedback in the hope that we might learn from our critics—including the ways our critics state that we have harmed Black women and others. We will continue to consider tangible ways to repair the harm and to make the changes necessary to avoid making the same mistakes. We humbly acknowledge that we failed Black women in particular, and we take full responsibility for the numerous failures of judgment that led to this moment. Our critics are right: we should have seen numerous red flags, including but not limited to the inappropriateness of a White theologian writing about the experience of Black women (the issue of cultural appropriation is pervasive, from cover to content), the lack of Black endorsers, and the apparent lack of relationship with Black scholars, especially those who originated the trap feminist discourse. We are deeply sorry to have published a book that has betrayed the trust of our authors and readers and that has damaged our ability to support work that we both value and believe is vitally important to the church and world at this time—especially the work of womanist and Black feminist theologians. We pledge to continue to listen, and we resolve to do better. —Wipf and Stock Publishers #trapfeminism #trapfeminist #womanism #womanisttheology #blacktheology #jenniferbuck[7]

The book's recall turned quite a few heads and raised accusations of selective censorship, with some dubbing it a victim of cancel culture. The recall was also characterized as an assault on academic freedom. Some who challenged the book argued that Buck, as a White woman, should not be writing about Black women. I disagree . . . there are several White women scholars who have published on Black women whose work is stellar. But I do believe it was a reasonable and responsible action by the press to pull the book because it failed the test of ethics and scholarly peer review—and this was a mistake by the press as much as by the author. It is unfortunate that the author was allowed to get that far in the publication process, but this was a teachable moment for all potential authors.

Examples of White women publishing about Black women are plentiful, from Jaqueline Jones's *Labor of Love, Labor of Sorrow* (Basic Books, 1985) to the more recent biography *Unceasing Militant: The Life of Mary Church Terrell* (U of North Carolina P, 2020) by Allison Parker. Both scholars were invested in securing prepublication input from Black women in their field to ensure their work would endure public scrutiny. Peer review is essential, not simply as a form of gatekeeping or bullying (though there is ample evidence those practices are rampant), but to catch glaring errors, maintain professional standards, protect those with less stature, and uphold intellectual accountability. Scholars who seek to publish books might consider peer review as a safeguard, ensuring that you have faced and met the challenge to address alternate viewpoints and included nuanced analyses that take into consideration the potentially negative impact of your work. It also ensures that you have honored the researchers who have come before, not with a simple bibliographic note but by participating in actual conversations with them.

Jones, for example, acknowledges Nell Irvin Painter, who "gave the entire manuscript a meticulous reading and encouraged me to think more carefully about the dynamics of class in relation to Afro-American history." Parker credits "some of the best minds in the field . . . for offering critiques and encouragement."[8] The four Black women scholars that Parker named Carol Anderson, Kimberly Wallace-Sanders, Rosetta E. Ross, and Jacqueline Rouse, are indeed stellar historians and exemplify the value of critical peer review—particularly for scholarship about marginalized communities.

There are some cases where Black women have noted that White women's work has received much more institutional support and professional credibility than their own. In addition, there have been several cases in the past few years of White women passing as women of color. The *Bad and Boujee* case was egregious because it displayed all the window dressing of scholarship, including Ivy League endorsement. The example of Dr. Buck's book was different than those who try to "pass" as women of color scholars, because the author situated herself as a White scholar deeply committed to community-based research. However, her engagement with Black women informants and research assistants actually concealed her lack of community building with Black women peers. In addition to formal peer review, authors can form their own professional peer mentoring circles to establish a group of knowledgeable colleagues who can serve as a sounding board for ideas.

Citation and engagement are both essential practices of academic publishing. *Bad and Bougee* failed to cite and engage authors of foundational work on the topic. References were missing that would validate the work. The author offered no acknowledgement of her scholarly debt to Black women, from recent work like Cecile Bowen's *Bad Fat Black Girl: Notes from a Trap Feminist* (2021) or Mikki Kendall's *Hood Feminism: Notes from the Women That a Movement Forgot* (2020) to other established works, including books by Joan Morgan and Brittney Cooper. To be clear, everyone needs to #CiteBlackWomen—including Black women—but the lengths Buck went to complete an extensive study, well-funded by a prominent university, without seriously engaging the leading theorists around her topic meant that her erasure of Black women was deliberate. The extents of her negligence can only be speculative, though, because the book is no longer for sale from the publisher.[9]

As scholars, we certainly must contextualize our work by offering statements of bias or reflective acknowledgments about how our position shades or shapes our analysis. But we also have a serious responsibility to acknowledge when we are writing about vulnerable populations. Doing so necessitates we demonstrate how our research benefits them more than simply advancing our career.

If you are only writing for tenure and promotion without duly inquiring what would materially and intellectually enrich our communities—especially communities you include in your study as data sets and sources of information—you are simply exploiting people. In addition to writing and publishing in community, it is imperative to take advantage of existing research guides that can help you double- and triple-check your research methods and select a scholarly press that takes seriously basic measures of professional ethics like requiring proof of Institutional Review Board (IRB) approval or the peer review process. Those who are chosen for peer reviewers for Black feminist books should be grounded in legacies of community-based scholarship. Asking a press to discuss their peer review process—especially a trade or independent press—may give you the answers you need to assess whether or not it is a fit for your work. Regardless of how the press handles peer review, know that various communities will access and review your work, so you should take steps to build academic community and ensure your work is vetted before it is released.

LEARN: Mary McCleod Bethune's Guide to Community Building

> I leave you a thirst for education. Knowledge is the prime need of the hour. More and more, Negroes are taking full advantage of hard-won opportunities for learning. . . . I leave you a responsibility to our young people. . . . Our children must never lose their zeal for building a better world. . . . Nor must they forget that the masses of our people are still underprivileged, ill-housed, impoverished, and victimized by discrimination. We have a powerful potential in our youth, and we must have the courage to change old ideas and practices so that we may direct their power towards good ends.
>
> —Mary McLeod Bethune, "Last Will and Testament"[10]

Black women's intellectual history is an exploration of ideas—specifically ideas about how to change and improve the world. Academic writing should add depth to the extant knowledge base by contributing to, as Mary McLeod Bethune writes, "building a better world." This work does not happen in a vacuum. Following the advice laid out in the first chapter, we must remember—and cite—past scholars. This practice will help us to engage in the public sphere with more confidence and conviction. It also will help us to organize in a way that sustains, formalizes, and institutionalizes our knowledge and experiences.

Bethune was explicit about the fact that her ideas of research, knowledge creation, and meaning making were informed by her cultural identity. She engaged in rigorous study for both personal and communal growth. She is widely regarded as a talented administrator and politico, and her collected speeches and written works enrich our definitions of research in ways relevant to contemporary academics. In addition to organizing the National Council of Negro Women (NCNW), she galvanized her resources to support academic research. In the journal article "Mary McLeod Bethune's Research Agenda: Thought Translated to Work," I traced Bethune's perception of academic research and contrasted it with the historic development of research in top-ranked institutions. She built an entire university in Florida to defy repressive state culture and the Sunshine State's long-standing moniker as a bastion of educational oppression. Her steadfast determination connected the youth of Florida to self-determination in the African diaspora.[11]

Mary Jane McLeod was born on July 10, 1875, in Mayesville, South Carolina, as the fifteenth of seventeen children and the first free of enslavement. She died in May 1955 at her "Retreat" on the Bethune-Cookman College campus in Daytona, Florida. In her youth, she labored in the cotton and cornfields to help keep her family afloat. In 1882, she attended Mayesville Industrial Institute at Trinity Presbyterian Church, graduating at twelve years old. She subsequently graduated Scotia Seminary (now Barber-Scotia College) in Concord, North Carolina, in 1894, as well as Chicago's Moody Bible Institute in 1895. After teaching eighth grade at Lucy Laney's Haines Institute in Augusta, Georgia, she moved to Daytona in 1904 to found what is now Bethune-Cookman College. Examples of her involvement include serving as president of the Florida Federation of Colored Women and president of the National Association of Colored Women (NACW) and founding the National Council of Negro Women (NCNW), an umbrella organization for Black women's clubs nationwide, where she served as president for more than a decade.

Bethune asserted that a university has three responsibilities: investigation, interpretation, and inspiration. In her life and work, she was aware of the complex and central role that cultural identity played in one's educational attainment. In her organizational addresses of the 1930s and 1940s, Bethune argued that education was a key component in fulfilling the promises of democracy, particularly for African Americans. In Logan's edited volume *What the Negro Wants* (1944), Bethune wrote a chapter, "In Pursuit of Unalienable Rights," in which she brainstorms with leading Black politicians to demand equity for her communities in Florida and across the country.[12]

Bethune was a forerunner in advocating for an Afrocentric education that would evolve into Black studies in the mid-twentieth century. She writes:

> When they learn the fairy tales of mythical king and queen and princess, we must let them hear, too, of the Pharaohs and African kings and brilliant pageantry of the Valley of the Nile; when they learn of Caesar and his legions, we must

teach them of Hannibal and his Africans; when they learn of Shakespeare and Goethe, we must teach them of Pushkin and Dumas. When they read of Columbus, we must introduce the Africans who touched the shores of America before Europeans emerged from savagery . . . With the Tragic Era we give them Black Reconstruction; with Edison, we give them Jan Matzeliger; with John Dewey, we place Booker T. Washington.[13]

Bethune charges us to center Black history and culture and has inspired efforts like the development of professional organizations, including Dr. Carter G. Woodson's Association for the Study of African American Life and History (ASALH), which was founded in 1915, and the National Council for Black Studies (NCBS), founded in 1968. Bethune led ASALH from 1936 to 1951 and is one of numerous Black women builders, most of whom are not as well known.[14]

The National Council for Black Studies was founded under the leadership of Dr. Bertha Maxwell-Roddey, along with other scholars, like Professor Malefi Asante and Maulana Karenga, and the organization has continued to thrive under the leadership of many women who remain active in organizational leadership. Though many know Woodson and Bethune, Maxwell-Roddey's legacy is only beginning to be commemorated. Sonya Ramsey's political biography *Bertha Maxwell-Roddey: A Modern-Day Race Woman and the Power of Black Leadership* (2022) details the educator's work in ways that align with Terborg-Penn's definition of African feminist values: self-care (in the areas of lifelong education, health, and spirituality); communal care (Maxwell-Roddey was a national president of Delta Sigma Theta); structural care (she led the Department of Africana Studies at University of North Carolina, Charlotte, and served as founding president of the National Council for Black Studies); and social justice (she fought for the desegregation of schools, businesses, organizations, and public spaces). When one talks about community-based research and building relationships for accountability on and off campus, Maxwell-Roddey was a model cut directly from Dr. Bethune's cloth. It is no surprise, then, that one of Maxwell-Roddey's earliest childhood memories was welcoming Bethune to a community gathering.

As academics, we must navigate public stressors in addition to institutional stressors. But public engagement is a central part of liberatory education. Whether in the classroom, in public lectures, in public policy hearings, or on social media, we can lean on the lessons of prior generations who were effective at gathering folks together to advance the cause of Black people (even when they vehemently disagreed). Sometimes, organizing for the public good means finding the people with whom you most enjoy working and creating spaces that inspire joy and purpose in ways that also result in academic productivity.

CREATE: 2007, Sisters of the Academy, Peer Networks, and Rights Pertaining Thereunto

The year my first book was published, I offered a presentation at the Sisters of the Academy (SOTA) Research BootCamp in Tallahassee, Florida, titled "Historical Sisters of the Academy: Using History as a Research and Publishing Tool." Since then, I have continued to write and mentor writers. At the boot camp, I was only one of a large team of senior scholars and I learned as much as a taught.

Academic writing is hard on one's ego. Learning to accept constant critique can cause mental duress if you are deeply invested in knowing everything, if you desire coddling, if you know more than everyone else in the room, or if you believe you are right all of the time. While you may want your writing to be relatable outside of the academy, you are still responsible for producing a manuscript that meets an academic standard. Some people are loud and wrong, but still insist on being loud. Some people have a high profile and produce work that is shoddy in conception, execution, or production. Some people surround themselves with sycophants. Some people aren't committed to writing well and refuse to learn to—even minimally—edit their own work. Don't be like some people. There are some seemingly harsh statements scattered in my writing. I hold no grudges and I'm not bitter about my experiences, but it is disingenuous to not alert those coming through the pipeline of "some people" they are likely to encounter.

Do not wait until your work is perfect to submit it to a press. Perfect is subjective and impossible. When it is finished turn it in and let it go. However, if you want to publish a credible book, you must edit your own work—again and again and again. Workshop your manuscript—selectively—in several writing circles. Make sure others are as accountable as you are for reading and writing. Hire professional editors so you can submit a (relatively) pristine final draft. Your manuscript does not have to be without error, but do not submit a raggedy draft to the press and expect a glowing reader report or smooth publishing process. You must be open to feedback that helps you reframe your argument or restructure your chapters. You must expand your vocabulary and fine-tune each paragraph.

If you want to publish, you must grow and you must grow up. You can't have it both ways. You cannot refuse to learn basic professional processes, then demand to be recognized as a peer with those who have earned the respect that the status as a published scholar confers. Yes, senior faculty, this applies to you too. You must continue to develop, no matter how many books you have already published.

Regardless of your professional status, do not measure yourself by the least of your peers. Neither fall into the trap of thinking that all that glitters is gold. Strip away the gilded scaffolding and some prized tablets turn to dust. In your writing journey, strive for competence, consistency, improvement, and innovation.

Surround yourself with people who are committed to lifelong learning not for status or recognition, but for consciousness and self-respect. Surely, some elder scholars have not had to meet the severe evaluative measures set by the modern corporate university. But they also had bigger battles to fight in order to establish spaces that younger scholars now enjoy.

Peer review is the lifeblood of academic publication, but sometimes that review process is harmful. The will to carry on is a condition of a sustainable publishing career. While you must acknowledge and address valid critique, you must also use discernment to trust your own instinct and know the yardsticks that are worthy measures for you.

Peer knowledge is as important as generational and ancestral knowledge, as evidenced by the NAACP Image Award-nominated survey *A Black Women's History of the United States*. As part of the process of editing the volume, the coauthors convened a series of critical discussions with top scholars in the field. Upon the book's release, Dr. Kali Gross shared a note of gratitude and pictures with the Association of Black Women Historians. The public Facebook post intimates the level of collective care taken in writing the book and ensuring its review before release:

> Friends we are so excited to share that, A Black Women's History of the United States (Beacon Press, 2020) is here! Kali Nicole Gross and Daina Ramey Berry have been honored and overwhelmed by the support and warm reception. This book has been a collective effort, by the co-authors but also by the scores of sister scholars who workshopped the manuscript and read

drafts and drafts of the work. Thank you: Deborah Gray White, Erica Armstrong Dunbar, Brittney Cooper, Donna Murch, Cheryl Hicks, Talitha LeFlouria, Stephanie E. Jones-Rogers, @SharonHarley, Tiffany Gill and @RhondaWilliams, LaShawn Harris, Ashley Farmer, Steven G Fullwood, Paula Giddings, @Jacqueline Jones, Pero Dagbovie, and Dr. Felicenne Ramey. We also must thank Gayatri Patnaik and our editors Cecelia Cancellaro and Cynthia Yaudes and the entire Beacon Press Team! Woo Hoo! Oh and you can buy it from Beacon Press or anywhere books are sold.

The photos provided glimpses of a roundtable discussion that reflects the joy that is possible when writing in community.

In 2021, Ashley Farmer and Tanisha Ford hosted a Writing and Publishing Black Women's Biography in the Black Lives Matter Era workshop, sponsored by the Radcliffe Institute at Harvard University. Daina Ramey Berry was among the collaborators along with A'Leila Bundles, Anastasia Curwood, K. T. Ewing, Alexa Pauline Gumbs, Sherry Johnson, Mary Phillips, Susana Morris, and Tiffany Florvil. They collectively produced a writing workbook that covers everything from selecting a subject and locating sources to setting the mood for writing, keeping a journal, and developing a writing routine. This online network exemplifies the ethos of collective self-care and producing work that helps guide others in their writing practice. Fittingly, Toni Morrison and her cat Zora grace the cover of the workbook.[15]

Given the importance of networks, it is incumbent upon senior scholars to create space for junior scholars to belong—on their own terms. I have heard too many stories about academic bullies who tolerate only groupies and who punish everyone else whom they deem not worthy, elite, or useful enough. There are also groups of younger scholars that conspire to defame those elders they deem unworthy. Networks should not devolve into cliques. Historical examples of Black women working together show that there was much derision, but work and collective support can happen despite not totally getting along with some folks. In short, Black feminist scholars can go farther if we work together . . . even if we decide we cannot be tightly aligned as individuals.

In the tradition of Bethune-Cookman University and National Council for Black Studies, the Sisters of the Academy (SOTA) is a national group of determined scholars who are organizing to prepare Black women researchers. For several decades, Black women's experiences on campuses have been chronicled, including in *Black Women in the Academy: Promises and Perils* (1997), edited by Lois Benjamin; *Sisters of the Academy: Emergent Black Women Scholars in Higher Education* (2001), edited by Reitumetse Obakeng Mabokela and Anna L. Green; and *Sistahs in College: Making a Way Out of No Way* (2001) by Juanita Johnson-Bailey. Volumes like these detail the "challenges and triumphs" that scholars have faced since the 1980s, when a critical mass of Black women faculty began to be employed at predominantly White campuses. A perusal of these narratives shows that the first-generation faculty have faced issues that remain pervasive.

Academic organizing has been a mainstay of Black women academics. The Sisters of the Academy Research BootCamp is a prime model of organizing a critical research collective. The organization, founded in 2001, quickly expanded to develop a signature boot camp that provides mentorship for scholars at several levels:

> The biennial Research BootCamp is an intense, one-week culturally responsive program designed to help doctoral students and junior scholars develop sound research projects. Senior Scholar Mentors serve as methodologists and theorists to facilitate workshops where doctoral students can conceptualize and design components of their dissertations (i.e., formulating research questions or hypotheses, developing literature review, selecting instrumentation, designing methodology, and completing data analysis). The Senior Scholar Mentors also assist junior scholars in the development of manuscripts for publication and advisement for tenure and promotion.
>
> BootCamp workshop topics include:
> Approaching the Dissertation Proposal
> Developing Research Questions and a Review of Literature
> Developing Research Questions Conceptual Framework
> Research Design
> Consultation/Writing
> Conceptual Framework
> Research Design Consultation
> Data Collection Strategies/Completion of Work Plan
> Data Analysis/Writing

Writing Your Research Results
Finishing Your Dissertation
Strategic Planning for the Academic
Designing Research Agenda
Developing the Tenure Binder
Dissertation to Manuscript
Qualitative Research Methods Overview
Quantitative Research Methods Overview
Publishing Your Research
Beyond the BootCamp: Career Trajectories and Success in the Academy
Using Technology for Research and Teaching
Qualitative Analysis Software Demonstration
Quantitative Analysis Demonstration
Self-Presentation and Skin Care
Self-Care[16]

SOTA is one of many programs designed to sustain scholars of color. Their network is built on the principles of academic excellence, but the leaders also understand the need to teach wellness, as evidenced by the inclusion of self-care on the list above.

The McNair Scholars Program I participated in as an undergraduate made a life-altering difference in my career. Programs like McNair, Mellon Fellows, and Ford Fellows teach scholars to seek out multiple communities and create a network of mentors so one is never working solo. These programs show scholars how to build a network of senior scholars and peer mentors so you are not dependent on a single source for intellectual nourishment or professional guidance. *Academic Pipeline Programs: Diversifying Pathways to the Professoriate* (2021), an open-access book written by my husband Dr. Curtis D. Byrd and his writing partner Dr. Rihanna Mason, identifies a wide-ranging map of programs, from high school and undergraduate to graduate and new faculty support. If you want to write a book that does more than sit on a shelf, then you must engage scholars in the academic pipeline and collaborate with others who make service, engagement, and community building central to their mission.

Engaging publics can be a source of vitality, inspiration, and energy. Reflect on the most positive conference experiences you have had and work to build relationships with other scholars that afford you more time to connect in professional spaces. Consider serving on an organization's book prize committee or in some other way that centers scholarship as a way to calibrate your work with new books that are being published. Most importantly, take every opportunity to work with students and junior colleagues to help them improve their writing. Teaching is an essential way to reassess your own work. Writing in community is another critical way to produce and review scholarship.

That said, I will end this section emphasizing that no one person or no one group should be the arbiter of style or access to resources. For instance, after his 1895 Atlanta Compromise speech and 1901 autobiography *Up from Slavery*, US presidents, educators, and business leaders considered Booker T. Washington the "go-to Negro" at the turn of the twentieth century. He often used his power to punish those whom he deemed enemies, which resulted in Anna Julia Cooper losing her job at M Street High School in 1906. After Washington visited the school and was shown the efficacy of her work in liberal arts education (instead of his vocational program model), she was mysteriously fired. Though she did not return to DC for five years, she went on to complete her doctorate and enjoy not only a lifetime of publishing, but a timeless legacy of intellectual impact. If your work is quality, it will reach a wide audience regardless of those who conspire against you.

Keep this in mind: although you are bound by professional peer review, that process should not stop you from moving forward with your work. Your research should not be beholden to those who anoint themselves thought police. There are several small circles that seem to deem themselves the sole authority of excellence. They recognize only those in the "in group," revealing a closed pipeline of power. In their mind, there are sides and you are either on their side or not. Ignore that. Write your work your way and build your collectives with cross sections of people who do not demand fealty.

Regardless of what collectives you create or who endorses your work (or doesn't), you will be judged and your book will be evaluated publicly. While you cannot control how your manuscript is reviewed, it is imperative that you follow professional guidelines of research methods, writing, and undergo peer review in an earnest effort to get honest feedback ahead of time. One way to prepare yourself for peer review is to immerse yourself in the literature and show you are familiar with Black feminist your scholars who research in your area.

TEACH: Collaborative Writing and Edited Volumes

Collaborative writing and publishing are important ways to mediate the impact of academic alienation, isolation, and bullying. Community building should not be developed for the purpose of creating an insular gang of bullies that require unquestioning allegiance. Quite the contrary, some of the most valuable and foundational critique can come from scholars in your close academic network and your clique can become an important model for others to organize and share resources with those not already affiliated with an in group. Editing books is an excellent way to grow your network. Editing alone is a monumental task. I have deeply enjoyed creating teams of editors to share the workload, to expand the reach of the call for contributors, and to magnify exponentially the opportunity to gather and share insights about closely related research.

Editing books is an act of labor-intensive service. You will be required to do a lot of behind-the-scenes work for other people that is neither acknowledged nor appreciated. You will work for the benefit of others—some of whom may be hard to please even as you complete numerous tasks on their behalf, often in ways they won't even know about. However, editing a volume does not have to be unpleasant. When undertaken with the right people, it can be an absolute joy. And you will certainly reap benefits in terms of recognition, creative control, and satisfaction of presenting a comprehensive volume that you could never write alone.

Gathering folks together to create, disseminate, and institutionalize Black-centered education can sometimes be an arduous task—but it can also feed the soul. For example, when I coedited a book on Black women's mental health, the two sister-scholars with whom I partnered, Kanika Bell and Nsenga Burton, were sources of inspiration and joy and remain so today. Part of our commitment to the writing process involved collective self-care. This took the form of editing each other's chapters, as well as spa visits and champagne brunches during the editing process.

My acknowledgement section for the *Black Women's Mental Health* tells a story: "Dr. Stephanie Evans would like to thank the co-editors Dr. Bell and Dr. Burton who were true partners in bringing this monumental work to fruition. She offers a special thank you to the authors who contributed chapters for bringing their 'best selves' to the project for the betterment of others. The process of collaborative wellness—especially the spa visits for editing parties—modeled a sisterhood that is definitely a 'best practice' for academic writing." The "sparty" (spa/party) took place at Chateau Elan, on the outskirts of Atlanta, Georgia, where we had massages, swam in the pool, relaxed in the jacuzzi, and snuck in cat naps on the chaise lounges. Though not fully adhering to Tricia Hersey's *Rest Is Resistance* manifesto, this restructuring of work as pleasure made a difference in the experience and the outcome.

While coediting the *Black Women's Mental Health* book, my stepmother passed away, and eight months later—within six weeks of each other—my mother and father also passed away. I was overwhelmed by funerals, resurfaced childhood trauma, and sorrow. My writing partners on the mental health book understood and supported me through the process of writing in real time about loss, grief, and healing. Mental health was not simply a cognitive concept in this book project; it was a collective, lived, and emotional experience.

Publishing a singled-authored monograph is stressful, but collaborating with others or leading a team through publication of an edited book increases the amount of pressure to stay on task even as your personal life flies off the rails. Collaborative work is good for the community, but it does have some drawbacks. As you move through the process of caring for other authors, make sure to find consistent ways to pay attention to your own emotional and physical needs. The best way to support your colleagues is to model self-care. Conversely, the more you care for yourself, the better position you will be in to support others. As you consider the tips below, understand you will have to experiment to find a balance that works for you.

Dr. E's Ten Tips for Publishing Coauthored or Coedited Volumes

1. **Clarify Roles, First Thing, In Writing.** When you begin an edited volume, be clear about the roles for each editor. Create a brief memorandum of understanding to clarify who will commit to taking on each task of publication (see the list in chapter 5) and put in writing the publication order and expectations of responsibility. If you have two editors, it is easier to share decision-making. When you have more than two, it is imperative to have clarity about who will have the final say if there is a disagreement. Ideally, get to know your coeditor(s) before committing

to a project so you don't have fundamental disagreements that can stall the project after the contract is signed. Be clear about what is really important to you and what decisions you are willing to surrender. Don't insist on having things a certain way if you are not willing to take the lead to make it happen (i.e., don't make up tasks for other people to do).

2. **Combine Targeted Invites and Open Calls for Chapters.** In my experience, I have seen the advantage of having a mixed submission process, meaning you should consider simultaneously inviting specific individuals to contribute chapters and, at the same time, publish an open call for chapters. You never know who is outside of your network and what brilliance they may offer to round out your project. While you want to invite folks within your academic community to contribute, make sure to set clear expectations early on. It is important for folks to know that if they do not submit appropriate chapters, their submission will not be included. Relay this information at the beginning of the process so they can manage their expectations and emotions if their chapter is not accepted.

3. **Streamline Communication with the Press.** Decide on who will be the point person for the press. While all editors should be copied on correspondence from the press, it is helpful if only one person responds . . . otherwise email inboxes will quickly be in shambles. The press should copy all on messages, the point person communicates offline with the editorial team, then the point person responds to the press (with a copy to all), so everyone stays in the information loop—but there are not endless email threads in twenty different directions.

4. **Provide Consistent Communication with Authors.** Decide early on who will be the point person for authors. See above point number three for the rationale. It is even more important that authors know to whom they should reach out with questions, because there will be dozens of folks with layers of questions. Dedicate one person to this task so authors are not burdened with communicating

with more than one person for critical answers. Many authors have not gone through the publishing process and, especially if they are relying on a publication to "count" for tenure or promotion, will be anxious about the timeline. If there is a significant delay in the process, reach out to authors so you can share updates. If one author contacts you with a question, chances are several others are wondering the same thing. If two authors inquire, best to send a group update. Pro tip: do not copy the full list. Instead, blind carbon copy (Bcc) everyone so folks don't spiral down an endless reply all hellscape.

5. **Be Up Front about Setting Deadlines and Conditions for Inclusion.** Move the project forward, even if that means losing someone special. It is not fair to hold up an entire book project for one or two people. Yes, it is wonderful to have the endorsement or contribution of a senior scholar, but if they cannot make the agreed-upon deadline or adhere to universal standards, they should be removed from the project. Of course, extend some measure of grace because things do come up that delay work. However, at some point, you must move forward, because their name does not outweigh the effort of dozens of people, many of whom do not have the privilege of recognition but have as much right to have their work produced. Set a viable timeline in advance and notify everyone in the project of the expectations to submit their work—and their revisions—in a timely manner or you will move forward without them. Offer alternatives: perhaps they might serve in another capacity as a partner on the project, such as reviewing the project or offering an endorsement. The global pandemic demonstrated that sometimes things don't move forward because of devastating circumstances that impact a few or all of us. Anticipate that there will always be catastrophic events that prevent or stall forward movement. Build in a communal commitment to the completion of the project and invite others to participate, understanding that, if they cannot move forward, the project will not stop. Everything happens for a reason and sometimes hearing "no, I cannot continue" from someone is a blessing for you and for them.

6. **Decide Whether to Accept Abstracts or Only Complete Chapters**. Abstracts allow you to begin to shape a project and provide an opportunity to interact with authors to help them develop their chapters. However, sometimes completed and edited chapters do not materialize. If you invite abstracts, notify authors that completed, polished chapters are required for full consideration. See the above note on the conditions for inclusion. It is fine to accept unedited placeholders as chapters if an author is trying to meet a deadline. However, extensions should only be offered on a temporary basis (with a clear deadline) because, again, it is not fair to other authors to hold up a project because of one or two people. Building community means understanding that not everyone has to (or will be able to) play the same role, and sometimes that opens the door for that person to contribute to the larger project in more impactful and interesting ways. For example, I invited a renowned senior scholar to write a foreword for a project. She initially accepted but was unable to meet the deadline, so we moved that particular project forward without her. Her schedule then opened up, and she participated as coeditor for a follow-up book in my *Black Women's Wellness* series. This was a markedly different—but much bigger role—than we had initially imagined. Be flexible and stay focused on moving the project forward for the benefit of the group. Where possible, keep the relationship intact, even as you make tough decisions.

7. **Commit to the Editing Process**. Editing books is largely a service to others. Even though, as an editor, you gain the benefit of primary name recognition, the workload and endless hidden tasks that you must undertake on behalf of others requires commitment. You are required to coordinate the team of editors and authors; secure the press contract and move through the publishing process; make the hard decisions not to include some folks if their work is not a good fit, completed, or polished; offer developmental feedback to authors and review pieces numerous times to catch small errors that may have been missed at

other points in the editing process; and, generally, make yourself available and accountable to others on a regular basis. Some of this work can be delegated or outsourced, but not if you desire to control the quality, vibrance, and viability of the book. As an editor, you must develop the skill to ask for help. You cannot do everything by yourself, so anticipate the enormity of the journey before agreeing to take the help. It is not necessary or professional to keep folks hanging on indefinitely when they entrust their work to you.

8. **Make the Decision Not to Include**. You will have to reject some work. Some people can be mentored and so you can make a case for their inclusion. Some pieces are not a good fit for the collection or won't be completed enough to include in the time available. As an author who spent much of my early years on the tenure track getting pieces rejected, it was devastating. After a three-hour mentoring session with a senior scholar, I was able to determine the (several) weak spots in my writing and work to correct them (and I'm still working on some things, lol). It is part of your job as a book editor to offer some guidance as to how the piece can be improved or where the author might find an alternate home for their work. One or two sentences goes a long way. Even if specific suggestions are not offered, a general recommendation for how to improve or a clear rationale about the criteria used to reject the piece can help the author understand the process (or, at least, your process) a bit better. Be kind. If you can't be kind, at least be professional. Timely rejections are best so the author can begin to look for another home for their work.

9. **Make the Decision Not to Move Forward with the Project—If Necessary**. I have served as the lead editor of five published books. I have served as the lead editor of at least that many book projects that did not see the light of day. In short, I've "failed" as often as I've succeeded in the publishing world. I hope that by being transparent, this helps people redefine failure. Some projects were great

ideas, but not enough people came forward to contribute or some contributions would not make it into the lineup (for example, a volume on Black women and sport or—my favorite failure—*Likka Stow: Alcohol in Black Life, History, and Culture*). Some projects were great ideas, but I was not the right person to see them to fruition. For example, my vision for a volume on Black women and music was not fully realized, but the online database can still be quite useful. As another unique example about the art of failing beautifully, I transferred my coedited book idea about Black women and dance to a much more capable and informed dance scholar who led the way for the project to be realized as a special-edition journal. She is an integral part of the dance community and moved forward with my full encouragement. Collaborative work is about the work. Collaborative work is not about one person. Keeping that in mind will help you to make difficult decisions. If a project is not going to move forward, it is best to make the decision to formally end the work and empower the authors to submit their work elsewhere. In some rare occasions, edited books take over five years, and, when released, are game changers. In other instances, transforming the book into another form (journal, web resource, etc.) is a way to move forward. But if the project is not going to be completed, it is best to close the door so everyone can move on.

10. **Build Community and Communal Ownership.** Colette Taylor, one of the coeditors of my first book *African American and Community Engagement,* also contributed a chapter to my latest book project, *Dear Department Chair.* Michelle Dunlap, another coeditor of *African American and Community Engagement,* served as a developmental editor for this book. I enjoy periodic happy hours with Nsenga Burton and Kanika Bell, coeditors for *Black Women's Mental Health,* and we still discuss the work of wellness. Ideally, edited books are opportunities to build relationships and develop sustained research collaboratives. These relationships may vary in depth and endurance,

but the wonderful thing about edited volumes is that you never know when you will have an opportunity to rekindle friendships (work-ships) at conferences, through interviews, or in service projects.

Bonus Tips to Build Community

Over the years, the most joyful part of book publishing has been creating community conversations around books. To celebrate the release of *Black Women in the Ivory Tower*, I hired a DJ and had a dance party with a book signing, including catered local snacks, where I cut a rug with students and colleagues alike.

Book clubs, classroom discussions, response panels, conferences, and release parties all function as celebration, dissemination, and collective enjoyment. They are especially meaningful when celebrating communal work like edited volumes. I share in the next chapter how Beverly Guy-Sheftall, Kimberlé Crenshaw, and others exemplify how to create community in ways that focus on public policy.

Book panel discussions are a significant source of joy and satisfaction in the publishing process. Whether in one-on-one conversations, on a small panel to discuss a single-authored book, or in a series of panels for an edited volume, talking about the book is where the action happens. Generally, engagement with people around your book is characterized as *marketing* and is portrayed as a way to "build your brand." Even though branding is an offensive holdover from enslavement and marketing every damn thing can function as a trap of capitalism, talking with people about your book does not have to be about making money. Public talks, like recorded online lectures, can be about building knowledge. Yes, selling books and receiving invites for paid book talks is part of claiming the worth of your labor, but worth is not reduced to monetary value. Sometimes the value is in how you are able to pass along a legacy. Working with former students to develop book projects and organizing faculty retreats (giving) are equally important as my honorarium (receiving). There must be a balance to build community that is not at your own expense, but that is sustained by your contribution as well.

Contributing to edited volumes offers an opportunity to partake in collaborative conversations. Several panel discussions for edited volumes by Black women scholars have been recorded for future discussions, including the one for *Black Women and Social Justice Education*, which was held virtually with scholars from around the country, well before the 2020 global pandemic. Think big. Think globally. I would challenge you to think about who you might engage from around the country and the world—whether in person or online—and build mutually beneficial relationships around your research interests.[17]

I could not attend the 2022 annual meeting of the Association of Black Women Historians (ABWH) due to a family illness. But as I watched on social media the dance party that occurred before the closing keynote by Dr. Treva Lindsey, I was transported to a nation of Black women sisterhood. The electric slide to Beyoncé's *Renaissance* showed the Living Legends Deborah Gray White, Paula Giddings, and Evelyn Higginbotham being honored at the event, alongside the outgoing president Erica Armstrong Dunbar and incoming president Shennette Garrett-Scott. Though they were not all dressed in Black, they swayed with the verve, power, and determination of Janet Jackson's *Rhythm Nation*.

Like thousands of Black women who experienced adolescence in the 1980s, I grew up inspired by Janet Jackson. I reflected on the character Penny in "Good Times" and moved out of my mother's house at the age of sixteen, at the same historical moment Ms. Jackson was taking *Control*. Unfortunately, I did not grow up in a tightknit family. I love my family, but our journeys have been marked by various types of violence, and, as a result, we have not traveled many of the same roads as a unit.

When the *Rhythm Nation* album was released, I had not yet found my crew. But, like Beyoncé's "Formation" would do later, Janet Jackson's music provided an example for me to gather folks together and sing for a better way of life. Janet's evolution was the revolution of my own life, and she has been one of the many artists whom collectives of Black women would celebrate together. Being a part of a nation of authors in race and gender studies is gratifying. When we unite with others in the commitment to educate others on human rights and social justice, we say, following Ms. Jackson's lead, we "want a better way of life" that transcends bigotry.

As part of a public practice, songs like "Rhythm Nation" remind us to gather with people who make us feel part of something bigger than ourselves. Faculty authors must address the responsibilities that we have not only to our readers but also to the subjects of our research. Unlike fiction writers or poets, our professional accountability extends beyond our circle, and the information we present as facts has far-reaching implications.

Reflection Questions

Question 18: What experience do you have with joint writing and collaborating on a joint publication? What space do you make to invite critique from people inside and outside of your inner circle?

Question 19: How can your work help "build a better world"? What nonprofit, policy, or government organizations might benefit from your research? What might community-based collaboration look like for you?

Practical Tasks

- Name people with whom you would like to write in community. Identify potential peer reviewers who will be supportive but also insightfully critical of your work. Share your work for informal peer review (share selectively).

- Create a small, short-term writing group with at least two others working on a book.

- Cite two edited volumes and read the introductions to get a sense of how the editors shape the collective discussion.

- Discuss chapter questions with a mentor or colleague.

- Share your chapter answer with a next-generation scholar.

7

Institution

Political Practice

Black feminist writing is a liberatory practice. My quest to maintain self-care in a hostile academy and to practice collective care in a hostile world is at once a continuation of a tradition and something of my own creation. Though I don't dive into public discussions that turn on a dime, I am deeply informed by public discourse. In this book, I embrace Black feminist writers—and those who write in this tradition—who have built writing communities. Perhaps more scholars outside of race and gender studies might follow our lead and embrace intellectual care, self-care, and collective care to guide their research so they not only produce a book but also create and develop mutually beneficial research agendas. Perhaps, together, we might endeavor to not only write books, but also write enough to educate, inform, and energize an ever-growing community of problem-solvers, dreamers, creators, and innovators. At the very least we can contribute to care and conversations of freedom-loving people.

Stay Woke:
The Never-Ending Attack on Black Women's Studies

> Freedom-loving people are certainly indebted to the decades-old work of Black feminist writers and scholars.
>
> —Beverly Guy-Sheftall, "The Essential Connection between Book Bans and Black Feminism," 2023

Black studies and women's studies have been demonized as woke because the goal of some campaigns is to ensure people stay asleep, confused, and overwhelmed so that the status quo—where a few people control all the resources—can continue unabated. Women have a long history of self-possession (despite generations of institutionalized gaslighting). Traditions of African American self-determination (despite generations of violent oppression) have resulted in effective clandestine self-education. It is no wonder that some entities have continuously sought to limit the access or impact of our emancipatory courses of study.

Academic research permeates public spaces. Whether through legislation, health care, K-12 education, business, or entertainment, scholarly research finds its way into language, culture, and policy. So not only should we be mindful of how research can influence structures, but we can also produce research in order to restructure higher education itself. While this book is about academic writing and publishing, throughout the text, I also draw your attention to implications of wellness work for academic institutions.

I served as a department chair for twelve consecutive years while also authoring or coediting nine books with three university presses. My experience is instructive for readers who are newly hired faculty members, struggling to understand how to publish despite institutional pressures and unforgiving timelines. The longevity of my career also supports senior faculty who desire to continue their writing journey despite administrative workloads. Regardless of the stage of your faculty career, writing can be a source of individual satisfaction and community connection. Administrators have a duty to protect academic freedom.

Democracy requires academic freedom. Threats to academic freedom abound. Threats to laws, leadership, literacy, and labor are of enduring concern. Each of the political barriers to higher education inform and are informed by Black feminist writing practices:

Laws:

- Undermining academic freedom for educators
- Normalizing laws against "divisive concepts"
- Instituting laws against Diversity, Equity, and Inclusion (DEI)
- Undermining tenure and guarantees against dismissal for political reasons

Leadership:

- Appointing politicians, businesspeople, and celebrities as administrators and board members for political reasons
- Overlooking tenured research faculty, teaching-based faculty, and other experienced educators for leadership and decision-making posts
- Administrators who do not defend human rights, free speech, or progressive scholar activism

Literacy:

- Diminishing access to information
- Undermining the validity of information and fact-checking
- Politics of standardizing information, AI, and politicized charges of plagiarism

Labor:

- Preventing union strikes for workers and the right to fair compensation
- Overcompensating administrators and instituting top-heavy administrative structures with limited transparency and lack of resources for faculty and graduate student researchers
- Undermining the equitable value of labor (full-time faculty, contingent faculty, and graduate student instructors)

In the words of Ella Baker, "we who believe in freedom cannot rest until it comes." Some people deem capitalism, colonialism, fascism, and war to be inevitable. While certainly they are enduring features of the human story, these destructive forces are historical. While I believe that evil is inevitable and evil people are a part of life, I do not believe that it is inevitable that evil will *dominate*. There is no one path to revolution; each must choose the journey to justice that resonates for them internally and organize with others on a similar path. To secure a future grounded in care and compassion, we must continue to study the past and act in the present.

Not everyone is invested in social justice, and many try to advance special interests to limit human rights in areas like equality in politics, economics, health, and education. For a long time, these four areas have impacted Black women's lives in particular—although, they are not alone in this. Black Women's Studies educators teach progressive pathways to secure political will (self-determination), work (benefitting from one's own labor and gaining economic stability), wellness (conditions that allow one to maintain holistic health), and wisdom (free access to information). Analyses, like Nancy MacLean's National Book Award finalist *Democracy in Chains: The Deep History of the Radical Right's Stealth Plan for America*, can identify and unpack the agendas that seek to manufacture the conditions that keep the masses powerless, poor, sick, and uneducated.

In September 2020, the forty-fifth president of the United States issued Executive Order 13950, "Banning Race and Sex Stereotyping," which sought to prohibit "divisive concepts." In part, the order claimed that teaching about race and gender promoted stereotypes:

> **Sec. 2.** *Definitions.* For the purposes of this order, phrase:
>
> (2) (a) "Divisive concepts" means the concepts that (1) one race or sex is inherently superior to another race or sex; (2) the United States is fundamentally racist or sexist; (3) an individual, by virtue of his or her race or sex, is inherently racist, sexist, or oppressive, whether consciously or unconsciously; (4) an individual should be discriminated against or receive adverse treatment solely or partly because of his or her race or sex; (5) members of one race or sex cannot and should not attempt to treat others without respect to race or sex; (6) an individual's moral character is necessarily determined by his or her race or sex; (7) an individual, by virtue of his or her race or sex, bears responsibility for actions committed in the past by other members of the same race or sex; (8) any individual should feel discomfort, guilt, anguish, or any other form of psychological distress on account of his or her race or sex; or (9) meritocracy or traits such as a hard work ethic are racist or sexist, or were created by a particular race to oppress another race. The term "divisive concepts" also includes any other form of race or sex stereotyping or any other form of race or sex scapegoating.[1]

In essence, this order functioned as a gag rule for race and gender studies or any course content that points out the histories of enslavement, oppression, discrimination, or bias—whether individual or systemic.

The Presidential Executive Order was one front in the battle for the control of resources and popular ideas about American history and world history. It was a calculated assault on education and academic freedom, designed by operatives in league with conservatives seeking to control policies around health, guns, and labor. As clearly outlined in *Democracy in Chains*, public and private university spaces have long been fertile ground for conservative think tanks like the Cato Institute, the Heritage Foundation, Citizens for a Sound Economy, Americans for Prosperity, FreedomWorks, the Club for Growth, the State Policy Network, the Competitive Enterprise Institute, the Tax Foundation, the Reason Foundation, the Leadership Institute, the Charles Koch Foundation, and Koch Industries.[2]

In 2023, Ron DeSantis, a presidential hopeful and the governor of Florida outlawed the teaching of African American studies in that state, effectively eliminating the freedom to teach and learn. Through a series of House Bills and fast-tracked legislation (HB 7 and "Stop the Wrongs to Our Kids and Employees, W.O.K.E." Act), particular books have been banned in K–12 schoolrooms because of supposed "indoctrination," or exposing students to concepts like queer theory, intersectionality, and abolition. The executive order did not mention Critical Race Theory (CRT) by name, but the order legitimized an orchestrated national attack on CRT in schools, libraries, and universities around the country.[3]

LEARN: Septima Clark's Guide to Problem-Solving

> My life has been devoted to the practical and the specific . . . I have been trying all my days to solve problems, and problems—brother—some ones, at any rate—are annoyingly specific.
>
> —Septima Clark (1962)

Septima Poinsette was born on May 3, 1898, in Charleston, South Carolina. Her mother, Victoria, was born free and raised in Haiti, and she worked as a laundress. Her father, Peter, was enslaved on the Poinsette's plantation in Charleston and later worked as a janitor. She was the second of eight children. In her 1962 autobiography, *Echo in My Soul*, Clark recalls her education, teaching career, activism, and hope for America's future. She began teaching at the Promise Land School on St. Johns Island, South Carolina, in 1916, at the age of eighteen. She taught writing to the men of the Odd Fellows, a Black fraternal organization, and participated in women's sewing circles. She did not view these activities as "service"; rather, she saw them as simply community engagement. In 1918, she moved back to the mainland and taught sixth grade at her former school, Avery Normal Institute. She married Nerie David Clark and had two children, but only her son survived. Nerie himself died in 1927. Septima taught in Columbia and Charleston, volunteered with the YWCA, mediated community relations between city officials and the police department, and was part of the campaign to equalize Black and White teachers' salaries. Her legacy epitomizes the town-gown relationships at the center of community engagement pedagogy and research.[4]

In January 1957, under the auspices of the Highlander Folk School, the first Citizenship School was opened on St. Johns Island, and Clark employed her cousin, Bernice Robinson, as head teacher. Robinson owned a beauty shop, and while she had no teaching experience or credentials, she was respected and trusted by the community. She spoke the local language Gullah, and she spent time talking and listening to community members. The Citizenship School's first students all passed the South Carolina literacy test, and the effectiveness of the program was duplicated in other Southern states. In 1959, police raided Highlander to enforce segregation policies, and, in 1961, the state of Tennessee forced Highlander out of the area. Again, Clark was out of a job. At the suggestion of Ella Baker, Clark moved the Citizenship School operation to Atlanta with the national Southern Christian Leadership Conference (SCLC). With the SCLC teacher-training program under her purview, Clark led the way for a national African American voter-registration drive.

The movement was furthered by the 1962 Voter Education Project, which involved a broad coalition of civil rights organizations. In the next four years, the coalition trained ten thousand teachers for Citizenship Schools and nonviolent resistance. By the eve of the 1965 Voting Rights Act, seven hundred thousand Black Americans had registered to vote. This movement was of monumental importance, as the Black population united and garnered unprecedented political power.[5] As a researcher, Clark painstakingly listed the many ways individuals, groups, and representatives of institutions operated to withhold rights to African Americans and poor people.[6]

Contributions by marginalized scholars of color can build on Clark's social justice legacy by not ignoring systemic inequities within and without the academy. Her legacy of community-based education is a model for how to write in ways that are fundamentally informed by those with whom you wish to build. Clark enrolled at Atlanta University to learn from W. E. B. Du Bois. In this same spirit, we must demonstrate how academic books in race and gender studies are relevant beyond the academy. This is especially important as political attacks on academic freedom increase.

CREATE: 2023, the Freedom to Learn Workshop

While Florida is a high-profile case of academic suppression, several other states are part of a coordinated and well-funded political attack. Texas is a notable example. The industry newspaper *Inside Higher Ed* reported on April 14, 2023, about "A Trilogy of Anti-DEI, Tenure Bills" that were orchestrated to deplatform scholars of race and gender studies and end the academic freedom that tenure is constructed to guarantee. Fortunately, national and institutional unions are fighting the repressive measures. Notably, scholars like Dr. Ashley Farmer, who labeled Texas and Florida as "two sides of the same coin," are actively resisting rollbacks in faculty rights. At an online teach-in, which was hosted by the voting-rights grassroots campaign Common Power, Farmer presented strategies for opposing encroachment on academic freedoms. Farmer recommended those interested in getting involved join the movement by leading teach-ins, testifying against bills, protesting, and participating in national days of action.[7]

I took several steps to protest the onslaught of ridiculous challenges to race and gender studies waged in education of all levels. I stayed focused on my writing. I supported lawyers of the HB 7 case by recommending several public-facing scholars to serve as expert witnesses. I signed an early petition of African American studies faculty against the College Board and Florida's decision around AP classes in Black history. And I amplified collective efforts by Khalil Gibran Muhammad, Carol Anderson, Beverly Guy-Sheftall, Kimberlé Crenshaw, Jelani Cobb, and others.

On Wednesday, May 3, 2023, the Freedom to Learn Coalition held a National Day of Action to defend truth and to protect the freedom to learn. Kimberlé Crenshaw, Khalil Gibran Mohammad, Beverly Guy-Sheftall, and education leaders from around the country formed the Freedom to Learn Coalition as a means to resist the repression of race and gender studies around the country: "Our collective emphatically oppose the attacks being waged on educational curricula in the United States and elsewhere against intersectionality, critical race theory, Black feminism, queer theory, and other frameworks that address structural inequality."[8] The group sponsored dozens of events on the chosen day and held numerous meetings via Zoom to share information, strategize, and offer resources and encouragement to support those invested in protecting the right to learn.

The coalition explained, "Now is the time to work to build a broad coalition of people to strengthen our democracy and our values of equity, inclusion and social justice. Through collective actions across the country, we will resist restrictions on the freedom to learn, fight the right's anti-woke disinformation campaigns, and demonstrate majoritarian support for equity in our schools, campuses, and workplaces." To pursue race and gender studies in the academy is challenging because, like the colonization of Africa, university systems are designed to block individual or collective progress while, at the same time, sending a message to marginalized scholars that if we are not thriving, it's our own fault.

On the National Day of Action, I held a teach-in that focused on writing books. While, at many events around the country, people read books that had been banned, I wanted to turn my attention to the next generation of scholars and support those books in the pipeline that are facing a headwind of censorship. The online workshop, titled "Write Me Down in History," an homage to Angelou's poem "Still I Rise" was designed as a space to mentor faculty in race and gender studies. Workshop registration prioritized the most vulnerable university educators in marginalized fields (like African American studies or women's, gender, and sexuality studies), where scholarship is under attack and devalued. The anti-woke censorship of African American studies, intersectionality, and Black feminism is designed to silence scholarship that unpacks the roots of oppression by having a chilling effect on any interest in reading, writing, and teaching critical history or theory. In short, censorship and intimidation are designed to keep us from doing our internal and external *work*.

Almost fifty people registered for that writing workshop from almost twenty locations: Alabama, California, Georgia, Delaware, North Carolina, Louisiana, Maine, Maryland, Missouri, New Jersey, New York, Oregon, Texas, Virginia, Vermont, Canada, England, Brazil, and St. Thomas. Those who attended submitted areas of interest and concerns about the publishing process, and the registration responses helped me to sharpen my offering for this book. In that workshop, I shared the lessons I have learned through my practice.

The one-hour online mentoring meeting supported instructional faculty working in higher education who may have felt especially uneasy in a time when race and gender studies are (again, as always) under a microscope. This is exactly the time when we must make our voices heard! If you are working on a book proposal or book-length manuscript in race and gender studies—particularly on projects informed by intersectionality and Black feminism—consider registering for workshops as well as creating your own groups.

To confirm duplicitous intents of conservatives (and what, exactly, are they conserving?) school districts in Houston, Texas, began to ban libraries and replace them with disciplinary facilities. I want to support research that not only exposes and reverses these trends, but that populates new libraries with forward thinking texts. I hope this book has helped you define writing for yourself and allows you to write in ways that resist intellectual violence.[9]

Political challenges to Black studies and women's studies that raged in the states of Florida and Texas could have been a challenge to me finishing this book. The main way I contributed to institutionalizing race and gender studies was to finish this book and to support others in their writing. Part of my service to the profession included reviewing five dossiers for tenure and promotion to full professor—because only those at rank can assess colleagues at this level.

Only two percent of full professors in the US are Black women. Me saying no to promotion reviews means there are few others to step up for professional service. I reviewed three manuscripts for university presses and participated in four manuscript review workshops, in addition to mentoring several scholars through submission of individual and edited volumes. Rather than participate in debates where terms are defined by antagonistic adversaries committed to distorting my words, I nurtured dialogue with those whom I felt would most appreciate my close attention and help us, collectively, address the issues that faculty face in higher education.

While part of me felt like a bystander for not being on television news, in the courtroom, in the statehouse, or on the protest lines, I understood that I can't do everything, so I chose to pay attention to growing areas that I could impact doing the work I loved to do most where I had been asked to serve.

Recent moves toward professionalization and institutionalization of BWST, and conversations surrounding these developments include several topics:

- varying definitions and traditions of womanism

- the relationship of newer developments, like Afropessimism and post-Blackness, to older or more established topics, like Afrocentrism, Black feminist thought, critical race theory, and intersectionality

- how to engage foundational scholars in Black Women's Studies (e.g., Patricia Bell-Scott, Barbara Smith, Beverly Guy-Sheftall) with Black women scholars in various disciplines (e.g., Hortense Spillers, English; Faye Harrison, anthropology; Darlene Clark Hine, history; Evelynn Hammonds, STEM), as well as scholars in Black studies (Carter G. Woodson, W. E. B. Du Bois, Sylvia Wynter, Walter Rodney), women's and gender studies (Simone de Beauvoir, Adrienne Rich, Alfred Kinsey), and adjacent fields (Michel Foucault, philosophy; Karl Marx, political science)

- the imperative to model Black feminist praxis that is inclusive of all queer, transgender women, and non-binary people

- the location of Black Women's Studies classes and faculty (or lack thereof) in Black studies departments versus women's studies departments

- the proximity of scholarship to activism—particularly in the wake of unmitigated personal, cultural, and structural violence against Black women and girls

- how deans and department chairs can create intellectually and physically inclusive spaces for Black Women's Studies to flourish

- how new media impact language, audience, dissemination, and preservation of scholarship and the vital role of librarians

- the responsibility of peer reviewers for journals, books, and other academic outlets to require submissions be revised if they do not cite relevant literature

Ultimately, these developments will show up in new research and we must address questions raised so that we may more clearly define what it means to say "I teach Black Women's Studies" in the twenty-first century. Meaning making about the future of feminism and of the field will happen in community.

Cultivating Compassion in the Global Academy: Writing and the Politics of Agency

> In sum, at some fundamental level all Black women historians are engaged in the process of historical reclamation. But it is not enough simply to reclaim those hidden and obscure facts and names of Black foremothers. . . . In synchrony with the reclaiming and narrating must be the development of an array of analytical frameworks which allow us to understand why Black women behave in certain ways and how they acquired agency.
>
> —Darlene Clark Hine, "Rape and the Inner Lives of Black Women in the Middle West: Preliminary Thoughts on the Culture of Dissemblance" (1989)

Academic writing—in and of itself—is not necessarily activism. Yet, writing books and teaching from published writing remain essential parts of human rights movements and are ways to both demonstrate and advocate for Black women's agency. For example, when mass violence and destruction erupted in Gaza in October 2023, I referenced Margo Okazawa-Rey's chapter "Solidarity with Palestinian Women: Notes from a Japanese-Black U.S. Feminist" in *Activist Scholarship: Antiracism, Feminism, and Social Change* (2009) to guide my thinking, speaking, and actions. Okazawa-Rey's memoir of anti-militarism activism and building networks of solidary across war-torn regions demonstrates the eternal gift of historical context that well-written and community-centered books can offer. Her work modeled agency, even in the face of horror. Scholar-activist Robin D. G. Kelly argues that the language of human rights often masks the imperative for self-determination. Yet, he and numerous other scholars have rightly taken a public stance to affirm Palestinian human rights. Dionne Brand's poem "prologue for now—Gaza" references media outlets referring to Palestinians as "human animals" (reminiscent of labels used during Jewish, Rwandan, Cambodian, and other genocidal horrors), so it is imperative to keep language of dehumanization and human rights central to Black feminist writing. Part of the power of positioning Black women's rights as human rights is it allows us to acknowledge that human rights are universal and you cannot argue for one group's rights without granting agency to all populations. Scholarship is one way to acknowledge the mandate to defy war mongering and affirm humanity beyond boundaries of race, gender, nation, religion, class, and other differences. We must continue calls for global ceasefires and divest from US people, policies, or organizations that are responsible for gun violence, structures built for killing death, and weapons of war at home and abroad.

Books can also educate us so we can confidently support organizations doing direct humanitarian work. Stanlie James's *Practical Audacity: Black Women and International Human Rights* (2021), profiles activist Jaribu Hill, who worked at the Center for Constitutional Rights (CCR). The CCR is at the forefront of several local, state, national and international human rights litigation. That is one organization but there are many others, like Doctors without Borders and CARE, doing lifesaving work in Gaza, Sudan, Congo, Haiti, Ukraine, and other areas torn by war and genocide. During times of multiple crises, it is necessary to both study and organize in real time by supporting folks who are already doing effective justice work.

The United Nations Universal Declaration of Human Rights (UDHR) set a benchmark in world history. Drafted by representatives from nine nations, the United Nations General Assembly formalized the UDHR in Paris on December 10, 1948.[10] During the Second World War, the world witnessed unprecedented destruction, and the declaration became a pact to ensure that devastation would not be repeated.[11] Eventually, however, the United Nations realized that rights were not sufficient to ensure peace. As a result, the organization produced a document in 2006 that acknowledged the need to actively advocate for social justice as supplemental to human rights. The committee conceded: "The concept of *social justice* and its relevance and application within the present context require a more detailed explanation. . . ." Following the revolutions that shook Europe in the mid-1800s, social justice became a rallying cry for progressive thinkers and political activists. Clearly, as war, conflict, genocide, and fascist leadership experience revival around the world, there is a global imperative to clearly define human rights and mandate actionable measurable steps toward social justice.[12]

A decade before this pairing of social justice with human rights in the United Nations, *Teaching for Diversity and Social Justice* (1997) was published to ground a pioneer program in social justice and higher education. All of these resources are important for facilitating a fuller understanding of the breadth of the contributions that Black women's narratives can bring to human rights and social justice literature and for reinforcing foundational concepts such as inclusion, oppression, privilege, and power.

Black Women in the Ivory Tower characterizes Black women's educational thought as a body of work that focuses on applied research. The goal of that book was explicitly to advance education as a human right and a civil right. That book, along with *Black Women and Social Justice Education*, centers ideas of Black women educators (historical and contemporary) and foregrounds what I call the "values of the ninety-four percent." Progressive education means embracing values and operating by ethics modeled by those ninety-four percent of Black women in the 2016 United States presidential election who opposed the regressive political candidate.

Black feminist writing is a problem-solving practice. To sustain race and gender studies means to center values and practices that do not dehumanize populations and that expand access to higher education. Institutionalizing Black feminist wellness means centering our views as the norm. Progressive writing means affirming mental health, human rights, and social justice.

Universal pressures like family, economy, and career are exacerbated by specific hate crimes that target Black women—especially queer and/or vocal Black women. Moya Bailey offers *misogynoir* as an important theoretical intervention to describe the pervasiveness of anti-Black misogyny. For Black women, the academy is a violent place. Rather than shielding Black scholars from emotional, physical, or intellectual pain, institutions often seek to rationalize suffering, blame victims, and make those who challenge oppressive conditions feel like they're insane. But this is a global phenomenon.[13]

European nations have systematically destabilized Africa. Part of the work of Western and European academics has been to cover up, excuse, or deny this fact in order to preserve economic dominance. The malicious role of academia in promoting racist, sexist, and empire-building "research"—whether overt, covert, or unintentional—is not hyperbole or paranoia, and scholars who write against the grain or challenge established canon are often punished.[14]

On October 14, 2015, the Sri Lankan economist Howard Nicholas delivered an explosive lecture hosted by Critical Collective at the International Institute of Social Studies in the Hague. By unpacking economic models, ideology, and the "doctrine of comparative advantage," he plainly uncovers the malice behind the colonial mentality and the use of universities to maintain white supremacy worldwide (both overtly and covertly). His economic model shows that, if Africa were to develop food and manufacturing self-sufficiency, it would cost "advanced countries" significantly, increasing the cost of living exponentially. To summarize, we overwhelmingly research, write grants, teach, and publish in a reality where our work is subsidized by the exploitation of human and natural resources in the African continent (and other regions in the Global South).

Nicholas, a scholar of Karl Marx, states, "Africa has a role to play, as a raw material producer. . . . We need Africa to be impoverished because we need those raw materials and we need them dirt cheap." This is an open secret. But what Nicholas also makes clear, a part that is too often denied, is that the Western academy in Europe and the United States (and now China) has a central role to play not only in obfuscating the truth of underdevelopment but also in pushing the ideologies that make Africans believe that poverty is their own fault rather than a systemic and purposeful effort by the West: "We are part of the producers of ideology. At universities and academic institutions we are complicit in this whole enterprise. So the job of many Western academics is to convince Africans they have to keep doing what they're doing and to show them, 'it's your fault that you're poor. It's not our fault.' This is what we do in academic institutions."[15] The same can be said of those who challenge the need to compensate Native populations for resources and to return stolen land. The academy is responsible for ideas and ideology that negatively impact people, land, animals, and all living beings. This holds true for the need to challenge environmental narratives that deny climate change. Ideas have consequences. Your ideas have consequences and, as Moya Bailey points out in *Misogynoir Transformed* (2021), Black women's writing is not inherently feminist.

Some scholars intentionally produce scholarship to keep the oppressive status quo intact. Some are invested in keeping power systems in place and try to make those who challenge the established order (academic whistleblowers) question themselves. In addition to the ordinary challenges of being an academic, any scholarship that seeks to undermine the status quo will draw blowback. But the work of destabilizing supremacist knowledge is both possible and necessary. I am not interested in supporting academic writing that results in individual advancement at the expense of those who are impoverished because of global greed. I believe that we can write our way to a better future in ways that do not require gross ethical negligence nor depend on our perpetual exhaustion. Here the work of Tricia Hersey is instructive. Her organization the Nap Ministry and book *Rest Is Resistance: A Manifesto* (2022) is grounded in womanist theology and leads the way to a more human approach to labor and rest.

Radical (meaning "root") observations by the Sierra Leonean and German social entrepreneur Mallence Bart-Williams and others model what liberatory work can look like outside the academy. In the viral Ted Talks "Change Your Channel" and "Africa Is not Poor," Bart-Williams gets to the point of how purposeful messaging can be to twist facts. Alternative works, like Julia Jordan-Zachery's *Erotic Testimonies: Black Women Daring to Be Wild and Free* (2022) and La Marr Jurelle Bruce's *How to Go Mad without Losing Your Mind: Madness and Black Radical Creativity* (2021), serve as beautiful examples of academic scholarship that challenge the epistemologies of white supremacy by embracing Black genius, while still exemplifying the rigors of modern scholarship. And they do this while still preserving their mental health in spite of the deadly mind games of the academy.[16]

For those, like me, who are survivors of sexual, cultural, and structural violence, the academy can be exponentially punishing because it harbors serial abusers and shames those who dare to challenge esteemed colleagues with known records of abuse. The chain of command of administrative protocol, professional mentorship, and scholarly authentication often places those climbing the professional ladder in a precarious position if they are inquisitive or defiant. But just like those who are born to an abusive family but who move on to construct supportive families, it is possible to create a network of support and mutual care, even while maintaining intellectual rigor, professionalism, and the relatively objective measures of excellence. The queer community, specifically the development of "houses" in ballroom culture, is a model for how to build your own "house" and find your chosen academic family. Writing is a way to build your own academic house in a way that can help reimagine the goals and norms of the academy. Your publications can reset the structure of the global academy.

TEACH: Epistemological Wellness and Ways to Sustain Black Women's Studies (REAL BAD NEWS)

Black women's writing often centers healing and offers clues about how to repair pain caused from violence. Consequently, Black women's memoirs constitute acts of personal and social defiance, often encouraging progressive action toward liberation, as espoused in Toni Cade Bambara's groundbreaking 1970 collection *The Black Woman*. African American intellectual history is steeped in the spiritual and social consciousness that undergirds Black women's pursuit of rights and justice. For example,

LeRhonda Manigault-Bryant's chapter, "I Had a Praying Grandmother: Religion, Prophetic Witness, and Black Women's Herstories" expands on the concept of intergenerational epistemologies of "wellbeing and survival" despite enduring inequalities, connecting identity and justice to foremother wisdom.

Like Manigault-Bryant's "grandmaternal knowledge" as an archival source, in my chapter in *The Black Intellectual Tradition,* I demonstrate how the study of memoir as epistolary writing expands how we identify and interpret primary source material on Black women's knowledge production. While narratives have always been considered one important source of historical analysis, looking closely at the expansive library of memoir and autobiography (rather than a select few of the more popular publications) broadens the scholarly landscape. Black women life writers form a dynamic, living network—one that depicts diverse experiences and shared knowledge creation. National and international voices are central to a deepened study of civil rights, human rights, social justice, and peace studies.

I view citation of Black women not as an obligation or as optional but as an indispensable part of Black feminist scholarship. Even though I know that I bring original questions, experience, and insights to my work, at no time have I written outside of my relationship with other scholars in my field, though I have also sought to connect to other disciplines as well. There are many scholars doing exemplary work—not knowing or citing their work would mean that my own scholarship is not as strong as it could be. It would also mean erasing entire encyclopedias of stories that reveal Black women's agency over time. The process of centering Black women's ideas in the institution is certainly a matter of time and energy.

SCHOLARS WITHOUT SOURCES ARE REAL BAD NEWS

Black feminist writing is a lifelong learning practice. Read everything. If you don't read, you will not write well. Your theoretical framework, research methodology, data collection methods, analysis, peer review, and audience should all be intimately intertwined. Your research should be informed by a wide variety of source types. Expand how you search for sources. By sources, I mean both the primary sources that provide the content for your argument (e.g., archives, memoirs, newspapers, interviews, focus groups), as well as the secondary sources you use to help evaluate those primary sources (e.g., journal articles, books, other published scholarship). Sources might also include knowledge gathered from community partners, organizations, artists, and activists. Strengthen the connection between where you gather information and where you plan to disseminate your scholarship.

You may envision producing a book on a narrow topic for a small panel of disciplinary experts. Your goal might be to share your work with a particular demographic or a community in a specific geographic location. Or you may want to create a manifesto for the wide world. Regardless of the type of book you want to publish, if you are writing an academic book, it is imperative to read broadly, analyze deeply, and consider your sources mindfully.

Too many colleagues miss the opportunity to communicate with artists, talk to youth and young students, learn from experts outside their area, or share the spotlight with other scholars outside their strata. Writing a book is often an isolating experience because we choose to isolate ourselves to show we are special. Then, we have the nerve to be taken aback when others fail to validate our specialness. You have no control over who likes your work, cites your work, or validates your work. Your energy is best spent working with those who want to work with you. Leave the rest alone.

The more you engage multiple source types and write within multiple communities, the less likely your work is to be insular, inaccurate, or irrelevant. Whether writing a single-authored or collected volume, it is critical to include a broad set of sources so you have multiple points of entry into discussion with diverse communities. The advent of crowd-sourced syllabi like #CharlestonSyllabus and #FergusonSyllabus has been helpful for college instructors, allowing us to locate sources and identify a broad range of source types that can inform students about crucial current events. But we should do much more to engage students with identifying reliable sources.[17]

I call engaging multiple source types "teaching from the source." Scholars who engage a wide variety of source types should not only validate their findings but provide points of entry into discussions with a broad readership. For example, by adding a music playlist to the interpretive structure (see the playlist in the appendix), I make my message more relatable to audiences outside of the ivory tower.[18]

Below is a detailed list of primary, secondary, and tertiary sources for you to develop a robust, well-cited book project. I organize diverse source types into an acronym to capture the limits of research that only uses books, articles, or random websites. Given the rapid growth of AI, it is imperative that researchers spend extra time fact checking, verifying a source, and extraordinary caution to verify a source by cross-checking references. Even senior scholars sometimes need to be reminded to move beyond books, articles, and archives to discover new touchstones that inspire our interpretation.

I created a maxim to encapsulate this idea: Scholars without sources are REAL BAD NEWS. The sources in the acronym are comprehensive:

Learning Source Types

- **R**eports, government documents, or databases
- **E**live sources, oral histories, interviews, videos, or podcasts
- **L**aw or legal journals
- **B**ooks (nonfiction, scholarly, or memoirs)
- **B**ook reviews
- **A**rticles (scholarly journals or magazines)
- **A**rchives, artworks, or museums
- **A**gencies, professional associations, or organizations
- **D**issertations or theses
- **D**ocumentaries or movies
- **N**ewspapers
- **N**ovels or short stories
- **E**ncyclopedias or bibliographies
- **W**ebsites, multimedia, blogs, or social media posts
- **S**ongs or poems

Since I began teaching in 2003, I've required *at least* ten source types in my students' final paper assignments. Some students may inevitably grumble, but I have held firm because it was my own undergraduate coursework that introduced me to sources like dissertations, documentaries, interviews, and book reviews—sources beyond books and articles and the then-emerging interwebs.

By exploring different source types throughout the semester, I teach the skill of information literacy. Taking the time to locate dissertations and archival work enables serious discussions about the validity of sources and the need to do background checks and clarify the provenance of published information. As you prepare your book manuscript, move beyond traditional source types to expand the range of your argument and the reach of your writing. Locate books and journal articles but also investigate social media, laws and legal journals, professional organizations, newspapers, and more. Surely this practice is intuitive to most scholars who do mixed-methods research. Yet, formalizing the practice of engaging a broad range of sources will improve your work exponentially.[19]

Critical thinking is a perennial mandate, so it is always necessary to cite a cross section of information in order to compare and contrast ideas. Discussing your work with other scholars and actively building intellectual community is one way to ensure your work is well-informed, vetted, and viable. But be forewarned, inner peace is not something that you will find outside of yourself. Community is messy, so you have to stay vigilant in managing your time and energy.

Agency in Practice:
Time and Energy Management

Two skills I adamantly worked on during the dozen years I served as department chair were time management and energy management. In essence, I became a master of agency. Time management is imperative, because without it, progress toward book publication is impossible. But energy management is equally essential. Some interactions can leave you emotionally, spiritually, or intellectual drained, even after a brief meeting. Learning to rebalance—or even *pre*-balance before stressful interactions—can make all the difference for a quick recovery that allows you to move on with your day after conflict or dreaded activities.

By carefully organizing my time, I have the energy and clarity to complete more writing tasks in my schedule. When I was an administrator, I had to prioritize in order to address major tasks of that job, take care of my students, address needs of my colleagues, and tame the beast that was my inbox. If I wanted to write, especially as department chair, I had to block schedule my calendar.

I make having time and space to think a regular priority. Through daily effort my projects come to fruition. While editing a volume on department chairs and managing stress as a department chair, focusing on the task at hand helped me to stay motivated and address the challenges I faced. Not only was I determined not to let the department chair job completely depress me, but I was also determined to name and address the unreasonable workload in an effort to change it for those who would take on the responsibility in the future. But determination is not enough. Over the years I have certainly benefitted from periodic counseling visits when the pressure became too much to bear.

One goal of your practice should be that writing become bearable and that the work does not cause mental harm. My focus on wellness is not only for individual benefit. Rather, wellness must be embraced as an institutional value. Supporting department chairs and fundamentally changing the structure of the academy and demographics of higher education leadership is my small contribution to build a better world. Anyone on campus can create a hostile work environment; conversely everyone can contribute to a humane work environment.

A decade after my graduation from the Du Bois Department of Afro-American Studies at the UMass-Amherst, I taught for eight years at Clark Atlanta University, the house that Du Bois built. It should then come as no surprise that his work has made an indelible mark on my own. In *The Souls of Black Folk*, Dr. Du Bois charges, "the thinker must think for truth, not for fame." Consequently, my obsession with Black women's intellectual history has been a constant journey to uncover truths espoused by educators before me, even as I discover and articulate my own truths in the process.

In my career, I have focused on how Black women write our lives to save our lives. By focusing on Black women's memoirs, I have been able to identify the life skills and academic skills that have advanced the lived and professional experiences of Black women. To "write for truth and not for fame" involves the pursuit of truth for universal equity. Justice requires that we change systems.

While Angelou describes memoirs as letters to her daughters, historian Darlene Clark Hine charges Black women historians with discovering Black women's agency. Combined, I add to these two thinkers by charging that Black feminist writers not only chart historical behaviors, but also that we identify strategies for empowerment. In essence, our work is to live and write in ways that connect lessons of the past to students of the future.

The questions I pose and the extended list of tasks in the appendix are created to spark longer conversations about how to identify strategies that work to calm the mind enough to write when everything else in the world is chaos. The question of mindfulness is useful for all who want to maintain balance, but it is especially necessary for those writing books that go against the academic grain. The constant attacks on race and gender studies indicate how concepts like critical race theory and intersectionality not only strike a nerve but strike fear in the hearts and minds of those invested in maintaining dominance. While several Black feminist writers (including Cathy Cohen and Beverly Guy-Sheftall) caution against romanticizing being on the banned book list, I do hope this book helps reverse conservative policies that disproportionately ban books by Black women.

Like a planet's ecology, BWST scholars are connected. We must nurture our spirits and give our energy to plant seeds of hope, love, truth, conviction, joy, and justice in others. The measure of an academic career should not simply be how much you publish but how much the publications positively impact the lives of others and how your books help improve the quality of life for others.

Laura Mvula, a British singer who has been generously transparent about her mental health challenges, collaborated with funk musician icon Nile Rogers to produce a song called "Overcome." She encourages those whose "heart is broken down" and whose "head don't reach the sky" to "take your broken wings and fly." The song, paced with rhythmic determination, encourages the listener to let the beat of the drums provide the will to carry on. The imagery in the music video includes a golden cage, an obvious reference to Maya Angelou's memoir *I Know Why the Caged Bird Sings*.

Publishing is a stressful endeavor, especially if you are a first-generation college student still figuring out the ways of academia, which some were born into or mentored through. If you were fortunate enough to attend a well-resourced institution, you may have had a developmental editor as an undergraduate student and have been exposed to a supportive network of mentors or sponsors that create a well-oiled pipeline for success. If you don't know anyone in publishing, attended lesser known or low ranked schools, or are confused about the inner workings of the ivory tower, it can be isolating. Yet, just like the closed power networks of Hollywood and the US government, there are more people working on the outside than the inside. The will to carry on is not a guarantee, especially if we understand how systemic barriers exacerbate the social inequities scholars of color have to face. However, without willpower, our voices will, in effect, be silenced.

When we expand our network to be genuinely meritorious and inclusive, our impact can be as great as those more well-known or well-financed scholars. Ultimately, only you can determine what makes your writing a success, by your own definition. And, given the limited availability of prizes, bestseller lists, and fellowships, writing regardless of those bonuses will help you to write for yourself and, regardless of the barriers, overcome. Collective care is a strategy to make sure that as you overcome challenges, you do not become a barrier for others to do the same.

Reflection Questions

Question 20: What specific problem are you working to solve? How does your work contribute to human rights and social justice education?

Question 21: How has your work resisted efforts to dismantle BWST? What steps have you taken to create pathways for future BWST scholars?

Practical Tasks

- Identify what classes, programs, or foundations may be interested in your book.

- Name your intended audience. Be clear about why you want to communicate with this group. identify people who are not your primary audience but who may benefit from your work nevertheless. Connect with scholars, friends, and community members who can inform your writing as your book takes shape.

- Connect with those whom you believe might be supported by your work. As you solidify and develop your book, engage with others. Don't wait for others to initiate. Reach out first. Actively mentor others who are interested in reading, researching, writing, teaching, and academic leadership. Reach out to others for help.

- Join a professional organization that centers Black Women's Studies. Work with a group to prepare a conference panel or community event. Volunteer to serve in an official capacity. Network at professional conferences, contribute to organizations, and meet informally with like-minded scholars to create space for teaching, learning, and writing.

8

Conclusion

Academic Wellness

Black feminist writing is a wellness practice.
Black feminist writing is a mindfulness practice.
Black feminist writing is a compassionate practice.
Black feminist writing is a mentoring practice.
Black feminist writing is an everyday practice.
Black feminist writing is a sankofa practice.
Black feminist writing is a peer review practice.
Black feminist writing is a soulful practice.
Black feminist writing is a creative practice.
Black feminist writing is a celebratory practice.
Black feminist writing is a courageous practice.
Black feminist writing is a caring practice.
Black feminist writing is a private practice.
Black feminist writing is a referential practice.
Black feminist writing is a generational practice.
Black feminist writing is a formal practice.
Black feminist writing is a relational practice.
Black feminist writing is a problem-solving practice.
Black feminist writing is a persistent practice.
Black feminist writing is a liberatory practice.
Black feminist writing is a lifelong learning practice.
Black feminist writing is a healing practice.
Black feminist writing is a rising practice.
Black feminist writing is a regenerative practice.
Black feminist writing is a working practice.

Human rights abuses regularly occur in higher education. The academy is not a safe place for Black women. There are no safe places for Black women. As chronicled in *The Sisterhood* in addition to writing by professors Monica A. Coleman and Lori Patton Davis, the academy has a nasty habit of killing Black women through overwork, disproportionate service, denial of leave, unreasonable expectations for mentoring, and any number of various means of invalidation, gaslighting, or suppression. Still, Black foremothers have gifted us with a legacy of regenerative writing. If we want to be well, we must work to become what Thorsson called "insurgent forces."

Healing yourself and supporting others in their healing journey are acts of insurgency. Black Women's Studies, the intersectional and interdisciplinary lens that shapes this work, critically examines how scholars can find their unique voice and also impact communities on campus and beyond campus walls. And still we rise.

LEARN: Writing Is Rising—Lessons of Survival and Self-Reliance in Networks

I am unwilling to cede academic space. I belong here. However, too often the culture of academe is inhumane. Most professional places are not healthy for Black women, trans women, queer people, women of color, and other marginalized communities. No wonder there is a regular exodus out of academe. Worse yet, so-called minority faculty are too often complicit in university exploitation or harassment. My work, then, is to change and transform the academy. I do so by centering compassion for myself and others.

My friend Sharon Burney says, "don't tell me what you're gonna do, tell me what you did." In other words, worry less about making pronouncements of your intentions to write and focus on writing, then celebrate the hell out of your work when it is complete and connect it to your larger vision for a better future. One of my closest colleagues in the field, Burney served as the administrator for African American Studies at the University of Florida. After leaving the position, she continued to flourish and serve the field as a leader in information science. Staff and librarians like Ms. Burney show that sometimes the smartest and most soulful people in the room don't have the most letters behind their name. When you create networks for self-reliance, don't build community based on prestige—connect with those who have the same worldview, spiritual commitments, and work ethic. Work with those who invest in saving Black women's lives.

I am writing for my life. What is good about my life I want to make better . . . and I want to make life better for everyone else. My writing feels inadequate in the face of global warfare and genocide happening in our own time. But I am not writing alone, so those whom I support make me feel connected to a life force bigger than myself. We need a global ceasefire. That seems impossible, given the almost giddy buildup of "World War III" talk on the eve of yet another election year that promises to be brutal on our gentle souls. Removing barriers to writing, joy, labor, and truth-telling seems time well spent. I write not only for my agency, but also to encourage those who will write long after I am gone.

I hope that my reflections can facilitate—literally *facil* (to make easier)—the process of scholarly book publishing, especially for Black feminist scholars. This writing practice demands that we stand on our own ideas, even as we strengthen relationships to others. Wellness, cultivating a healthy academic family tree to increase our collective agency, is inherently collaborative.[1]

I have imagined myself writing my freedom papers, and writing this book has become one way to emancipate myself from systemic exploitation. I want to do one thing well—one thing that I love. I do one thing: I write. Mainly, I write as a reflection of Black feminist ethics. This work can and should inform all disciplines and should permeate all areas of higher education research, teaching, and service.

Above all, this practice should help you do your work in ways that let you control your time and energy. The following lessons are insights that I learned from my teachers and those I share with my students.

Gifts of Agency from My Teachers (Lessons Learned)

1. You will survive. You are not the center of the universe (Annette Edmonds, Mother)
2. Figure it out! Learn. Practice. Teach. Repeat (Pam Copley-Grube)
3. Become an active learner (Fanny Jackson Coppin)
4. Regenerate: Look backward, inward, and forward (Anna Julia Cooper)

5. Investigate, interpret, inspire (Mary McLeod Bethune)

6. Solve specific problems (like dehumanization in the ivory tower). Build the road by walking (Septima Poinsette Clark)

7. Announce you are working. Prioritize your wellness (Toni Cade Bambara)

8. Say no. No is a complete sentence (Byllye Avery)

Gifts of Agency for My Students (Lessons for Next Generation Scholars)

1. You can rewrite the academy for future generations (*Black Women in the Ivory Tower*)

2. Connect your writing to teaching and community work (*African Americans and Community Engagement*)

3. Identify and develop a robust archive of primary sources (*Black Passports*)

4. Learn to BREATHE through writing (*Black Women's Mental Health*)

5. Amplify activist voices (*Black Women and Social Justice Education*)

6. Name your theory and method ("Letters to My Daughters" in *The Black Intellectual Tradition*)

7. Give flowers to your foremothers and mentors while they are alive (*Black Women and Public Health*)

8. Organize to restructure the academy (*Palimpsest Journal*)

9. Don't have a boss and don't be one. Don't just manage your time—own it. Serve others, but still maintain your boundaries (*Dear Department Chair*)

10. Learn, Create, and Teach (*Black Feminist Writing*)

11. Tell the truth and share tea with your crew to improve health (*Africana Tea*)

Black feminist writing is a rising practice. Maya Angelou's poem "And Still I Rise" shines a light on how writing can help us rise. And we rise to rewrite the bitter, twisted lies of history.

I imagine "rise" as an acronym: Rest, Immerse, Study, and Engage. These four practices—collectively representing everyday writing—map efforts needed to transform epistemological power structures. RISE is a summation of the five locations of practice.

Rest in the Moment (Personal Practice)

Find your voice. This requires that you rest in the present moment and take time to reflect on personal writing goals. Consider whether you are only writing a book for promotion or if you are writing to satisfy an internal goal you have set for yourself.

Immerse Yourself in Gratitude (Professional Practice)

State your argument. Immerse yourself in historical foundations and extant scholarship. Locate cultural ancestors in your profession to demystify academia. Find gratitude in the work done before you and use intellectual history (like early dissertations in your academic discipline) as a guide to understand the ways thinking has evolved over time.

Study Resilience (Publishing Practice)

Organize your structure and edit your manuscript. Study and prepare for the tasks required to publish a professional book. Use guides to prepare you for the long journey of academic publishing and dive deep into the editorial process in order to fully shape your contribution and polish your work even before submitting it for professional processing.

Engage Community (Public Practice and Political Practice)

Check your sources. Use your scholarship to enjoy and build community inside and beyond higher education institutions. If you take time to share your work in peer review and interrogate your data collection methods, you may relieve anxiety around how your book will be received when released. Critical peer review is a blessing. Consider your readership as a community (rather than an audience who consumes your product). This might result in a more satisfying outcome for your research. Purposefully construct your work in ways that uplift other scholars and contribute to the advancement of Black Women's Studies.

My academic family tree is part of a living, thriving ecological system that sustains me and affords me time and energy to share the deepest parts of myself with others. That truly is an awesome inheritance. Frankly, I feel like my writing is somewhat predictable—everyone knows that I'm writing about Black women, memoir, and wellness. But, for me, that consistency has enabled me to explore an ever-expanding diasporic multiverse about not only our pasts but also our futures. More than anything, cultivating your family tree and growing your writing practice requires a commitment to lifelong learning.

CREATE: 2022, Inner Peace Is Not a Group Project

In June 2022, the love of my life faced a life-threatening health challenge. I was a loving, attentive caretaker, even though my heart was heavy, my legs stiff, and feet dragging. I was fortunate, perhaps, to be teaching online that fall semester. But holding classes while in the hospital was not the least bit ideal. FMLA (Family and Medical Leave Act) hardly seemed an option as several other political dynamics were also at play that made it seem not viable for me to take time off and I did not want to leave my students adrift. Given my exhaustion and mildly depressive state, I had to hold on to my meditation, yoga, and tea practices and to resist the temptation to escape from this spirit-breaking circumstance by falling to pieces.

Every day during the 2022–2023 academic year was a fight not to give in to forces that would sap my energy and dilute my focus. Toni Cade Bambara advocated for herself by simply announcing she was working. She'd say "leave me alone and get out of my face." The determination to work through devastation and destruction not only takes willpower but it also takes—you guessed it—practice. In addition to professional and familial issues, one space in particular presented a challenge for me to navigate and keep on track with my writing goals: social media.[2]

Twitter was one of the most influential social media platforms. As it spiraled out of control under new ownership in 2022 and 2023, "Black women" continued to trend. The "attention industry" is an irresistible and gruesome reality where deadly and damaging stereotypes are pushed to the top of the algorithm and where many folks desire to be an "influ-

purpose. The more you tap into your inner motivation, the more effective you can be when engaging others.[3]

In disciplines like psychology and human development, "managing self" is known as self-regulation. Introspection and self-regulation are measures to gauge your inner peace. Universities routinely espouse core values. Inner peace, which is a measure of wellness, is my core value.[4]

In the essay "How Can Values Be Taught in the University?," Toni Morrison affirms that values are ever-present and that academic objectivity is a myth. She observes, "Explicitly or implicitly, the university has always taught (by which I mean examined, evaluated, posited, reinforced) values . . . We teach values by having them."[5] Like care, social justice requires balancing individual needs with collective needs. For marginalized scholars in the academy, social justice is often self-advocacy and applying the demands you secure for yourself to benefit others as well.[6]

In *We Want to Do More than Survive: Abolitionist Teaching and the Pursuit of Educational Freedom* (2019), Bettina L. Love focuses on schools and communities working together to move beyond pedantic approaches to educating Black and Brown children. She problematizes mere survival and bolsters the argument that mere survival is not a worthy goal. In her newest work, *Punished for Dreaming: How School Reform Harms Black Children and How We Heal* (2023), she holds systems accountable for damage and suggests ways forward to healing through restorative justice.[7]

Time management is essential, but I have also worked hard at energy management and attention management. Focus is certainly a Black feminist practice. You cannot fully support others if you do not take time for yourself. Healing from historical trauma is a marvelous and terrible phenomenon. While every individual must overcome seemingly insurmountable stress, the unending tsunami of destruction to Black women's minds, bodies, and spirits is psychically exhausting. Collectively, memoirs and monographs constitute an individual and a structural understanding of Black women's conviction in each era to do more than survive.

TEACH: Five Ways to Care for Your Academic Mental Health and Collective Well-Being

We have a right to prioritize our own health and purge anyone from our inner circle who endangers our self, healing, or well-being. If we desire to have a fruitful career, we also have the right—and the necessity—to prioritize our writing practices. The universe responds to clarity, so we must clearly define our professional goals and make concrete, attainable, and measurable plans to develop our writing. This includes carving out time to read deeply and broadly.

I challenge you to cultivate spaces where you can strengthen your individual writing practice but also facilitate spaces where others can benefit from communal writing exercises.

Personal Health: Make Time Out of No Time

Self-empowerment as a model for living was a pervasive character trait for twentieth-century elders. Several Black women who lived long lives took the time to write their memoirs and tell their stories, leaving ample material to better understand the balance between self-care as an individual ethic and self-help as a community imperative. Harriet Jacobs's story is one of the earliest examples of self-empowerment narratives explicitly about sexual violence. Her story exemplifies self-ownership and "healthy self-possession" in ways that are echoed by hundreds of authors who followed in her path.[8]

Harriet Jacobs was born enslaved in Edenton, North Carolina, on February 11, 1813. She recalls living with her mother Delilah, father Elijah, loving grandmother Molly, and several aunts and uncles, until her mother passed away in 1819, when Harriet was six years old. Harriet then lived with a "kind mistress," Margaret Horniblow, who was in her early twenties and sickly at the time and who taught her how to read and sew. It was an unusual fortune that Harriet, then called "Hatty," would be companion to someone who shared learning with her. After Horniblow died, six years later when Harriet was twelve, James Norcom conspired to produce an addendum to the will, which moved Harriet's ownership from Horniblow's mother to Norcom's daughter (a three-year-old girl), making him the de facto owner. Norcom began to torment Harriet, refusing to let her marry a free Black man with whom she was in love. He began to compel her to obey his every command—including his sexual advances—and Norcom's young second wife added to her misery by jealously haunting Jacobs in her sleep and overworking her as an added form of spite.

To reject Norcom's vile advances, fifteen-year-old Harriet chose a White local lawyer named Samuel Tredwell Sawyer as a lover and bore him two children, Joseph and Louisa Matilda. In June 1835, in her early twenties, she could no longer bear the rule of Norcom and torture of Norcom's wife. She had been banished to Auburn plantation, six miles from her mother's home, and upon hearing her children were to be sent to the fields, she chose to escape in a desperate act to save them. The father of her children refused to free them or purchase them (especially after marrying his White wife), so Harriet escaped, hoping to save both herself and her children. For a brief time, she hid in people's houses, then in a swamp; finally, she stayed in a crawl space in her grandmother's attic, which had been made livable by her uncle Phillip, a carpenter. She lay in hiding in that space above a storage area and porch for six years and eleven months. After being close to her two children, only to see them raised by her grandmother, Harriet made arrangements to send them north. She then chose to escape after it was clear her presence was putting her family in continued danger. Harriet Jacobs escaped in 1842, the same year she turned twenty-nine. She spent the next seven years in deep contemplation—while working as a domestic for a family—and penned her painful life story.

As historian La'Neice Littleton explains, long before antiliteracy laws sprang up following rebellions like Nat Turner's Virginia revolt of 1831, Jacobs had the good fortune of learning to read. This would guide her hand to produce one of the only self-written accounts of slavery by a woman. Harriet Jacobs died on March 7, 1897, at the age of eighty-four, and was buried in Mount Auburn Cemetery, Cambridge, Massachusetts—in the same resting place as Nathaniel Parker Willis and his family. She is buried next to her brother, who died in 1873, and her daughter Louisa.[9]

If enslaved women like Sojourner Truth, Harriet Tubman, and Harriet Jacobs had listened to their family or so-called owners, they would have remained enslaved. Because they asserted their humanity, they were able to free themselves from the structural oppression of enslavement and directly free their family and children, even encouraging others to escape as well. To effectively deal with their stress, Black women must insist that we be recognized as human beings, not mules. We must also be disabused of the idea that suffering is a birthright or that "strong" is a compliment.

Harriet Tubman did not join John Brown in his raid on Harper's Ferry. Read that sentence again. Although we must struggle and join the revolution for Black liberation, women's liberation, and liberation for all oppressed people, that does not mean that we must agree to be on the front lines of every fight, everywhere. If writing is your means of struggle, don't sacrifice that for someone else's vision. It is in the spirit of what Congresswoman Maxine Waters calls "reclaiming my time" that Black women's writing can take the form of self-determination.[10]

I worked with Dr. Littleton at Clark Atlanta University, where the institutional motto is Making a Way Out of No Way. It is there that I penned sketches of what would become *Black Women's Yoga History*, which features the story of Harriet Jacobs. It was at Clark Atlanta, where I was chair of three academic units while carrying a regular teaching load, that I learned to "make time out of no time." That was possible because I remained focused on the sacrifice and determination of women like Jacobs, and the indelible mark she left on me and legions of others.

Professional Health: Weather Academia

There is a popular saying about Black women's aging, which indicates the positive impact that melanin seems to have on our outside appearance: "Black don't crack." While many Black women, like Angela Bassett (sixty-two) and Cicely Tyson (who passed away at age ninety-six), are lauded for their stunning beauty, African-American women are, on the whole, aging faster on the inside. This phenomenon is called "weathering." In the article "Do US Black Women Experience Stress-Related Accelerated Biological Aging?," for example, University of Michigan researchers note the health disadvantages that Black women face.[11] Similarly, the Black Women's Health Imperative has observed:

> Applying this estimate as a rough metric suggests that black women in the study sample experienced an accelerated biological aging of approximately 7.5 years compared with white women of the same chronological age. . . . We found evidence that stressors associated with perceived stress, poverty, and WHR [waist-to-hip ratio] contributed to black-white differences in telomere length. Differences by race in the probability of being poor or of having a higher WHR were strongly correlated with each other as well as accounting for the largest shares of the racial difference in telomere length in terms of base pairs.

Historically, the "weather" of social environment has always been bad for Black women. Our ability to navigate storms is essential, but, given the historically disproportionate amount of violence as the root cause of our stress and suffering, it is imperative to fight for control over our environment. Freedom struggles are constant, as seen in the narratives of Harriet Jacobs, Sadie and Bessie Delany, and Eartha Kitt. Stress also shows up in our DNA.

Weathering the storm for Black women has meant turning inward to take control of our lives. Inner peace and listening to one's own voice are the hallmarks of wellness. Weathering academe has also meant creating curricular space to earn degrees in BWST. Universities like University of Maryland, Clark Atlanta University, Michigan State University, University of Illinois, University of Washington, Spelman College, Howard University, and several others have developed degrees, programs, and certificates. These spaces should be supported and more programs are needed.[12]

By connecting to Black women's intellectual history, we can more effectively expand human rights, civil rights, and global social justice. Like Anna Julia Cooper, we must engage in progressive peace, restorative justice, and regenerative education. Like Sonia Sanchez, we must continue to find creative ways to sustain a healthy struggle for peace.

Publishing Health: Tend the Roots, Spill the Tea, and Harvest the Fruit

On November 7, 2022, at the Atlanta History Center, a small group of Black women historians in the state of Georgia came together to "Spill Tea in the Living Library." Dr. La'Neice Littleton was appointed as the community liaison for the Keenan Research Center. Her work on behalf of the ancestors is a source of pride and inspiration. The day-long retreat consisted of a tour of the historical acreage, including the "living library" of a diverse agricultural garden, an orientation to the research facilities and staff, and a keynote lecture I offered titled "Black Women's Tea History."

I was grateful for the positive and lively engagement from colleagues about my new research on Black women's tea history, and, like all my research endeavors, I presented my work to groups of scholars who knew enough to challenge me to expand, clarify, and sharpen my work, while also offering me professional care and emotional support to fully realize my vision.

The abstract for the project (highlighted in chapter 5) demonstrates how a cornerstone of one book project (*Black Women's Mental Health*) can become a building block for a second project (*Africana Tea: A Global*

but, instead, to find the strength to fight against the dehumanization of the prison–industrial complex.

In 1987, Angela Davis delivered a speech at Bennett College entitled "Sick and Tired of Being Sick and Tired: The Politics of Black Women's Health." The speech takes its title from Mississippi Civil Rights Movement activist Fannie Lou Hamer who delivered the speech in Harlem with Malcolm X (Hamer, 1964). In her talk, Davis details the health disparities experienced by Black women, like heart disease, arthritis, hypertension, diabetes, cancer, and AIDS, and how these issues are exacerbated by poverty and political disenfranchisement. In the speech, which was later published in *The Black Women's Health Book: Speaking for Ourselves* (edited by Evelyn White), Davis offers a clear and straightforward look at the six fundamental elements of Black women's experience: body, mind, and spirit (health), as well as social, economic, and political (emancipation).

The Black Women's Health Handbook is just one publication that builds on the legacy of Byllye Avery and the decades-long relationship between Davis and Avery. However, that influential edited volume signifies the best possible relationship of individual and collective self-care in Black women's scholar-activism.

Political Health: Study the Power of Black Women's Healing Traditions

While Angela Davis is a very visible figure in the Black Power Movement of the 1960s, another scholar activist of note is Ericka Huggins. Scholar Mary Phillips has a forthcoming book; *Black Panther Woman: The Politics and Spiritual Life of Ericka Huggins*, which will be published by New York UP, in the Black Power series. This will be the first biography of one of the most fascinating and elusive members of the Black Panther Party. It is not hyperbole to say that this book is eagerly awaited. Mary's book on Huggins soothes the soul and stirs the conviction to advance human rights in its broadest possible conceptualization. The research leading up to *Black Panther Woman* has moved the needle on scholarship about the ongoing Black freedom struggle, women's contributions to human rights, and offer a much-needed critical assessment of contemporary wellness studies that too often devolves in to commercial and cultural self-promotion.

Huggins, a member of the Black Panther Party for fourteen years, centers love, healing, and meditation in her activism, which advocates for prison abolition while also including aspects of mental health and environmentalism. The collaboration between Phillips and Huggins is another primary example of Black women's wellness, scholar-activism, and how to realize the power of collective self-care. This collaboration highlights how Black feminist writing is both a spiritual and a mindful practice.[13]

The writers of the *Health First!* guide echo this sentiment: "Become courageous enough to confront your fears because they are often the sources of great power. As you become a more enlightened person your power and love will spread and influence others around you. In the words of Byllye Avery, 'This is your life, and you deserve to live it as powerfully as possible!' "[14] Black women's narrative definitions of power are different from mainstream White and male definitions, which define power as domination. A paradigm of this definition of power is Robert Greene's *The 48 Laws of Power*, which puts forth a Machiavellian model of control that is not only unobtainable by most women, but also unsustainable as a human form of communication. Akasha Gloria Hull's work, in turn, directly refutes Greene's ideas of power.

My charge for Black feminist writing, then, is to sustain our wellness practices. One way to sustain Black women's wellness is to centralize Black women's wellness in all of our work—academic and otherwise. I have never had the luxury of not working—not if I wanted to eat. So, I have been determined to define work in my own image. That is why my series at SUNY is called Black Women's Wellness. And I will try to find other ways to sustain this work.

As I was completing the final edits for this book, I was pleased to be invited to serve on the committee for the Byllye Avery Sexual and Reproductive Justice Endowed Professorship at the CUNY School of Public Health. Along with Linda Goler Blount of the Black Women's Health Imperative, I celebrate Mama Avery while she is living and ensure that her name and her work are centered in the halls of higher education.[15]

This book is a love letter is for those who feel like they are on rented time and space. I have been fortunate to take up space in academe and have been granted access to university press publishing. I understand my opportunity to take up space on library shelves and digital libraries is not because I am exceptional but because others who came before me paved the way—so that I can make the way for others. Let us weigh professional writing on the scales of human history and not be found wanting. Like the iconic lead song from the Broadway show *Rent*, I hope my career is measured in love.

Discussion Question 22:
How Do You Measure an Academic Career?

The summer of 1999, after I graduated with my bachelor's degree, I took a cross-country road trip with my good friend Mike. We were both on our way to graduate school—him in Washington, DC, and me in Massachusetts. As we left California, we listened to the soundtrack from the Broadway musical *Rent*, and we were filled with emotion about the challenges we'd each overcome, the hope we had for the next phase of our lives, and the promises that advanced education offered. We cried and sang and sang, crying about love, fear, hope, determination, and justice. I have kept the refrain of the song in mind each step I have taken in my career: measure your life in love.

I have seen the musical *Rent* several times and the soundtrack continues to resonate with me. It feels like I've written 525,600 words—a word for every minute of the year. My actual word count is around that number, when you count four single-authored books, the introductions to five coedited books, and over a dozen journal articles or book chapters. After struggling through my master's thesis and dissertation, I have had a fruitful publishing career, which has been most productive since I earned tenure. Though I have published over a dozen journal articles and have enjoyed creating multiple websites as resources, my passion is academic books.

I am not the most productive Black studies or women's studies scholar I know (professors like bell hooks, Farah Griffin, Tracy Sharpley-Whiting, Mark Anthony Neal, Alexis Pauline Gumbs, Keisha Blain and, of course, Gerald Horne come to mind). I am not the most soulful writer (Imani Perry, Daniel Black, Regina Bradley, and Josh Myers are inspirations), nor the most impactful feminist or womanist theorist (this list includes Beverly Guy-Sheftall, Layli Maparyan, Monica A. Coleman, Jennifer Nash, Brittney Cooper, Christen A. Smith, Sherie Randolph, Erica Edwards, and Moya Bailey). I am certainly not the most radical writer (Carol Anderson, Kimberlé Crenshaw, Robin Spencer, Ashley Farmer, Robin D. G. Kelly, Keeanga-Yamahtta Taylor, Jeanne Theoharis, Davarian Baldwin, Bettina Love, and Charisse Burden-Stelly personify this important tradition). But I weigh my contribution to BWST among these thinkers.

Among the many problems I've observed in higher education is the tendency to conflate ego with intellect. Some of those who publicly deem themselves racial, gender, or radical purists also often enjoy profound professional and financial security based on the labor of staff and administrators they publicly disavow but privately depend on to process their requests for resources. As in all other professions, too many academics are mean-spirited, and their "critical" work is a thinly guised nastiness that no doubt masks their own fear, unresolved trauma, or guilt. Often, when threatened, this type of scholar lashes out and when wounded narcissists have a chance (especially as administrators), they punish without mercy. On the other end of the spectrum, other senior scholars with status and resources routinely leverage their name, time, and expertise for the benefit of others—even if they only act anonymously.

Tennis champion and scholar-activist Arthur Ashe once derided the physical violence of South African apartheid, but he also fought against "intellectual violence." He shamed those who professed Christianity but upheld racism at home and abroad. As in the church, some in academia employ rhetoric of equity but raise their voices to keep systems in place or to block the scholarship of their "adversaries" because they believe it upsets the established order. Some become insufferable gatekeepers once they have ascended to a throne of popular, disciplinary, professional, or elite prominence. I have found "climbing" unsatisfying but have a deep respect for those who are committing themselves to pursue ethical leadership. You will have to compromise, make concessions, and grow beyond your current habits, but your success should not require abasement or professional prostration.

Writing a lot does not mean writing well. Yet, without constant writing and editing your work will not improve. Also, just because you have an outstanding book that is critically celebrated by the top scholars in your field, this does not translate into you being a person who treats others well. After thirty years in higher education (ten as a student and twenty as faculty), yes, I have published several books. But, as in the musical *Rent*, I measure my life and my career in love. And, like everyone else, I still have much work to do to perfect that practice.

Final Point. Compassion Is Work for the Soul: Writing Is Hard Work—So Work It!

Beverly Guy-Sheftall defines Black feminism as a commitment to liberation. A commitment like writing requires work. Writing is soul work—it both emanates from and feeds the soul.

Like Rihanna sings "he say me haffi work, work, work, work, work." I have never had the luxury of not working. But I refuse to work myself to death. While working on the final edits for this book, I created a work playlist (included as an appendix). Listening to Vanessa Williams, Missy Elliot, Jon Batiste, Vivian Green, Prince, Bob Marley, Maxwell, Michael Jackson, and others gave me enough energy to get me over the finish line. In 2023, the fiftieth anniversary of hip-hop, it was fitting that Missy Elliott was inducted into the Rock & Roll Hall of Fame. After all, Missy not only taught us how to work it, but also how to put that thing down, flip it, and reverse it.

Academic writing is nothing if not work. Celebrate your work. Find courage through your work. Care for your work. As a writer, you can facilitate change and transformation. If you want your writing life to grow, you must cultivate it, study it, nurture it, and share it. I will not lie and say that you can complete an academic book without putting in serious, sustained, and arduous work. I will, however, offer an alternative to sacrificing your health to labor merely for the wavering favor of a few folks at your institution or in your field. You can define writing work for yourself. And you can define your writing work as rest, play, joy, justice, or in any way you like. Let your writing liberate you and write to liberate others. Writers from Phillis Wheatley to Toni Morrison have shown us that, when you work as a writer, you can experience a modicum of freedom, despite the worldly chains that are fashioned to bind you.

Black feminist writing is a regenerative practice. Writing is learning self-care. Writing is creating self-care. Writing is teaching self-care. Every day that the morning star rises, you have another chance to do the hard work of writing and the harder work of being well.

> Black feminist writing is a wellness practice . . . every day.
> Black feminist writing is a wellness practice . . . every day.
> Black feminist writing is a wellness practice . . . every day.

I wish you well in your practice.

Coda

Feeling Good

> The longer you can pull yourself out of a kind of rat race and out of an economic kind of depravation and can sit still and let your mind flow freely, then the better the world will be for everybody.
>
> —John H. Bracey, Jr. (2017)[1]

When Professor Bracey joined the Ancestors on February 5, 2023 (during Black History Month, of course), he was widely heralded by those who knew him. While the world busied itself with war, entertainment, politics, sex, scandal, and other predilections, Bracey's passing gave me pause. A mighty oak had fallen.[2]

For the remainder of the year, listening to John Coltrane while writing brought me closer to Bracey's memory. I needed some time, as the group Arrested Development sang, to ease my mind. Taking time to "sit still and let my mind flow freely," also allowed me to reflect on lessons I learned from teachers throughout my lifetime, especially Ms. Copley. *Black Women in the Ivory Tower* was dedicated to Pam Copley-Grube, my eighth-grade dance teacher who was the first educator to help me begin to heal my body and my mind. Through dancing, my soul could fly free. Ms. Copley, who regularly offered a master class in compassion, had high expectations of her students and challenged us to "figure it out." I've had to figure out how to write and though much has been through instruction, I have developed as a writer through trial and error, bouncing sound off bandmates, creating compilations, samples, or collaborations, tinkering with and strengthening my voice, book by book. Improvising. Just like jazz.

Bracey's article in the *Massachusetts Review* Music Issue, "The Coming of John, with Apologies to W. E. B. Du Bois and Amus Mor," is my favorite piece of writing because the bebop tone most closely mirrors the swinging spirit of his oral teaching voice. His stories, gestures, and joyful brilliance demanded that students pay close attention in order to keep up and master the craft of our work. Like John Coltrane inspired a dutiful appreciation of sound, Bracey inspired a dutiful appreciation of reading, writing, learning, and teaching. Bracey embodied a love of Black soul.

For me, the Earth stopped for a moment when Bracey passed. I was in the final days of completing a very rough first draft of this manuscript, already dedicated to him. For the days following his passing, I simply sat still, listened to Coltrane, his favorite musician, and let my mind flow freely over his pictures, writing, and speeches. As Karla Holloway wrote in her dirge, *Passed On: African American Mourning Stories* (2002), I filtered through the "ephemera" of a life. The music helped me be present to my feelings of loss, yes, but equally so to become immersed in my feelings of gratitude for the privilege to witness a Black life lived well.[3]

I am still working on finding the right balance in my care for self and others. Completing this book has been an opportunity to claim a bit more agency while also seeking to support those who are struggling. This book has cost me something—time and energy—but I believe the gift to those long after I am gone will be worth the price. In the meantime, I'm going to take more time to breathe. I will practice equanimity.

A New Life for Me:
Futurity and Finding My Favorite Things

Despite numerous challenges, Nina Simone sang about the hope of a new dawn, a new day, a new life, and feeling good. The song has been covered by everyone from Lauren Hill, Jennifer Hudson, Ledisi, and Chlöe to George Michael and Michael Bublé. Feeling good does not mean the absence of pain, sorrow, empathy, horror, rage, or grief. To the contrary, flourishing is about feeling the full range of emotions, facing each new dawn, and committing to your practice each new day in spite of life's struggles.

Books—whether in libraries or bookstores—are among my favorite things. Books have brought me closer to my ancestors, to myself, my students, my colleagues, and my loved ones. Gramms not only gave me a letter, but she also gave me a lifeline. Writing is a passion not only because it helps me feel like I'm fulfilling my life purpose, but also because it contributes to the human library. When I'm in the presence of books, I feel alive. Books, music, wine, food, tea, travel, and love—all of these are my favorite things to experience and share. As I close this book, I'm recommitting to claiming time to pull myself out of the rat race and spend time doing what I love. Though I will continue to write, I want to do so in ways that incorporate all of the other things I love and enable me to breathe more slowly.

Music has made me feel good enough to write. I come from a long line of music lovers. In her heyday, Gramms performed at the Howard Theatre in Washington, DC, as did my grandfather, Charles Dix Edmonds Harris (King). It is no wonder that I recognize music as integral to Black writing traditions. Usually when I draft or sketch new ideas, I write in silence. I will print out a draft of the manuscript and mark my edits in silence. But when I enter my corrections, I listen to music. Depending on the mood, it might be jazz, mediation, or chill Afrobeat. André 3000's *New Blue Sun* dropped just in time to mellow me out when I needed it. Music helps me tap the keyboard like a piano and I can swing into the morning, noon, or night, bopping my head to the beat or swaying slowly like a breeze. The closer I get to finishing the final draft (sometimes after going through two dozen or so full manuscript edits), the harder I swing. I know I'm getting close to finishing when I kick my feet up and spin around in my chair. And, of course, wine. Hey! Let's go! Chair dancing, fingers popping, body swaying. Sometimes, I'll have a whole one-person Soul Train line in my office. Even when I'm swinging low (either over some trifling issue at my job or in despair at the cruelty of this murderous world), the blues feeds my soul to help me get back to my work. Often, I write through tears.

Writing is the one thing that has helped me heal from my past (which is an ongoing process). But writing helps me to imagine and create my future in new, positive, and powerful ways. In *Keywords for American Cultural Studies* (2020), Rebecca Wanzo defines "Futurity" as ways to "imagine worlds." She writes, "By framing futurity in ways that recognize historical injuries and deromanticize narratives of progress, many theorists of the future work to imagine worlds in which justice—and survival itself—is possible." Writing has helped me imagine a new academic world and also imagine myself in new ways.[4]

As a symbolic example, while in the throes of completing this book, I shaved my head. I imagined a different, creative future for myself by letting go of my image as it was. My locks, which I started at the age of twenty-eight, began to thin and wither. I did not show my hair enough attention so, predictably, it did not grow. The combination of stress and alopecia left me with hair that was . . . let's just call it, um, less than vibrant. I had the option to spend an exorbitant amount of time, energy, and money on figuring out how to revive my hair, which was absolutely viable given effective treatments available. My other option was to cut it off. I chose the latter. More time for writing, right? I realized that I would rather write than fix my hair. No regrets.

Fortunately, my husband, who loves my Black soul, volunteered to shave off my hair for me. It was a tender and very sexy moment . . . but that's not your business. His love, compassion, and care made me feel courageous, even during the awkward first few months. I love the way my bald head looks and feels so there's no turning back.

I found inspiration for my bald life in several places: in Congresswoman Ayanna Pressley, the Shaolin monks of karate movies I endlessly watched as a young girl, and the Dora Malaje of the *Black Panther* movie. Ytasha Womack, credited for her worldmaking book *Afrofuturism: The World of Black Sci-Fi and Fantasy Culture* (2013) reached out to me when she saw my social media posts that featured photos of my new look (in fabulous pictures taken by my talented cousin Minta Wood). Ytasha helped me celebrate and make meaning of "the big chop" by featuring me in her book *Black Panther: A Cultural Exploration* (2023). My cousin's encouragement and Ytasha's inclusion of my big chop further illustrates the communal aspect of Black women's healing traditions. I'm ever grateful for the multitude of sistren who have uplifted me over the years—through their writing or otherwise. Resistance can be beautiful, fun, and communal. If joy were not so effective, there would not be so many global mandates to curb or outlaw dancing, singing, art, and other expression by those fighting oppression, marginalization, and erasure.[5]

When you imagine your future, dare to believe in your ability to write. If you want to publish an academic book, writing is the one thing required. If you are a writer, you keep writing. As you write, imagine other worlds. Then, reimagine. Then write, rewrite, work for freedom, and imagine again. Imagine what a new life might feel like for you and yours. In the final moments of my writing, I imagine the books that *Black Feminist Writing* might help midwife—ideas and practices of life and love to alleviate or prevent the harm of death and hate. Celebration and care take practice. Courage takes practice. It takes courage to love something as stressful as writing. But even if you don't love writing, I hope that you cultivate a practice that helps you manage the inevitable stressors so you can finish your book. When you finish typing, hit "send," and work with to your editor to handle the minutia required to get your book in print, you will undoubtedly be in the tight grip of one stressor or another. But I hope when you finish your book, you cultivate time and space for swinging to your favorite music or doing something else that brings you joy.

As the old folks say, trouble don't last always. As I finished final edits on this manuscript, I was notified that my fourth application for a research leave was approved and that my application for a Distinguished Fulbright Scholar award had made it past the first round of peer review. Though I did not ultimately receive the award, I know this book will do much important work on many shores. You will win some, you will lose some, but keep writing yourself toward wellness. Black women's ideas showed me how to solve my problem of anxiety and mental malaise. Black women's ideas helped me develop a sustainable wellness practice. Black women's ideas also offer insight into how we can, collectively, address global problems. I hope your writing practice helps you overcome challenges you face and that your published book paves the way for others to do the same. I will keep writing and working for Black women's wellness. And when I'm writing, I'll be thinking of you. I hope that you, too, can make time to think. And I hope that every day you rise and salute the sun that you cultivate a practice of writing and feeling good.

Breathe.

Acknowledgments

Thank you, Dr. Rebecca Colesworthy, for encouraging me to keep writing about Black women's wellness and supporting my series to expand this area. Thanks especially for the hands-on treatment for this particular manuscript. Thank you to the entire SUNY Press team for ensuring my work is produced with courage, care, and quality. I'm grateful to "Reviewer A" who shared a ten-page single-spaced series of comments that helped me restructure this project.

Thank you, Dr. Michelle Dunlap, for additional developmental editing support. I'm grateful that we have been vibing for decades now and continue to support each other as we work in ways that allow us to practice our values of intellectual healing and collective wellness at the deepest levels. Thank you also to Matthew John Phillips for copyediting, correcting citations, and fine tuning. Your continued services are much needed and appreciated. Thank you, Dr. Jennie Burnet, director of the Georgia State University Institute for Women's, Gender, and Sexuality Studies (WGSS). You have been immeasurably supportive. You stepped into the department chair role when I left to fill gaps in faculty appointments, and I could not have asked for a more prepared, sincere, knowledgeable, and committed colleague to take administrative leadership seriously. I was happy to support you in your transition and I am forever grateful for the peer mentoring and resource support you provided that enabled me to complete this project in a timely manner.

Thank you to Dr. Beverly Guy-Sheftall for an early read and affirmation of this book. I remain grateful for the way you have modeled making one's life work joyful and committing to Black feminist worldmaking. Thank you to two former students, Dr. La'Neice Littleton (Atlanta History Center) and Angela Thorpe Mason (Pauli Murray Research Center) for staying connected and guiding my thoughts about how this book can enhance our communities in real time. Thank you to all who have partnered with me over the years to create a vibrant library of Black community-building books. Thank you also to my colleague and co-chair of Chair at the Table Network, Dr. Tracy Sharpley-Whiting (Vanderbilt University), for supporting conversations with colleagues across the pond in the When in Higher Education Network (WHEN). Also, thank you to Dr. Jenny Douglas and colleagues of the 100 Black Women Professors Now program for showing what creating community looks like in the Diaspora.

Thank you to the three outstanding graduate students, Parker Foster, Raina Brown, and Rosalynn Duff who offered insightful, relevant, and critical feedback to make this work more legible to readers whom I most wanted to reach.

Thank you, always, to my fabulous husband, Dr. Curtis D. Byrd, for marrying a Black feminist writer and loving me through thick, think, strong, weak, and everything in between. Happy fifteenth anniversary and cheers to all the years ahead of us in this beautiful thing called life.

Appendix A

List of Reflection Questions

Question 1: What does flourishing look like for you?

Question 2: What types of educational stress have you faced? What has been your main source of stress in the writing process?

Question 3: How do you want your writing to change institutions and policy and transform the quality of life for you and others around you?

Question 4: Personal Practice. How would you characterize your writing voice? Do you identify as a feminist? What personal experiences have impacted your research focus? What are you afraid of?

Question 5: Professional Practice. What are the writing requirements of your job? How does your job get in the way of writing? What scholars most impact your writing? Who are you agreeing with and disagreeing with?

Question 6: Publishing Practice. Why did you decide to write your book? What questions do you have about publishing? What makes you most excited or nervous about the publishing process?

Question 7: Public Practice. Who is part of your academic family tree? Who do you work with in your community? Do you have a writing group or accountability partners? Who is your scholarship intended to help besides yourself?

Question 8: Political Practice. In what ways does your work affirm extant scholarship in BWST? How might your book disrupt norms of traditional discipline(s)? How do you learn, create, and teach BWST?

Question 9: What was your earliest piece of academic writing? How did it impact your research trajectory? What song or poem best characterizes messages conveyed in your writing?

Question 10: How would you describe the tone of your voice? What is your message? What lies have you told yourself during the writing process?

Question 11: How do you practice mindfulness and compassion? How do you declutter your mind? What are your barriers to mindful work? How will you manage your time to get more rest (even a little bit)? Can you manage your space to ensure at least five minutes a day to sit with yourself?

Question 12: When and where were your academic disciplines established? What have Black women written in dissertations about your topic?

Question 13: What are the foundations/evolutions of a major disciplinary theory? What interdisciplinary iterations have emerged over time?

Question 14: What is the problem (or question/idea) your research addresses? What argument are you contributing to advance your field? Whom do you cite as relevant comparison authors and why?

Question 15: Why do you want to publish an academic book? How do you imagine this current project in the big picture of your career and holistic research agenda?

Question 16: What are the key steps in the academic book publishing process that you are most excited about? Which key steps intimidate you most?

Question 17: Which top five books do you cite as relevant comparison texts? What presses published them? What top three publishers appear most often in your manuscript bibliography?

Question 18: What experience do you have with joint writing and collaborating on a joint publication? What space do you make to invite critique from people inside and outside of your inner circle?

Question 19: How can your work help "build a better world"? What nonprofit, policy, or government organizations might benefit from your research? What might community-based collaboration look like for you?

Question 20: What specific problem are you working to solve? How does your work contribute to human rights and social justice education?

Appendix B

List of Practical Tasks

CHAPTER 1: INTRODUCTION

- Assess your career path thus far. Decide which direction you would like to move after publishing your book. Identify campus, inter-campus, local, national, and international publics who might benefit from discussions about your work.

- What recurring questions do you want to explore in more depth. How are you creating a research plan in ways that are emotionally and intellectually sustainable?

- Read a source—from cover to cover—that takes your mindfulness practice to the next level.

- Review existing scholarship on your topic. Read historical research as well as new contributions. What are the patterns that have remained consistent or changed over time?

- Name a historical scholar who is a publishing inspiration. Identify gifts your intellectual ancestors granted you. Name a writing tradition you are carrying forward.

CHAPTER 2: REGENERATIVE WRITING

- Attend or plan a virtual or in-person writing retreat.

- Name your big idea (theory). Decide on a working title, data set, method, argument, and chapter organization. Give your rationale for chapter organization.

- Identify your publishing goal. Start developing your routine. Set aside a bit of time every day for one week to write (or read or edit). Change to a different schedule the following week. See which works best and go with that as the centerpiece of your plan. Do not create a schedule at the expense of your health and well-being. Find a balance between regularity and exhaustion.

- Create a playlist of main themes in your research. Name inspirational artists (in music, poetry, literature, etc.) that connect with the main messages you want to convey.

- Cite three comparative books that most impact your project. Contact one author to let them know their impact on your work.

- Discuss project goals and calendar with a colleague or mentor.

- Share the concept of an academic family tree with a next-generation scholar.

Chapter 3: Personal Practice

- Name two sources of your stress and name a longtime wellness practice. Create a five-minute daily practice to address stress and sustain it for one week. Cite a source that takes your mindfulness practice to the next level.

- Arrange your writing to preserve it for posterity. Consider writing a memoir and, perhaps, writing a memoir.

- Organize a writing calendar. List regular activities and block out "focus time" (FT)—at least one hour every day for six days per week. Increase the amount of time and schedule around that time. Focus for at least one hour per day: fifteen minutes breathing and forty-five minutes writing. "Pay yourself first."

- Discuss your questions with a mentor or colleague.

- Share answers to questions with a next-generation scholar. Share your mindfulness practice with a friend or family member.

Chapter 4: Professional Practice

- Name three major figures in higher education history that have contributed impactful concepts. Identify three professional role models in your academic discipline and one outside of your discipline.

- Compare three academic disciplines. What are the advantages/drawbacks of their theories and methods?

- Cite foundational Black feminist research in your area (books and articles). Locate archives, newspapers, oral histories, and other resources related to your discipline.

- Discuss these chapter questions with a mentor or colleague.

- Share your chapter answers with a next-generation scholar.

Chapter 5: Publishing Practice

- Read at least three additional "how to publish" guides (see bibliography for options).

- Create a project calendar and timeline. Be realistic about expectations. Gift yourself the grace of flexibility then move forward with diligence. Create a draft proposal outline.

- Using a publishing guide (definitely consider *The Book Proposal Book*), draft an interest inquiry letter for two presses. Evaluate what rationale you offer for each press about why your work is a good fit for their catalog.

- Discuss chapter questions with a mentor or colleague.

- Share your chapter answers with a next-generation scholar.

Chapter 6: Public Practice

- Name people with whom you would like to write in community. Identify potential peer reviewers who will be supportive but also insightfully critical of your work. Share your work for informal peer review (share selectively).

- Create a small, short-term writing group with at least two others working on a book.
- Cite two edited volumes and read the introductions to get a sense of how the editors shape the collective discussion.
- Discuss chapter questions with a mentor or colleague.
- Share your chapter answer with a next-generation scholar.

Chapter 7: Political Practice

- Identify what classes, programs, or foundations may be interested in your book.
- Name your intended audience. Be clear about why you want to communicate with this group. identify people who are not your primary audience but who may benefit from your work nevertheless. Connect with scholars, friends, and community members who can inform your writing as your book takes shape.
- Connect with those whom you believe might be supported by your work. As you solidify and develop your book, engage with others. Don't wait for others to initiate. Reach out first. Actively mentor others who are interested in reading, researching, writing, teaching, and academic leadership. Reach out to others for help.
- Join a professional organization that centers Black Women's Studies. Work with a group to prepare a conference panel or community event. Volunteer to serve in an official capacity. Network at professional conferences, contribute to organizations, and meet informally with like-minded scholars to create space for teaching, learning, and writing.

Appendix C

Playlists

Chapter Playlist

My use of the term *creative resistance* places heavy emphasis on creative. One way that Black feminists have connected inner peace (self-definition) to outer peace (resistance) is to enjoy music. This sample playlist below pairs music choices with each chapter to exemplify the power of including music and other artistic genres to shape your intellectual work.

If you do not have time or inclination to create a playlist, consider a free streaming service. I often work to Afrobeat, classical, jazz, or neo soul stations that keep my fingers clicking on the keys until my work is done. Breathe.

Preface: "I Know," Dionne Farris
Chapter 2. "Appletree," Erykah Badu
Chapter 3. "Wild World," Maxi Priest; "Elevation," Mayah Dyson
Chapter 4. "A Long Walk," Jill Scott
Chapter 5. "Overcome," Laura Mvula
Chapter 6. "Rhythm Nation," Janet Jackson
Chapter 7. "Seasons of Love," from *Rent*, covered by Stevie Wonder
Chapter 8. "1Thing," Amerie
Coda. "Feeling Good," Nina Simone

Dr. E's Writer's "Work" Playlist

Professor Sonia Sanchez insists that writers acknowledge our privilege and make full use of the gift of a "literate, educated, and self-sustaining" life our ancestors willed. As seen in the collection *Black Women Writers at Work*, generations of writers before me have taken the time to write *for* me. Intellectual care is the act of taking time to engage the ideas of those who have come before, adding our own perspective, and writing for the next generation. This is a playlist I listen to when I'm working out on the Peloton, walking, or stretching, to get me hyped up for the work of writing.

- "Work," Bob Marley & The Wailers
- "We Can Work It Out," Stevie Wonder
- "Let's Work," Prince
- "Workin' Day and Night," Michael Jackson
- "Work to Do," Vanessa Williams
- "You Make Me Work," Cameo
- "Work It," Missy Elliott
- "Work," Rihanna
- "The Work, Pt. 1," Prince
- "The Work," De La Soul
- "This Woman's Work," Maxwell
- "Work," Vivian Green
- "Work," Kelly Rowland
- "Work," Gang Starr
- "Work It Out," Jon Batiste
- "Work," Charlotte Day Wilson

Notes

Preface

1. "Five Questions with John Bracey," Stony Brook U, February 2, 2017, video, 4:41, https://youtu.be/oRNfwc5AHu8.

2. Professor John Bracey and his wife, Dr. Ingrid Bracey, are both featured in *Diverse Issues in Higher Education*. February 13, 2018. https://www.diverseeducation.com/latest-news/article/15102004/black-scholars-matter-series-celebrates-academicians-and-their-work-part-1. Accessed November 16, 2023. See also, John H. Bracey, Jr., "Afro-American Women: A Brief Guide to Writings from Historical and Feminist Perspectives." *Contributions in Black Studies: A Journal of African and Afro-American Studies*, no. 8, 1986–1987, pp. 106–11.

3. Toni Morrison, "In Her Own Words: Toni Morrison on Writing, Editing, and Teaching," interview by Kathy Neustadt, *Bryn Mawr Alumnae Bulletin*, Summer 2019, https://www.brynmawr.edu/bulletin/her-own-words-toni-morrison-writing-editing-teaching.

4. In the year I earned tenure and promotion to associate professor at University of Florida (2010), I reflected on the meaning of my work to that point—I wrote a poem. The poem was reprinted in *Passports*.

Chapter 1

1. Kerry Ann Rockquemore and Tracey Laszloffy, *The Black Academic's Guide to Winning Tenure—Without Losing Your Soul* (Lynne Rienner, 2008).

2. Emily J. Lordi, "Soul," in *Keywords for African American Studies*, pp. 206–09.

3. Betinna Love chronicles how this happens in K–12 education and reference Patricia Williams's use of spirit murder. https://www.tandfonline.com/doi/full/10.1080/15505170.2016.1138258. Accessed December 3, 2023.

4. For more on the Black Super Woman, read the edited volume *Mental Health*.

5. Bernice Johnson Reagon's "Coalition Politics: Turning the Century" in Barbara Smith's *Home Girls: A Black Feminist Anthology*. Kitchen Table Press, 1983, pp. 357–68.

6. For details on editorial resources, visit https://blackfeministwriting.net/resources. Accessed November 25, 2023. Note: The invite came from Pompeu Fabra University in Barcelona, though I had to decline due to scheduling conflict.

7. Layli Maparyan and Barbara McCaskill. *Signs*, Summer 1995, vol. 20, no. 4, "Postcolonial, Emergent, and Indigenous Feminisms" (Summer, 1995), pp. 1007–18.

8. Toni Cade Bambara in Claudia Tate, *Black Women Writers at Work*.

9. Adinkra symbols http://www.adinkra.org/htmls/adinkra/sesa.htm. Accessed November 28, 2023.

10. I established the "learn, create, teach" framework independently, based on Anna Julia Cooper's articulation of regeneration in her article, "Womanhood: A Vital Element in the Regeneration and Progress of a Race" (1886). Searching the term, I found a book about art education with that title, so I cite Clara Lieu accordingly. Similarly, there is an online Regenerative Writing Institute. https://www.regenerativewritinginstitute.com/. I began publicly thinking about regenerative writing in 2013 in a presentation titled, "Black Passports: Connecting Sankofa and Afrofuturism in African American Travel Memoirs, A Tradition in Regeneration," given at Texas A & M University. I first published my ideas on regenerative writing in 2014 in the book *Black Passports* (SUNY Press) and again in 2017 in the "From Worthless to Wellness" chapter of *Black Women's Mental Health* (SUNY Press). In "From Worthless to Wellness," I explained how regeneration as a Black women's framework signified growth and health. I wrote, "Black women's life writing is regenerative. Narratives speak on a time continuum: they look backward, inward, and forward. Memoirs reflect wisdom of the past, reveal inward strengths of the present, and project courage to generate a hopeful future. In addition to call and response and resistance—oft-cited themes in African American literature—these narratives invoke themes of sankofa (go back and get it), contemplation (meditation), and improvisation (making a way out of no way)" (p. 117). Though I am using the term "regenerative writing," in line with my own thinking, I acknowledge I am not the only one to use the term that is the title of chapter two. I make the same acknowledgment regarding the term #HistoricalWellness, which I came up with independently, but when I checked social media, found one reference. Lastly, I acknowledge effective wellness writing programs, like Michelle Boyds's Inkwell, Marita Golden's Hurston/Wright retreats, and Cave Canem for poets. My work with regenerative writing practice and sankofa writing joins these community-building efforts.

11. Locating root causes of my academic anxiety and untangling the knotty aspects of my own stressors has helped me clarify what—exactly—is getting on my nerves when I write. I acknowledge, for example, my compulsive search for Black women's wisdom stems from the need to recover from an abusive relation-

ship with my mother. Specializing in BWST helped me not only name the source of my pain—a mother wound—but also helped me better understand the forces that restricted and her limited options. Even if you have a loving relationship with your mother, you may struggle with the demands of academic writing: personal and professional stress are not the same thing but, unchecked, they can negatively reinforce each other. "Mother Wound," *Psychology Today*. October 25, 2019. https://www.psychologytoday.com/us/blog/addiction-and-recovery/201910/the-mother-wound. For more on recovery from childhood trauma, see Stacey Patton, *Spare the Kids: Why Wupping Children Won't Save Black America* (2017). Factoring in my mother's own struggles not only helped me understand and forgive her, but also to recognize patterns and name, as Stacey Patton does in her work, that naming dehumanization wherever we find it (even in our homes). This is essential to addressing issues that Black women face.

12. My use of *liminal* here was deeply informed by a tea shop discussion with Parker Foster. Foster, a graduate student in education, is interested in sexuality and development in middle school—literally learning how to navigate the middle spaces of identity in the middle of adolescence development.

Chapter 2

1. Recognizing memoirs as a vital part of Black women's intellectual history allows readers to learn from reflections of historical experiences for several purposes: to re-create effective practices of personal and collective peace activism (retrospection), to define identity in ways that promote health and healing (introspection), and to engender a politics of resistance that allows for a model of sustainable well-being (prospection). In this article, "Letters to Our Daughters: Black Women's Memoirs as Epistles of Human Rights, Healing, and Inner Peace," I show how subjective writing constitutes a central tenant of traditions of this progressive scholarly practice. In *The Black Intellectual Tradition* (New Black Studies Series). U of Illinois P, 2021.

2. Moya Bailey and Trudy, "On Misogynoir: Citation, Erasure, and Plagiarism" (2018). On misogynoir: citation, erasure, and plagiarism, Feminist Media Studies, 18:4, 762–68 and Moya Bailey, *Misogynoir Transformed: Black Women's Digital Resistance* New York UP, 2021.

3. For a comprehensive list of Black women radicals, see https://www.blackwomenradicals.com/database.

4. Layli Maparyan, *The Womanist Idea*. Routledge, 2011, p. 3.

5. For a deeper sense of programs training next generation scholars, read *Academic Pipeline Programs: Diversifying Pathways from the Bachelor's to the Professoriate*, edited by Curtis D. Byrd and Rhiana S. Mason. Lever Press, 2021. Also visit the Academic Pipeline Project resource website https://academicpipelineproject.com/.

6. Historian John Hope Franklin's observation about historiography offers a useful entry point into understanding Black women's intellectual history and foundations of Black feminist writing. See John Hope Franklin, "On the Evolution of Scholarship in Afro-American History" (1986), Franklin delineated several stages of scholarship (including manuscripts on Africans' first arrivals to the Americas and research on "slave revolts").

7. Deborah Gray White, *Telling Histories: Black Women Historians in the Ivory Tower*. U of North Carolina, 2008, p. 21.

8. Rosalyn Terborg-Penn, *Women in Africa and the African Diaspora: A Reader*. Howard UP, 1997, emphasis added.

9. Anna Julia Cooper, "The Early Years in Washington: Reminiscences of Life with the Grimkés (1951)," in *The Voice of Anna Julia Cooper*, edited by Charles Lemert and Esme Bhan. Rowman & Littlefield, 1998, pp. 310–19.

10. Cooper, *A Voice from the South*. Aldine, 1892, p.121.

11. For more on spirit-murdering, see Nichole Margarita Garcia, "Spiring-Murdering in Academia," *Diverse Issues in Higher Education*, February 26, 2020, https://www.diverseeducation.com/opinion/article/15106340/spirit-murdering-in-academia. Toi Derricotte, "The Telly Cycle," *Rattle*, no. 31, summer 2009. Stephanie Y. Evans, "Living Legacies: Black Women, Educational Philosophies, and Community Service, 1865–1965." (Dissertation, University of Massachusetts, 2003).

12. Maya Angelou, "Still I Rise," in *And Still I Rise*. Random House, 1978.

13. Charlene A. Carruthers, *Unapologetic: A Black, Queer, and Feminist Mandate for Radical Movements*. Beacon Press, 2018, p. 140.

14. Daniel Black, "Rhythm in Writing," in *How We Do It*. Harper Collins, 2023, p.10.

15. Rita Dove, "Seven Brides for Seven Mothers," in *How We Do It*. Harper Collins, 2023, p.109.

16. My use of historical wellness as a concept is original; searches in books, journal articles, and social media turn up only one reference prior to today: A Twitter post about the value of essential oils by Angie Goderich in March 2017. I am establishing and developing the concept as an academic guidepost. Though I came to this idea independently, the idea is the culmination of decades of studying Black women's memoirs, and the term is a direct beneficiary of existing scholarship by Black women academics in history, African American studies, women's studies, and, certainly, Africana women's studies.

17. Maya Angelou, *Letter to My Daughter*. Random House Publishing Group, 2008, p. 89.

18. Jon Kabat-Zinn, *Full Catastrophe Living: Using the Wisdom of Your Body and Mind to Face Stress, Pain, and Illness*. Random House, 2013 (revised edition).

19. Olúfẹ́mi O. Táíwò, *Elite Capture: How the Powerful Took Over Identity Politics (and Everything Else)*. Haymarket, 2022, p. 110.

20. Rececca Wanzo, *The Suffering Will Not Be Televised: African American Women and Sentimental Political Storytelling*. State U of New York P, 2009.

21. Moya Bailey and Trudy, *Feminist Media Studies*. Mar. 2018. https://www.tandfonline.com/doi/abs/10.1080/14680777.2018.1447395. Accessed December 11, 2023.

22. Works by Tanisha Jackson and Norma Burgess and Ernestine Brown are useful here.

23. There is an online community called the Academic Family Tree that connects scholars in various disciplinary groups. "The Academic Family Tree" is an online network that tracks scholarly relationships of mentors and mentees through an interactive website. Examples in the "History Family Tree" include Darlene Clark Hine of Michigan State and Northwestern University, who mentored scholars like Randall Jelks and Kennetta H. Perry. The current list is not complete and does not include the likes of Pero Dagbovie and Eric Duke, but it is a useful idea to begin to identify the relationships and impacts of training. The Association of Black Women Historians offers a valuable case study in how scholars like Deborah Gray White, Paula Giddings, and Evelyn Higginbotham (all honored at the 2022 ABWH Living Legends Luncheon at University of Southern California) formally mentor many students but also impact a large number of scholars, whether personally, through informal mentoring, or through their books. This online academic family tree also identifies scholars, like Hine and Higginbotham, who have been targeted by book bans or political exclusion from curriculum. "Darlene Clark Hine," Academic Family Tree, https://academictree.org/history/tree.php?pid=566165, accessed December 8, 2022; Association of Black Women Historians, https://abwh.org/.

24. The chapter sections fashioned into the family tree mirrors Layli Maparyan's "learning ladder" for identifying effective practices to remedy stress and build community. In *The Womanist Idea*, Maparyan delineates the learning ladder, where Black women's ways of knowing involves stages of gathering information, formulating knowledge, steeping in wisdom through experience, and attaining enlightenment. My work takes this conceptualization one step further by clarifying the historical and ancestral sources of information and extending the learning ladder to explicitly include those in the next generation. In essence, my learning ladder is a tree (figure 2), where we trace learning from the roots of history to the fruits of the future.

Figure 2.

TREE PART		FAMILY	SECTIONS	TASKS
1.	Landscape	Book Lovers	Work of...	Assess
		Editor	Self-Editing	Checklist
2.	Roots	Ancestors	Gift of...	Name
		Peer Scholars	Research	Cite
3.	Trunk	Self	Introspection	Create
4.	Branches	Community	Questions	Discuss
		Next Gen Scholars	Tasks	Share
5.	Planting Seeds	Artists	Playlist	Inspiration

My reflection on cognitive processes also expands on Benjamin Bloom's pyramid of learning, which moves from knowledge, comprehension, and analysis to application, evaluation, and creation. Bloom's taxonomy underlies most learning objectives articulated in higher education frameworks, is a regular feature of learning outcomes for course syllabi, and is used, for example, by university offices of teaching and learning for the purpose of accreditation. My work joins Maparyan in scaling these learning measures to reflect the ontologies and cosmologies of Black women.

Howard Gardner's "multiple intelligences" allows for the various ways people experience the meaning-making process. One of the most valuable uses I have found for Gardner's work is the understanding that measures of "genius" and "intelligence" can mean many things, only a few of which appear on so-called standardized tests. The skill of introspection, for example, is something that institutions would do well to teach—self-awareness and emotional maturity are clearly lacking in large swaths of society, but those cognitive functions are not always presented as an essential part of the curriculum. Prioritizing self-care is important, but practicing collective self-care involves recognizing oneself in direct relation to others. Howard Gardner, *Frames of Mind: The Theory of Multiple Intelligences*. Basic Books, 2011.

25. Tillie Olson, "Foreword," in *Black Women Writers at Work*, edited by Claudia Tate. Haymarket Books, 2023.

26. Sagirah Shahid, "Killing Us Softly: Chronic Stress and the Health of Black Women," Minnesota Women's Press, October 1, 2018, https://www.womenspress.com/6018/.

Chapter 3

1. La'Neice Littleton, "Great Influence on My Mind: African American Literacy and Slave Rebellion in the Antebellum South," Clark Atlanta University, 2020, pp. 50, 180. https://radar.auctr.edu/islandora/object/cau.td%3A2020_littleton_laneice_m?search=littleton. Accessed November 25, 2023.

2. Patricia Hill Collins, *Black Feminist Thought: Knowledge, Consciousness, and the Politics of Empowerment*. Routledge, 2000, p. 210.

3. Frederick Douglass, *Narrative of the Life of Frederick Douglass*. Dover Edition, p. 52.

4. Sonia Sanchez and Yolanda Wisher, editors, *Peace Is a Haiku Song*. City of Philadelphia Mural Arts Program, 2013.

5. Keeanga-Yamahtta Taylor, editor, *How We Get Free: Black Feminism and the Combahee River Collective*. Haymarket Books, 2017.

6. American Psychological Association, *Stress in America: The State of Our Nation*, Stress in America Survey, 2017, https://www.apa.org/news/press/releases/stress/2017/state-nation.pdf.

7. U of California P, "Demystifying Book Publishing for First-Gen Scholars," UC Press Blog, January 27, 2022, https://www.ucpress.edu/blog/58132/webinar-demystifying-book-publishing-for-first-gen-scholars/.

8. Robert M. Sapolsky, *Why Zebras Don't Get Ulcers*. Henry Holt, 2004, pp. 404–5.

9. Sapolsky, pp. 414–15. See also Kanika Bell, "Sisters on Sisters: Inner Peace from the Black Woman Mental Health Professional Perspective," in *Black Women's Mental Health*, pp. 23–42.

10. Amit Sood, *The Mayo Clinic Guide to Stress-Free Living*. Da Capo Press, 2013, p. 82.

11. For more on the epistolary tradition, read Stephanie Y. Evans, "Letters to Our Daughters: Black Women's Memoirs as Epistles of Human Rights, Healing, and Inner Peace," in *The Black Intellectual Tradition: African American Thought in the Twentieth Century*, edited by Derrick P. Alridge, Cornelius L. Bynum, and James B. Stewart. U of Illinois, 2021, pp. 100–8. Epistolary writing is widely recognized to mean letters or documents written as correspondence. These letters may be published or not, but epistles are, in an ancient form, prose of communication, as can be seen in some biblical verse.... Memoirs are mentors.... Empowerment through literature can be a multigenerational experience ... I read Africana memoirs as collected letters, documents, and missives written to pass on wisdom. Even when narratives are not explicit about the audiences they address, many readers are clear about how they read life stories for more than comprehension; they read for evaluation and application. They read and can be changed.

12. Maya Angelou, "Shades and Slashes of Light," in *Black Women Writers (1950–1980): A Critical Evaluation*, edited by Mari Evans. Anchor Books, 1983, p. 4.

13. Stephanie Y. Evans, *The Department Chair Journal*.

14. Stephanie Y. Evans, *Black Women's Yoga History*, 203–4.

15. Stephanie Y. Evans, "Mother Vines," https://mother-vines.net/research.

Chapter 4

1. Leonard Pitts. "Honorary Whiteness Must Be a Powerful Drug." *The Baltimore Sun*. July 25, 2019. https://www.baltimoresun.com/opinion/op-ed/bs-ed-op-0725-pitts-whiteness-20190725-scptfi5vcbhrleczah3l5utwru-story.html. Accessed November 17, 2023.

2. Beverly Guy-Sheftall. *Words of Fire: An Anthology of African-American Feminist Thought*. The New Press, 1995, p. 586.

3. For a list of Black professional organizations, visit "Founding Dates of Black Professional Associations," in Joyce Bell. 2014. *The Black Power Movement and American Social Work*. Columbia UP, p. 188. Online at https://www.degruyter.com/document/doi/10.7312/bell16260-012/pdf.

4. *Black Women's Studies Booklist*. Online resource, https://bwstbooklist.net/.

5. Allen Repko. *Interdisciplinary Research: Process and Theory*. SAGE Publications, 2008; Kimberlé Crenshaw. "Mapping the Margins: Intersectionality, Identity Politics, and Violence against Women of Color." *Stanford Law Review*, vol. 43, no. 6, July 1991, pp. 1241–99. The Atlanta University Africana Women's Center's *Africana Women's Studies Series* was provided by Dr. Shelby Lewis. It has been digitized and made available online at http://www.professorevans.net/teaching.html. Accessed January 5, 2019.

6. Sherie M. Randolph. "Projects." http://www.sheriemrandolph.com/projects.

7. Darlene Clark Hine. "Doing and Making History: Black Women Historians in the Academy." Rutgers University, 18:45, June 26, 2009, https://youtu.be/026pggYAeBs.

8. Stephanie Y. Evans. *Black Women in the Ivory Tower*. p. 125

9. Stephanie Y. Evans. *Black Women in the Ivory Tower*. p. 137. Their approaches and conclusions both complemented and contradicted each other. Each manuscript held broader implications for African Americans and women. The expanded opportunities created by World War I explains the granting of three degrees in the same year. The phenomenon of three degrees being granted in one year at different institutions and in different disciplines allows for fascinating comparisons.

10. Deirdre Cooper Owens. *Medical Bondage: Race, Gender, and the Origins of American Gynecology*. U of Georgia P, 2017.

11. Barbra Ehrenreich and Deirdre English. *Complaints and Disorders: The Sexual Politics of Sickness*. Feminist Press, 1973.

12. My use of calorimeter here is a nod to Anna Julia Cooper, who offered early assessment of the intersection of race and gender in Black women's experiences.

13. See Evans, *Black Women in the Ivory Tower*, pp. 172–73. Carter G. Woodson, *The Mis-Education of the Negro*. The Associated Publishers, 1933; Paulo Freire, *Pedagogy of the Oppressed*. Continuum, 2000[1970].

14. Stephanie Y. Evans, "Living Legacies: Black Women, Educational Philosophies, and Community Service, 1865–1965." PhD dissertation. University of Massachusetts Amherst, 2003.

15. Stephanie Y. Evans. *Black Women's Yoga History*. p. 361.

16. Jacob Lassner. *Demonizing the Queen of Sheba: Boundaries of Gender and Culture in Postbiblical Judaism and Medieval Islam*. U of Chicago P, 1993.

17. Ivan Van Sertima, editor. *Black Women in Antiquity*. Transaction Books, 1984.

18. Significantly, Kidjo also performed a song "Burning Down the House," with the women's and non-binary artist-activist singing group, The Resistance Revival, further connecting themes of Africana history and creative resistance https://www.resistancerevivalchorus.com/.

19. "This dissertation is an exploration into African American women's intellectual history in an effort to inform current educational philosophies and pedagogical practices." Stephanie Y. Evans "Living Legacies: Black Women, Educational Philosophies, and Community Service, 1865–1965." PhD dissertation. University of Massachusetts Amherst, 2003. "Black women's intellectual history allows readers to learn . . . effective practices of personal and collective peace activism." Stephanie Y. Evans, "Letters to Our Daughters: Black Women's Memoirs as Epistles of Human Rights, Healing, and Inner Peace." In *The Black Intellectual Tradition* (New Black Studies Series). U of Illinois P, 2021.

Chapter 5

1. Beacon Press, http://www.beacon.org/A-Black-Womens-History-of-the-United-States-P1524.aspx.

2. Janice Dean Willis. *Dreaming Me: Black, Baptist, and Buddhist: One Woman's Spiritual Journey*. Wisdom, 2008.

3. Toni Morrison. *The Source of Self-Regard: Selected Essays, Speeches, and Meditations*. Alfred A. Knopf, 2019, pp. 280–81.

4. Morrison. *The Source of Self-Regard*. p. 283.

5. Dan Sinykin. "Why Toni Morrison Left Publishing." Literary Hub. https://lithub.com/why-toni-morrison-left-publishing/. Accessed November 12, 2023.

6. Stephanie Y. Evans. *Black Women in the Ivory Tower*.

7. For the review, visit: Elisabeth I. Perry (Department of History, Saint Louis University), "Perry on Evans, 'Black Women in the Ivory Tower, 1850–1954: An Intellectual History,'" H-SHGAPE (April 2008), https://networks.h-net.org/node/20317/reviews/21447/perry-evans-black-women-ivory-tower-1850-1954-intellectual-history.

8. Collins. *Black Feminist Thought*. p. 34.

9. Rebecca Colesworthy. "Why I'm Wary of Publishing Advice, but Will Offer It Anyway." *Chronicle of Higher Education*. Sep. 20, 2023. https://www.chronicle.com/article/why-im-wary-of-publishing-advice-but-will-offer-it-anyway?-cid=gen_sign_in. Accessed November 13, 2023.

10. In addition, when it comes to peer review processes, keep in mind there is a severe labor issue where academics provide free or cheap service for some publishers that are highly profitable. While some trade presses turn a profit, public university presses sometimes do not. As a result, the wait time for UPs can sometimes be longer. Also note the price of hardcover books is high to encourage library purchase to help the press recoup some costs. Pay close attention to conditions of a paper, electronic, or audiobook release if you desire a general audience.

228 | Notes to Chapter 6

11. For examples, see Michelle Dunlap. "Retail Racism: Shopping While Black & Brown in America." Parent Support Video Resource Page, YouTube, 1:20, April 29, 2023, https://youtu.be/oE4H3cNk1Fs; and Bettina Love. "Punished for Dreaming." YouTube, 3:01, May 1, 2023, https://youtu.be/1VXp1nzDiiM.

Chapter 6

1. Stephanie Y. Evans, Stephanie Shonekan, and Stephanie G. Adams. *Dear Department Chair: Letters from Black Women Leaders to the Next Generation of Academic Leaders*. Wayne State UP, 2023.

2. Stephanie Y. Evans, "Black Women in the Ivory Tower," YouTube, 2:26, July 12, 2008, https://youtu.be/bbjcjwIQ_Iw; and "Learners and Teachers of Men, Black American Men in Higher Education: Diminishing Proportions," YouTube, 4:15, March 17, 2009, https://youtu.be/TZW5WYB16ic.

3. See also https://citeasista.com.

4. Black Women's Studies Association, "About," https://www.blackwomensstudies.com/about-us/.

5. See Black Women's Studies Association, https://www.blackwomensstudies.com/.

6. Alexandra Alter and Elizabeth A. Harris. "A White Author's Book about Black Feminism Was Pulled after a Social Media Outcry." *The New York Times*, Apr. 15, 2022, https://www.nytimes.com/2022/04/15/arts/jennifer-buck-bad-and-boujee-book-pulled.html; Archuleta Chisolm. "A White Author's Gaze on Black Feminism." *Black Girl Nerds*, https://blackgirlnerds.com/a-white-authors-gaze-on-black-feminism/; Wipf and Stock Publishers, "Our Story," https://wipfandstock.com/our-story/.

7. Wipf and Stock Publishers, Twitter post, April 15, 2022, 1:31 PM, https://twitter.com/wipfandstock/status/1515020040294133764.

8. Jacqueline Jones. *Labor of Love, Labor of Sorrow: Black Women, Work, and the Family, from Slavery to the Present*. Basic Books, 2010, xii; Alison M. Parker. *Unceasing Militant: The Life of Mary Church Terrell*. U of North Carolina P, 2020, p. 298.

9. Azuza Pacific's website lists a $10,000 grant awarded in 2017 for a Junior Faculty Summer Research Grant from the Yale Center for Faith and Culture at Yale Divinity School: https://www.apu.edu/researchandgrants/facultynotes/25705/.

10. Mary McLeod Bethune. "Dr. Bethune's Last Will and Testament," https://www.cookman.edu/history/last-will-testament.html.

11. Stephanie Y. Evans. "Mary McLeod Bethune's Research Agenda: Thought Translated to Work." *African American Research Perspectives*, vol. 12, no. 1, 2008, pp. 22–39.

12. See Evans, *Black Women in the Ivory Tower*.

13. Mary McLeod Bethune. "Clarifying Our Vision with the Facts." *Journal of Negro History*, Jan. 23, 1938, pp. 10–15.

14. Association for the Study of African American Life and History (ASALH). "Mary McLeod Bethune Service Award," https://asalh.org/awards/mary-mcleod-bethune-service-award/.

15. See workbook at https://issuu.com/blackwomensbiographygenius/docs/black_women_s_biography_writing_kit_revised_3_

16. Sisters of the Academy. "Signature Research BootCamp," https://sistersoftheacademy.org/signature-research-bootcamp/.

17. *Social Justice Ed* Conference, Clark Atlanta University, March 29, 2019, https://blackwomensocialjusticeed.net/conference.

Chapter 7

1. Executive Order 13950. "Combating Race and Sex Stereotyping," https://|www.federalregister.gov/documents/2020/09/28/2020-21534/combating-race-and-sex-stereotyping.

2. Nancy MacLean. *Democracy in Chains: The Deep History of the Radical Right's Stealth Plan for America*. Penguin, 2017.

3. Juliana Kim. "Florida Says AP Class Teaches Critical Race Theory. Here's What's Really in the Course." NPR, January 22, 2023, https://www.npr.org/2023/01/22/1150259944/florida-rejects-ap-class-african-american-studies.

4. See Stephanie Y. Evans, Colette M. Taylor, Michelle R. Dunlap, and DeMond S. Miller, editors. *African Americans and Community Engagement*: SUNY Press, 2009.

5. Evans. xiv.

6. Evans. xvii–xviii.

7. Ryan Quinn. "A Texas Trilogy of Anti-DEI, Tenure Bills." *Inside Higher Ed*, April 14, 2023, https://www.insidehighered.com/news/faculty-issues/tenure/2023/04/14/texas-trilogy-anti-dei-tenure-bills.

8. See Freedom to Learn, https://freedomtolearn.net/.

9. NPR. "Houston's Plan to Convert Some School Libraries into Discipline Centers Is Criticized." https://www.npr.org/2023/08/02/1191519700/houstons-plan-to-convert-some-school-libraries.

10. United Nations Universal Declaration of Human Rights. http://www.un.org/en/universal-declaration-human-rights/.

11. United Nations Universal Declaration of Human Rights. "History of the Document," http://www.un.org/en/sections/universal-declaration/history-document/index.html.

12. United Nations, Department of Economic and Social Affairs, Division for Social Policy and Development. *Social Justice in an Open World: The Role of the*

United Nations. United Nations, 2006, http://www.un.org/esa/socdev/documents/ifsd/SocialJustice.pdf, pp. 11–12.

13. Moya Bailey and Trudy. "On Misogynoir: Citation, Erasure, and Plagiarism." *Feminist Media Studies*, vol. 18, no. 4, Jul. 4, 2018, pp. 762–68.

14. Stephanie Y. Evans. "Gender Research and the African Academy: 'Moving against the Grain' in the Global Ivory Tower." *Black Women, Gender, + Families*, vol. 2, no. 2, 2008, pp. 31–52.

15. Howard Nicholas. "'Underdevelopment' in Africa—What's the Real Story?." *Critical Collective*, YouTube, 29:37, October 22, 2015, https://www.youtube.com/watch?v=SaqgQvLn5sQ, view minutes 1:00–4:24. Professor Nicholas is a Marxist scholar; a senior lecturer in economics; a convenor of MA in Economics of Development in International Institute of Social Studies, Erasmus University of Rotterdam; and an associate professor at ISS. See also richardshabazz, "We must understand why they need Africa to be poor," Instagram Reels, December 6, 2022, https://www.instagram.com/reel/Cl0u2B3KKPQ/; Walter Rodney. *How Europe Underdeveloped Africa*. Verso Books, 2018.

16. Mallence Bart-Williams.

17. In 2022, my first year free from administrative duties in over a decade, I turned, with a clear mind and new enthusiasm, to prepare my class syllabi. Every year I tweak them, but that year, I completely restructured my syllabi. I structured my classes to maximize my effort to teach students about different types of sources—from the known (books and articles) to the rarely cited (dissertations, archives, and creative texts). As an affirmation of the approach, the professional magazine *Inside Higher Education* published an article on the topic.

18. Stephanie Y. Evans. "Teaching from the Source." *Inside Higher Ed*, Oct. 11, 2022. https://www.insidehighered.com/advice/2022/10/12/teaching-students-how-use-variety-research-sources-opinion.

19. Let's pause here for one important note when considering creative sources and publishing: it is often difficult to get permission to cite poems or song lyrics within the text of your books. When anticipating using creative sources like lyrics or images, make sure to check out what will be required for use before you assume it will be included in your published text. As much as possible, gather your sources before you make major decisions about the final direction of your publication. That said, try to incorporate art, poetry, and music as much as possible in your work—they are sources of oxygen to breathe life into your work.

Chapter 8

1. Maparyan's edited volume *The Womanist Reader: The First Quarter Century of Womanist Thought* (2006) demonstrates how Black women have offered

several alternative paradigms with which to structure academic contributions. The reader also underscores the inevitability of diverse interpretations of any one idea.

2. CT: "How do you fit writing into your life?" Bambara: "But to answer the question—I just flat out announce I'm working, leave me alone and get out of my face." In Tate, *Black Women Writers at Work*, p. 49.

3. Frederick T. Evers, James Cameron Rush, and Iris Berdrow. *The Bases of Competence: Skills for Lifelong Learning and Employability*. Jossey-Bass, 1998.

4. See Kanika Bell. "Sisters on Sisters." in *Mental Health*, pp. 23–42; and Michelle R. Dunlap, *Reaching Out to Children and Families: Students Model Effective Community Service*. Rowman & Littlefield, 2000.

5. Toni Morrison. "How Can Values Be Taught in the University?" *Michigan Quarterly Review*, vol. 40, no. 2, 2001, p. 273.

6. Kimberly Miloch, Christopher T. Ray, and Abigail Tilton. "Values-Based Leadership: Culture versus Strategy." *The Department Chair*, vol. 31, no. 1, 2020, pp. 1–3. In the searing article "Identifying White Mediocrity and Know-Your-Place Aggression: A Form of Self-Care" (2018), Koritha Mitchell chronicles how mediating microaggressions and managing energy in workspaces is an essential way to care for oneself. Conversely, Donna Nicol's academic narrative "Chairing as Self-Care: Strategies for Combatting the Cultural Identity Taxation Trap for Black Women Chairs" outlines how taking control of your professional career can be an empowering act. Koritha Mitchell. "Identifying White Mediocrity and Know-Your-Place Aggression: A Form of Self-Care." *African American Review*, vol. 51, no. 4, 2018, pp. 253–62; Donna J. Nicol. "Chairing as Self-Care: Strategies for Combatting the Cultural Identity Taxation Trap for Black Women Chairs." *Palimpsest: A Journal on Women, Gender, and the Black International*, vol. 10, no. 2, 2021, pp. 179–88. Kesho Yvonne Scott argues that mere survival is not the goal. Her book *The Habit of Surviving* traces the lives of five Black women, including her two daughters. She reveals several harsh truths that recur in Black women's writing: not all Black women survive. Those who do survive may not experience true liberation, and those who are liberated in one way or another may not enjoy a sustained experience of freedom. And, surely, intersectional oppressions have not and may never disappear. Kesho Y. Scott. *The Habit of Surviving: Black Women's Strategies for Life*. Ballantine Books, 1992.

7. Bettina L. Love. *We Want to Do More than Survive: Abolitionist Teaching and the Pursuit of Educational Freedom*. Beacon Press, 2019.

8. Stephanie Y. Evans. *Black Women's Yoga History*, p. 179.

9. Harriet A. Jacobs. *Incidents in the Life of a Slave Girl*, edited by Nell Irvin Painter. Penguin Books, 2000.

10. Paul Bowers. "When Harriet Tubman Met John Brown." *Jacobin*. June 19, 2022. https://jacobin.com/2022/06/juneteenth-john-brown-harriet-tubman-abolitionist-slavery-south-emancipation. Accessed November 16, 2023.

11. Arline T. Geronimus, Margaret T. Hicken, Jay A. Pearson, Sarah J. Seashols, Kelly L. Brown, and Tracey Dawson Cruz. "Do US Black Women Experience Stress-Related Accelerated Biological Aging? A Novel Theory and First Population-Based Test of Black-White Differences in Telomere Length." *Human Nature*, vol. 21, no. 1, Mar. 2010, pp. 19–38.

12. See Historian Speaks https://historianspeaks.org/f/black-womens-studies. Accessed December 5, 20223

13. Ericka Huggins, https://www.erickahuggins.com/

14. Evans. *Black Women's Yoga History*, p. 343.

15. Byllye Avery Endowed Professor at CUNY School of Public Health https://foundation.sph.cuny.edu/byllye-avery/.

Coda

1. "Five Questions with John Bracey," Stony Brook U, February 2, 2017, video, 4:41, https://youtu.be/oRNfwc5AHu8.

2. For a collective reflection, see *Journal of African American Studies*, vol. 108, no. 4, fall 2023, pp. 765–91.

3. Karla Holloway. *Passed On: African American Mourning Stories* Duke UP, 2002, pp. 17, 265.

4. Rebecca Wanzo. "Futurity." *Keywords for American Cultural Studies*, third edition, edited by Bruce Burgett and Glenn Hendler. New York UP, 2020, p. 122.

5. Ytasha Womack. *Black Panther: A Cultural Exploration*. Becker & Mayer Books, 2023, pp. 119–20.

Select Bibliography

Alridge, Derrick P., Cornelius L. Bynum, and James B. Stewart, editors. The Black Intellectual Tradition: African American Thought in the Twentieth Century. U of Illinois P, 2021.

American Psychological Association. Stress in America: The State of Our Nation. Stress in America Survey. 2017. https://www.apa.org/news/press/releases/stress/2017/state-nation.pdf.

Angelou, Maya. And Still I Rise. Random House, 1978.

Bailey, Moya. Misogynoir Transformed: Black Women's Digital Resistance. New York UP, 2021.

Bailey, Moya, and Trudy. "On Misogynoir: Citation, Erasure, and Plagiarism." Feminist Media Studies, vol. 18, no. 4, July 4, 2018, pp. 762–68.

Belcher, Wendy Laura. Writing Your Journal Article in 12 Weeks: A Guide to Academic Publishing Success. U of Chicago P, 2019.

Benjamin, Lois, editor. Black Women in the Academy: Promises and Perils. UP of Florida, 1997.

Berry, Daina Ramey, and Kali Nicole Gross. A Black Women's History of the United States. Beacon Press, 2020.

Bethune, Mary McLeod. "Clarifying Our Vision with the Facts." Journal of Negro History, Jan. 23, 1938, pp. 10–15.

Bracey, John H., Jr. Foreword to Truth and Revolution: A History of the Sojourner Truth Organization, Michael Staudenmaier, v–vii. AK Press, 2012.

Bruce, La Marr Jurelle. How to Go Mad without Losing Your Mind: Madness and Black Radical Creativity. Duke UP, 2021.

Burgett, Bruce, and Glenn Hendler, editors. Keywords for American Cultural Studies. 3rd ed., New York UP, 2020.

Byrd, Curtis D., and Rihanna S. Mason. Academic Pipeline Programs: Diversifying Pathways to the Professoriate. Lever Press, 2021.

Carruthers, Charlene A. Unapologetic: A Black, Queer, and Feminist Mandate for Radical Movements. Beacon Press, 2018.

Clark, Septima. *Echo in My Soul*. Dutton, 1962.
Collins, Patricia Hill. *Black Feminist Thought: Knowledge, Consciousness, and the Politics of Empowerment*. Routledge, 2000.
Cooper, Anna Julia. *The Voice of Anna Julia Cooper: Including "A Voice from the South" and Other Important Essays, Papers, and Letters*. Edited by Charles Lemert and Esme Bhan. Rowman & Littlefield, 1998.
Coppin, Fanny Jackson. *Reminiscences of a School Life and Hints on Teaching*. A. M. E. Book Concern, 1913.
Crenshaw, Kimberlé. "Mapping the Margins: Intersectionality, Identity Politics, and Violence against Women of Color." *Stanford Law Review*, vol. 43, no. 6, July 1991, pp. 1241–99.
Dunlap, Michelle R. *Reaching Out to Children and Families: Students Model Effective Community Service*. Rowman & Littlefield, 2000.
Ehrenreich, Barbara, and Deirdre English. *Complaints and Disorders: The Sexual Politics of Sickness*. Feminist Press, 1973.
Evans, Mari, editor. *Black Women Writers (1950–1980): A Critical Evaluation*. Anchor Books, 1983.
Evans, Stephanie Y. *Black Women in the Ivory Tower, 1850–1954*. UP of Florida, 2007.
Evans, Stephanie Y. *Black Women's Yoga History: Memoirs of Inner Peace*. State U of New York P, 2021.
Evans, Stephanie Y. "Gender and Research in the African Academy: 'Moving against the Grain' in the Global Ivory Tower." *Black Women, Gender + Families*, vol. 2, no. 2, 2008, pp. 31–52. https://www.jstor.org/stable/10.5406/blacwomegendfami.2.2.0031.
Evans, Stephanie Y. "Letters to Our Daughters: Black Women's Memoirs as Epistles of Human Rights, Healing, and Inner Peace." In *The Black Intellectual Tradition: African American Thought in the Twentieth Century*, edited by Derrick P. Alridge, Cornelius L. Bynum, and James B. Stewart. U of Illinois P, 2021, pp. *100–26*.
Evans, Stephanie Y. "Living Legacies: Black Women, Educational Philosophies, and Community Service, 1865–1965." PhD dissertation. University of Massachusetts Amherst, 2003.
Evans, Stephanie Y. "Teaching from the Source." *Inside Higher Ed*, Oct. 11, 2022. https://www.insidehighered.com/advice/2022/10/12/teaching-students-how-use-variety-research-sources-opinion.
Evans, Stephanie Y. "We've Been Lovers on a Mission." *Palimpsest Journal: A Journal on Women, Gender, and the Black International*, vol. 10, no. 2, 2021, vi–xii.
Evans, Stephanie Y., Colette M. Taylor, Michelle R. Dunlap, and DeMond S. Miller, editors. *African Americans and Community Engagement: Community Service, Service-Learning, and Community-Based Research*. State U of New York P, 2009.

Evans, Stephanie Y., Kanika Bell, and Nsenga K. Burton. *Black Women's Mental Health: Balancing Strength and Vulnerability*. State U of New York P, 2017.

Evers, Frederick T., James Cameron Rush, and Iris Berdrow. *The Bases of Competence: Skills for Lifelong Learning and Employability*. Jossey-Bass, 1998.

"Five Questions with John Bracey," Stony Brook University, February 2, 2017, video, 4:41, https://youtu.be/oRNfwc5AHu8.

Garcia, Nichole Margarita. "Spiring-Murdering in Academia." *Diverse Issues in Higher Education*, Feb. 26, 2020. https://www.diverseeducation.com/opinion/article/15106340/spirit-murdering-in-academia.

Gardner, Howard. *Frames of Mind: The Theory of Multiple Intelligences*. Basic Books, 2011.

Geronimus, Arline T., Margaret T. Hicken, Jay A. Pearson, Sarah J. Seashols, Kelly L. Brown, and Tracey Dawson Cruz. "Do US Black Women Experience Stress-Related Accelerated Biological Aging? A Novel Theory and First Population-Based Test of Black-White Differences in Telomere Length." *Human Nature*, vol. 21, no. 1, Mar. 2010, pp. 19–38.

Greene, Robert. *The 48 Laws of Power*. Penguin Books, 1998.

Griffin, Farah Jasmine. *Read until You Understand: The Profound Wisdom of Black Life and Literature*. W. W. Norton, 2021.

Guy-Sheftall, Beverly. *Words of Fire: An Anthology of African-American Feminist Thought*. The New Press, 1995.

Hamer, Fannie Lou. "I'm Sick and Tired of Being Sick and Tired." In *Megan Parker Brooks, the Speeches of Fannie Lou Hamer: To Tell It Like It Is*. UP of Mississippi, 1964, pp. 57–64.

Hull, Akasha (Gloria T.), Patricia Bell Scott, and Barbara Smith. *All the Women Are White, All the Blacks Are Men, but Some of Us Are Brave: Black Women's Studies*. Feminist Press, 1982.

Jacobs, Harriet A. *Incidents in the Life of a Slave Girl*. Edited by Nell Irvin Painter. Penguin Books, 2000.

Johnson-Bailey, Juanita, editor. *Sistahs in College: Making a Way Out of No Way*. Krieger, 2001.

Jones, Jacqueline. *Labor of Love, Labor of Sorrow: Black Women, Work, and the Family, from Slavery to the Present*. Basic Books, 2010.

Jordan-Zachary, Julia. *Erotic Testimonies: Black Women Daring to Be Wild and Free*. State U of New York P, 2022.

Kabat-Zinn, Jon. *Full Catastrophe Living: Using the Wisdom of Your Body and Mind to Face Stress, Pain, and Illness*. Bantam Dell, 2013.

Lassner, Jacob. *Demonizing the Queen of Sheba: Boundaries of Gender and Culture in Postbiblical Judaism and Medieval Islam*. U of Chicago P, 1993.

Lieu, Clara. *Learn, Create, Teach: A Guide to Building a Creative Life*. CreateSpace Independent Publishing Platform, 2013.

Love, Bettina L. *We Want to Do More than Survive: Abolitionist Teaching and the Pursuit of Educational Freedom*. Beacon Press, 2019.
Mabokela, Reitumetse Obakeng, and Anna L. Green, editors. *Sisters of the Academy: Emergent Black Women Scholars in Higher Education*. Stylus Publishing, 2001.
MacLean, Nancy. *Democracy in Chains: The Deep History of the Radical Right's Stealth Plan for America*. Penguin, 2017.
Miloch, Kimberly, Christopher T. Ray, and Abigail Tilton. "Values-Based Leadership: Culture versus Strategy." *The Department Chair*, vol. 31, no. 1, 2020, pp. 13.
Mitchell, Koritha. "Identifying White Mediocrity and Know-Your-Place Aggression: A Form of Self-Care." *African American Review*, vol. 51, no. 4, 2018, pp. 253–62.
Morrison, Toni. "How Can Values Be Taught in the University?" *Michigan Quarterly Review*, vol. 40, no. 2, 2001, pp. 273–78.
Morrison, Toni. "In Her Own Words: Toni Morrison on Writing, Editing, and Teaching." By Kathy Neustadt. *Bryn Mawr Alumnae Bulletin* (Summer 2019). https://www.brynmawr.edu/bulletin/her-own-words-toni-morrison-writing-editing-teaching.
Morrison, Toni. *The Source of Self-Regard: Selected Essays, Speeches, and Meditations*. Alfred A. Knopf, 2019.
Nicol, Donna J. "Chairing as Self-Care: Strategies for Combatting the Cultural Identity Taxation Trap for Black Women Chairs." *Palimpsest: A Journal on Women, Gender, and the Black International*, vol. 10, no. 2, 2021, pp. 179–88.
Parker, Alison M. *Unceasing Militant: The Life of Mary Church Terrell*. U of North Carolina P, 2020.
Portwood-Stacer, Laura. *The Book Proposal Book: A Guide for Scholarly Authors*. Princeton UP, 2021.
Ramsey, Sonya. *Bertha Maxwell-Roddey: A Modern-Day Race Woman and the Power of Black Leadership*. UP of Florida, 2022.
Repko, Allen. *Interdisciplinary Research: Process and Theory*. SAGE Publications, 2008.
Rockquemore, Kerry Ann, and Tracey Laszloffy. *The Black Academic's Guide to Winning Tenure—Without Losing Your Soul*. Lynne Rienner, 2008.
Rodney, Walter. *How Europe Underdeveloped Africa*. Verso Books, 2018.
Rudolph, Frederick. *The American College and University: A History*. U of Georgia P, 1990[1962].
Sanchez, Sonia, and Yolanda Wisher, editors. *Peace Is a Haiku Song*. City of Philadelphia Mural Arts Program, 2013.
Sapolsky, Robert M. *Why Zebras Don't Get Ulcers: A Guide to Stress, Stress-Related Diseases, and Coping*. Henry Holt, 2004.
Scott, Kesho Y. *The Habit of Surviving: Black Women's Strategies for Life*. Ballantine Books, 1992.

Shahid, Sagirah. "Killing Us Softly: Chronic Stress and the Health of Black Women." Minnesota Women's Press. Oct. 1, 2018. https://www.womenspress.com/6018/.
Sood, Amit. *The Mayo Clinic Guide to Stress-Free Living*. Da Capo Press, 2013.
Staudenmaier, Michael. *Truth and Revolution: A History of the Sojourner Truth Organization*. AK Press, 2012.
Tate, Claudia, editor. *Black Women Writers at Work*. Haymarket Books, 2023.
Taylor, Foluke. *Unruly Therapeutic: Black Feminist Writings and Practices in Living Room*. Norton, 2023.
Taylor, Keeanga-Yamahtta, editor. *How We Get Free: Black Feminism and the Combahee River Collective*. Haymarket Books, 2017.
Terborg-Penn, Rosalyn. *Women in Africa and the African Diaspora: A Reader*. Howard UP, 1996.
United Nations, Department of Economic and Social Affairs, Division for Social Policy and Development. *Social Justice in an Open World: The Role of the United Nations*. United Nations, 2006. http://www.un.org/esa/socdev/documents/ifsd/SocialJustice.pdf.
Van Sertima, Ivan, editor. *Black Women in Antiquity*. Transaction Books, 1984.
White, Evelyn. *The Black Women's Health Book: Speaking for Ourselves*. Da Capo Press, 1990.
Willis, Janice Dean. *Dreaming Me: Black, Baptist, and Buddhist: One Woman's Spiritual Journey*. Wisdom, 2008.
World Health Organization. *Mental Health Action Plan, 2013–2020*. World Health Organization, 2013.

Index

abundance, 29–30
academic hypocrisy, 3, 99, 131
academic presses. *See* university presses
access, accessibility, 36, 38, 145; to higher education, 42, 49, 131, 157–58, 169; open, 104–5; scholarship and, 100
accountability, 39, 86–87, 121–22, 132, 135, 139–41, 150–51
Achebe, Chinua, 107–8
activism: Black feminist writing as, 25–27, 29–31, 32, 60; scholarship as, 77, 80, 81, 167–68, 195–97; social media campaigns, 128; wellness and, 196–97
Adichie, Chimamanda, 25
Adinkra, 16–17
administration: Black women in, 1–2, 8–9, 96–97, 171; time burden of, 1–2, 43, 62, 68–69, 126–27, 158, 175
adult reentry students, xiii–xiv, 5
advocating, 8, 25–26, 62–65, 100–101, 138–39, 167–68, 186–89
African American Intellectual History Society (AAIHS), 130
African American Policy Forum, 128
African feminism, 10, 15, 18–19, 27–28, 33, 42, 82, 92–93, 139. *See also* Black feminism

African Methodist Episcopal (AME) Church, 88
Africana Women's Studies, 82, 93–94. *See also* Black Women's Studies; Women's Studies
agency: Black women's history and, 59, 61, 172, 176–77; time management and, 175–77; writing and, xiv–xv, 167–68, 183–86, 202
alienation, 95, 146
Alpha Kappa Alpha Sorority, 86
American Economic Association, 85
American Educational Research Association (AERA), 128–29
American Historical Association, 85
American Philological Association, 85
American Psychological Association (APA), 50–51
American Sociological Association, 125–26
American Studies Association (ASA), 130
Americans for Prosperity, 161
Amerie, 123
ancestor acknowledgments, xvi, 17–18, 27–31, 85, 89, 185
Anderson, Carol, 58, 135, 163, 198
Anderson, Marian, 34
André 3000, 203

Angelou, Maya, xiii, 31, 41, 53–56, 93, 176–77, 185
anti-imperialism, 129
antimilitarism, 26, 167–68
anxiety, xiii, 50, 59, 64, 120–21, 148–49, 185–86, 205
appropriation, 133–35
Aptheker, Bettina, 81–82
archives, 37, 40, 129, 172–75
argument, 17, 73–76; active learning and, 87–88; clarifying, 94–96, 185; context and, 80–81, 94–95, 172–75; revising, 118–19, 140–41
Arrested Development, 201
artificial intelligence (AI), 48, 173–74, 187–88
Asante, Malefi, 139
Ashe, Arthur, 199
Association for the Study of African American Life and History (ASALH), 130, 138–39
Association for the Study of Negro Life and History, 86
Association for the Study of the Worldwide African Diaspora (ASWAD), 130
Association of Black Women Historians, (ABWH), 27, 141–42, 154
Atlanta History Center, 193
Atlanta University Africana Women's Center series, 82
attention, 10, 14, 38–39, 47–48, 51, 63–64, 102–3, 147, 165, 186–89
audience: community and, 125–26, 185–86, 194–95; identifying, 41–44, 125–26; outside of academia, 15, 33, 70, 74; scholarship and, xii, 74, 91, 113, 117–19, 172–73
Avery, Byllye, 61–62, 67, 92, 195–97

Badu, Erykah, 44

Bailey, Moya, 24, 75, 95, 169–70, 198. *See also* misogynoir
Baker, Ella, 159, 162
balance, 31–32, 53, 60, 68, 71, 147, 153, 175, 177, 189–90, 202
Baldwin, Davarian, 198
Baldwin, Mary Louise, 86
Bambara, Toni Cade, xiii, 2, 14, 24, 36, 120–21, 171–72, 186
Barrett, Janie Porter, 86
Bart-Williams, Mallence, 170–71
Bassett, Angela, 192–93
Batiste, Jon, 200
Bay, Mia, 80–81
Beckham, Ruth Howard, 53
Belcher, Wendy Laura, 51–52
Bell-Scott, Patricia, 32
Bell, Kanika, 35, 62, 146–47, 152–53
Benjamin, Lois, 142–43
Berry, Daina Ramey, 103, 142
Bethune, Mary McLeod, 25–26, 86, 90, 94, 111, 137–39
Bethune-Cookman College, 138, 142–43
Beyoncé, 154
bias, 111–12, 121–22, 136
Bill of Rights (US), 58
Black Arts, 2
Black feminism, 24–26; Black Women's Studies and, 86–87; community and, xi–xii, 27–28, 73, 86–87; compassion and, 27–28; freedom and, 11–12; after intersectionality, 76; joy and, 30–32; justice and, xiv–xv; liberation and, 25, 199–200; as practical, everyday approach, 11–12; sharing and, 10; as transnational, 25; wellness and, 61–62
Black Feminist Summer Institute, 128
Black Feminist Theory Project (Brown University), 82

Black Feminist Think Tank, 82–83, 128
Black feminist writing: in academia, 9; agency and, 175–77, 190–92; Black womanhood and, xv–xvi, 26; care and, 24, 31–33, 39–41, 64–65; as celebratory, 30–34; challenges of, 6, 17–18; as courageous, 31, 34–39; as community-centered, 1, 10, 33, 39, 86–87; as deconstructive and constructive, 26; as everyday approach, 11–13; freedom and, 26, 44, 47–48, 110, 170–72; historical lineage of, 10, 24, 31–32, 34, 58–59; human rights and, 33, 167–72; methods of, 100; as practice, xi, xiii, 9, 19, 23–26, 31–41, 47–48, 73–74, 99–100, 125, 157, 169, 181, 185–86, 200; progress and, 75; regeneration and, 29–31, 44, 110, 200; resistance and, 37; as resource, 54–55, 59, 65–66, 112; space of, 26–27; themes of, 17–18; wellness and, xi, xiii, 9, 23–24, 74, 93–94, 108, 171–72, 197
Black Lives Matter, 50–51, 142
Black Panther Party, 196–97
Black Power Movement, 2, 195–96
Black Studies (BST), 28, 48–49, 79, 81–82, 89–90, 92, 130–31, 158. *See also* Black Women's Studies; race and gender studies; Women's Studies
Black Super Woman myth, 5
Black Women Oral History Project (Harvard University), 82
Black women: are not saviors, 96; attacks on, 99, 169; centering, 26, 47–49, 58–59, 61, 108–10, 128–30, 138–39, 196; diversity of, 96–97; in education, xiv–xv, 1–2, 9, 25, 28, 31–32, 42, 47–51, 56–59, 70–71, 73–74, 76–97, 103–4, 111–12, 114, 126–32, 138–39, 142–44, 165, 168–69, 181–82; erasure of, 136; health disparities, 196; knowledge production by, 171–72; in leadership positions, 126–27; in literature, 108–9; in medical field, 86; in publishing, 107; service and, 5; stress and, 4–8, 38–39, 50, 62, 192–93, 204; tea and, 67–68; violence against, xiii–xiv, 4–5, 48–49, 57–60, 86, 90, 112, 128, 154, 165–66, 169–71, 192–93; wine and, 66–67
Black Women's Health Imperative (BWHI), 43–44, 92, 94, 127, 192–93, 195–97
Black Women's Health Project, 195
Black Women's Mental Health Institute, 43–44, 94, 127
Black Women's Studies (BWST): attacks on, 3, 83, 94–95, 156–66, 177; change and transformation in, 16–17, 57–58, 77, 137; citation and, 15, 80–81, 128–32, 136–37, 172–75; community and, 128–31, 154–55; everyday and, 11; global and diasporic awareness in, 81–82; history of, 11, 48–49, 76–83, 92–94, 97; human rights and, 90, 159–60, 167–72, 182; as interdisciplinary, 28, 42, 80, 82–83, 129–30; Makedaic tradition of, 18–19, 92–94; problem-solving and, 92; professionalization of, 165–66; programs in, 193; as resource, 75–76, 112
Black Women's Studies Booklist, 77, 80–81
Black Women's Studies Association (BWSA), 128–30
Black Women's Wellness series (SUNY Press), 100–101, 197

Black, Daniel, 32–33, 198
#BlackGirlMagic, 110, 128
#BlackGirlsMatter, 128–29
#BlackInTheIvory, 122–23
Blain, Keisha, 130, 198
Blay, Yaba, 128
Blount, Linda Goler, 197
Bolles, A. Lynn, 129
Bond, Beverly, 128
Booth, Wayne, 104
Bouchet, Edward, 84
boundaries, 5, 60, 184
Bowen, Cecile, 136
Bracey, John H., Jr., xi–xiii, 15, 89–90, 187–88, 201–2
Bradley, Regina, 198
Brand, Dionne, 167–68
Brooks, Gwendolyn, 102
Brown v. Board of Education, 53, 85
Brown, Charlotte Hawkins, 86
Brown, Hallie Quinn, 24, 86
Brown, James, 2
Brown, Jericho, 32
Brown, John, 191–92
Brown, Raina, 194–95
Bruce, La Marr Jurelle, 170–71
Bublé, Michael, 202
Buck, Jennifer, 132–37
bullying, 3, 135, 146
Bundles, A'Leila, 142
Burden-Stelly, Charisse, 75–76, 198
Burney, Sharon, 182–83
burnout, 188. *See also* stress
Burroughs, Nannie Hellen, 86
Burton, Nsenga, 35, 146–47, 152–53
Byrd, Brandon, 130
Byrd, Curtis D., 144

Cameron, Christopher, 130
cancel culture, 134–35
Candia-Bailey, Antoinette, 3

Canty, Jayme, 194
capitalism, 9, 24, 26, 100, 153, 159
care, 19, 100–101; communal, 27–29, 32–34, 39–41, 82–83, 115, 139, 141–42, 157, 178, 189, 193–97, 200, 202, 204; gender and, 5; politics of, 76; for self, 23–24, 27–28, 32–34, 44, 139, 157, 189, 193–97, 200, 202; structural, 139; writing and, 14, 24, 31, 115, 200, 204–5
Cato Institute, 161
celebration, 30–34, 153
censorship, 134–35, 165
Center for Black Women's Wellness (CBWW), 43–44, 127, 195
Center for Constitutional Rights (CCR), 168
Chair at the Table Network, 64–65, 122–23, 126–27
change, 16–17, 25, 38–39, 55, 57–58, 77, 137
Charles Koch Foundation, 161
#CharlestonSyllabus, 172–73
ChatGPT, 188. *See also* artificial intelligence
Chlöe, 202
Christian, Barbara, 81–82
Chronicle of Higher Education, 100–101, 115
citation, 15, 28–30, 37, 80–81, 85, 87–88, 100, 121, 125, 128–32, 136–37; REAL BAD NEWS and, 172–75
#CiteASista, 128–29, 131–32
#CiteBlackWomen, 128–32, 136
Citizens for a Sound Economy, 161
Citizenship Schools, 162
Clapp, Nicholas, 92–93
clarity, 13, 17, 80, 96, 106–7, 110, 114, 147–48, 189–90, 193
Clark Atlanta University, 192
Clark, Mamie Phipps, 53

Clark, Septima Poinsette, 90, 94, 161–63
classification, 18, 95–96
Cleopatra, 93
climate change, 170
Club for Growth, 161
club movement, 131, 138
Cobb, Jelani, 163
Cohen, Cathy, 177
Cole, Natalie, 66–67
Coleman, Monica A., 3, 182
Colesworthy, Rebecca, 100–101, 115
collaboration, xi–xii, 39, 126, 144, 146–54, 193–94. *See also* community
collective. *See* community
Collier, Joan, 128–29
Collins, Patricia Hill, 11–12, 23–24, 31, 47–48, 61–62, 82, 114–15, 125–26
colonialism, 24–25, 36, 68, 113, 159, 169–70
Coltrane, John, 201–2
Columbia University Press, 102
Combahee River Collective, 26–27, 49, 81
Common Power, 163
community: building, 17, 37–39, 86–87, 94, 122–23, 125–31, 136–37, 141–55, 182–83; care for, 27–29, 32–34, 39–41, 82–83, 115, 139, 141–42, 157, 178, 189, 193–97, 200, 202, 204; engaging, xiii–xiv, 139, 161–63, 185–86; knowledge and, 73; scholarship and, 94, 135–36, 139; social media and, 187; stress and, 10–11; writing and, xi, 1, 10, 13–14, 33, 39, 86–87 115, 136–37, 142–54, 172–73
compassion, xiv–xv, 8, 15, 23–24, 27–29, 31, 35–36, 44, 159, 167–70, 181–82, 199–200

Compassion-Based Cognitive Therapy (CBCT), 35–36
Competitive Enterprise Institute, 161
conferences, 9, 13, 101; community and, 39–40, 113, 128–31, 144–45, 152–53; presenting at, 121
consciousness-raising, 92
conservativism, 24, 58–59, 75, 161, 165, 177
context: disciplinary, 29, 59, 74–76, 80, 83, 90, 94–96; historical, 31, 29, 80, 85, 167–68; wellness and, 6–8, 31; writing in, xii, 2, 24, 29, 31, 75–76, 94–96, 136
contract, 43, 102–5, 117–18, 150–51
cooking, 5
Cooper, Anna Julia, 19, 24–26, 29–30, 57, 67, 84–85, 90, 94, 108, 145, 193
Cooper, Brittney, 136, 198
Copley-Grube, Pam, 201
Coppin, Fanny Muriel Jackson, 86–90, 94
courage, 8, 204–5; care and, 34–39, 44; Black feminist writing and, 6, 17–18, 26, 30–31, 181, 200
Covey, Stephen, 69
COVID-19 pandemic, 7–8, 50–51, 120–21, 153–54
craft, 32–33, 68–69, 202
Crenshaw, Kimberlé, 80, 95, 128, 153, 163–64, 198
critical legal theory, 80
critical race theory (CRT), 36–37, 49, 79, 128, 131, 161, 163–66, 177
cause and effect, 95–96
cultural studies, 42
Curwood, Anastasia, 142

dance, 201
Daniel, Sadie Iola, 24, 86
Darling, Marsha, 81–82

data, 12, 17, 61, 65–66, 67, 74, 100, 103, 121, 185–86
Davis, Angela, 27–28, 107–8, 195–96
Davis, Lori Patton, 3, 182
De La Soul, 48
deadlines, 7–8, 41, 120–21, 149–50
decolonialism, 25
defining, definition, 12, 25–27, 61, 74, 94, 95–96, 165–66, 197, 200
dehumanization, xv–xvi, 61, 86, 90, 96, 167–69, 184, 187–88, 195–96
Delany, Sadie and Bessie, 34, 192–93
Dennie, Nneka, 129–30
Derricotte, Toi, 30–31
DeSantis, Ron, 161
Deschamps, Alexandrina, 4–5
description, 95–96
diaspora, 65–66, 75–76, 81–82, 137–38, 186
disciplinary process, 28, 38, 42, 73–76, 79–80, 87, 96–96, 185
digital humanities, 127
Dill, Bonnie Thornton, 112
discussion, 13, 29, 35, 80, 95–96, 117–18, 153–54, 173, 175
dissertation, 9–10, 42–43; argument and, 74–75, 90–91; historical, 89, 93–94, 174–75, 185; revising for book publication, 74–75, 91, 94; stress and, 84
diversity: academic family tree and, 44; of Black women's experiences, 67–68, 86–87, 96–97; in education, 56, 94; in publishing, 3, 100, 104, 107, 132; of sources, 173–74
Diversity, Equity, and Inclusion (DEI), 158
Doctors without Borders, 168
Douglass, Frederick, 36–37, 47–48
Dove, Rita, 32–34, 102
Du Bois, W. E. B., 2, 67, 82, 89–90, 94, 162–63, 176

Duff, Rosalynn, 194–95
Dunbar, Erica Armstrong, 154
Duncan, Natanya, 130
Dunlap, Michelle, 152–53
Dykes, Eva, B. 3, 24, 85
Dyson, Mayah, 71

Edim, Glory, 128
edited volumes, 131, 146–54
editing, 99–100, 106–7, 110, 118–19, 140–41, 150–51
editors, 116–21, 140–41; acquisition, 40–41, 104–6, 117–19; copy, 102–3, 105, 106; developmental, 10–11, 14, 43, 106, 119, 152–53, 177–78; proofreader, 106
education: academic freedom and, 158–66; attacks on, 114–15, 161–66, 177; Black women in, xiv–xv, 1–2, 9, 25, 28, 31–32, 42, 47–51, 56–59, 70–71, 73–74, 76–97, 103–4, 111–12, 114, 126–32, 138–39, 142–44, 165, 168–69, 181–82; colonialism and, 169–70; community and, 29–30, 162–63, 185–86; inequity in, 28; progressive, 30, 58–59, 138–40, 168–69, 193; as self-education, 37, 47–48, 88, 99–100, 158; space of, 26–27, 31–32; stress and, 68–71, 87; time and, 187–88; values in, 189; violence in, 169–71, 182, 198–99; wellness in, 36, 49, 158
Edwards, Erica R., 82–83, 96, 128, 198
Ehrenreich, Barbra, 86
elite capture, 36
elitism, 32, 36–38, 89, 96, 114–15, 142
Elliot, Missy, 200
energy management, 175–77. *See also under* time
English, Deirdre, 86
environmentalism, 196–97

Epps, JoAnne, 3
equality, xiv–xv, 15, 25–26, 42, 159–60, 163–64
erasure, 18–19, 34–35, 92–93, 107, 111, 136, 204
ethics: Black feminist, 24, 31, 44, 168–69, 182–83; of care, 31, 44, 100–101; of professional writing and publishing, 99, 105, 118–19, 131–37, 145
Euclidean math, 74–75
Evans, Mari, 32, 55–56
Everett, Edward, 84
Evers, Frederick, 56
everyday, 11–12, 61–62
Ewing, K. T., 142
exemplification, xi, 84, 120–21, 126, 135, 142, 153, 170–71, 190
exercise, 13, 34–35, 62–64. *See also* meditation; yoga

Family and Medical Leave Act, 186
family tree, 18, 29–30, 37–38, 39, 44, 128, 183, 186
Farmer, Ashley, 130, 142, 163, 198
Farris, Dionne, 20
feedback, 10–11, 14, 100–103, 140–41, 145, 150–51, 194–95
Feminist Press, 102
#FergusonSyllabus, 172–73
Fichte, Johann, 84
Figueroa-Vasquez, Yomaira C., 25
first-generation scholars and students, xiii–xiv, 5, 36–39, 88–89, 94, 142–43, 177–78
fit, 100–101
Flemming, Sheila, 113
Florvil, Tiffany, 142
flourishing, 1–4, 8, 10, 27–28, 33, 38, 166, 202
for-profit presses, 3
Ford Fellows, 144

Ford, Tanisha, 142
Foster, Parker, 194–95
Franklin, Aretha, 2
freedom, xiv–xvi, 11–12, 15, 18, 30, 44, 47–48, 50–51, 109–10, 114–15, 158–66, 204–5
Freedom to Learn Coalition, National Day of Action, 163–65
FreedomWorks, 161
Freire, Paulo, 88
futurity, 17–18, 44, 69–70, 159, 170, 182–84, 186, 203–5

Gainesville Women's Health Center, 195
Gardner, Howard, 56, 188–89
Garrett-Scott, Shennette, 154
gatekeeping, 100, 107, 111–12, 135, 199
Gay, Claudine, 3
Gay, Roxanne, 24
genealogy, 29–31. *See also* family tree
Georgia State University Humanities Center Faculty Fellowship, 10–11
Giddings, Paula, 82, 154
Gillespie, Dizzy, 63–64
global, 30, 42, 58, 81, 153–54, 168–71, 205
goals, 70, 102–3, 173, 185
Gottlieb, Robert, 110
Gramms (Mary Edmonds), xiii–xiv, 202–3
gratitude, 35–36, 89, 185, 202
Great Books curriculum, 57–58
Green, Anna L., 142–43
Green, Vivian, 200
Greene, Robert, 197
Grier, Pam, 93
Griffin, Farah, 80–81, 103, 198
Gross, Kali, 103, 141–42
Gumbs, Alexis Pauline, 142, 198

246 | INDEX

Guy-Sheftall, Beverly, 11–12, 24, 61–62, 77, 81–83, 112–13, 153, 163–64, 177, 198–200

hair loss, 204
Hamer, Fannie Lou, 196
Hannah-Jones, Nichole, 3
Harley, Sharon, 81–82
HarperCollins, 102
Harris (King), Charles Dix Edmonds, 203
Hathaway, Lalah, 4–, 63–64
Haymarket Books, 101–2
healing: Black women's traditions of, 65–68, 90, 92, 171–72, 181–82, 189, 196–97, 204; self-care and, 20, 23, 34, 54–55, 189–90; space of, 19; writing and, xiii, 23–24, 54–55, 59–62, 147, 171–72, 181
health. *See* wellness
Healy, Patrick, 84
Heritage Foundation, 161
Hersey, Tricia, 146–47, 170
Higginbotham, Evelyn, 154
Hill, Anita, 59
Hill, Jaribu, 168
Hill, Lauren, 202
Hine, Darlene Clark, 83, 91, 176–77
Historically Black Colleges and Universities (HBCUs), 39–40, 48–49
history: of Black women, 5, 11–12, 23–24, 26–27, 29, 31–34, 56–59, 65–68, 79–87, 95–97, 108–9, 112, 138–39, 171–72, 176; community and, 125–27; contextualizing, 8, 29; wellness and, 14–15, 31–34, 67–68, 79, 95–96
Holloway, Karla, 202
hooks, bell, 24, 36, 58–59, 198
hope, 4–5, 29, 177, 198
Hopkinson, Nalo. 93

Horne, Gerald, 198
Howard University, 102
Hudson-Weems, Clenora, 25
Hudson, Jennifer, 202
Huggins, Ericka, 196–97
Hull, Akasha (Gloria T.), 2, 81–82, 197
human rights, 3, 26–27, 33, 49, 58, 90, 159–60, 167–72, 182, 193
Hunter, Jane Edna, 86
Hurston, Zora Neale, 120–21
hypnotherapy, 63–64

identity: Black women's, 26, 32, 48, 87, 137–38, 172–73; wellness, 172–73; writing and, 32, 48, 87
India Arie, 71
individualism, 37–38
Institute for Colored Youth (ICY), 88
Institutional Review Board (IRB), 136–37
intelligences, 56, 188–89
interdisciplinary studies, 28, 42, 57–58, 79–80, 84–87, 100–101, 130
International Institute of Social Studies, 169–70
intersectionality, 36–37, 76, 80, 95, 177
intervention, 17, 60, 73–74
introspection, 29, 31, 189
Irvin, Dona, 34
isolation, 33, 39, 146, 173, 177–78

Jackson, Janet, 154–55
Jackson, Michael, 200
Jacobs, Harriet, 36–37, 60, 190–93
James, Joy, 187
James, Stanlie, 168
January 6 insurgency, 50–51
jazz, 37, 202
Jesús, Ursula de, 66–67
Johnson-Bailey, Juanita, 32, 142–43
Johnson, Jessica, 130

Johnson, Sherry, 142
Jones, Grace, 66–67
Jones, Jaqueline, 135
Jones, Martha, 80–81, 130
Jordan-Zachery, Julia, 170–71
Jordan, June, 32
journaling, 142
journal reviews, 121–22
joy, 2, 19, 30–31, 51, 53–54, 55, 68, 139–40, 153, 177, 183, 200, 202, 204–5
justice, xiv–xv, 30; restorative, 189, 193; social, 3, 13–14, 139, 159–60, 162–63, 168–72, 189, 193

Kabat-Zinn, Jon, 35–36
Karenga, Maulana, 139
Keeling, Ida, 34, 66–67
Keenan Research Center, 193
Kelly, Robin D. G., 167–68, 198
Kendall, Mikki, 136
Kidjo, Angelique, 93
King, Tiffany, 75–76
Kirk, Gwen, 15–16
Kitt, Eartha, 75, 192–93
knowledge: Black feminist, 73, 128–29, 137–38, 171–73; community and, 114–15, 172–73; creation, 30, 73–74, 137–38; peer, 141–42; value of, 95–96
Koch Industries, 161

labor: academia and, 43, 158–61, 198–200; gendered, 5; publishing as, 3, 105, 113–14, 117–18, 146, 153; social justice and, 50–51, 170, 183
Laney, Lucy Craft, 86
language: degrees in, 84–85; human rights and, 167–68; violence and, 86; writing and, 32–33, 69–70, 100, 109–10, 165–66

Lassner, Jacob, 92–93
Laszloffy, Tracey, 1
Leadership Institute, 161
learning: academia and, 90–91, 107, 112, 140–41, 194; active, xiv–xv, 87–88, 183; African traditions of, 18–19, 92–93; applied, xiv–xv, 16–17, 42, 87–88, 94, 168–69; community and, xi, xiv–xv, 10–11, 37–38, 115, 125, 179, 186; freedom and, 50–51, 161, 163–66; as interdisciplinary, 28; self-learning, 37–38, 56, 188–89; time for, xii; unlearning, 36; wellness and, 8, 19–20, 31, 34–36, 60, 62–65, 84, 175, 184, 200
Ledisi, 202
Lee, Annie, 66
Leedy, Paul D., 104
Lewis, Edna, 66–67
Lewis, Shelby, 82
liberalism, 24–25
liberation, 23, 25–27, 37, 44, 110, 157, 170–72, 199–200
life writing. *See* memoir
Lindsey, Treva, 154
literacy, 14, 47–48, 158–59, 162, 175, 191
Literary Conversations series (University of Mississippi Press), 102
literature review, 73, 87–88
Littleton, La'Neice, 47–48, 191–94
Lorde, Audre, xii–xiii, 2, 15, 23–24, 36, 38–39, 102
Lordi, Emily, 2
love, 55, 58–59, 177, 196–99, 202–5
Love, Bettina L., 189, 198

Maathi, Wangari, 25
Mabokela, Reitumetse Obakeng, 142–43

MacLean, Nancy, 159–60
Macmillan, 102
Makeba, Miriam, 2
Makeda (Queen of Sheba), 18–19, 92–94
Malaje, Dora, 204
Malcolm X, 196
Manigault-Bryant, LeRhonda, 171–72
Mann, Rowena, 84
Maparyan, Layli, 11, 26, 61–62, 198
marginalization: academia and, 4, 9, 15, 32, 42, 61, 90, 94–95, 131–32, 162–64, 182, 189; Black feminism and, 25–26, 94–95, 204; history and, 58–59
Marley, Bob, 200
Marx, Karl, 170
Mason, Rihanna, 144
Maxwell, 200
Maxwell-Roddey, Bertha, 139
McCaskill, Barbara, 11
meditation, xv, 13, 34–36, 61–64, 108, 110, 186, 195–97
Mellon Fellows, 144
memoir, 24, 32, 35–37, 54–55, 59, 61, 65–68, 88, 90–91, 93, 172, 176–77, 189, 190
mental health. *See* wellness
M.E.N.T.A.L. health strategies, 62–63
mentoring, xi, 1, 4–5, 27–28, 89, 143–44, 164–65, 193–95; peer, 126, 195–96
Michael, George, 202
mindfulness, 15, 24, 108, 110
Mindfulness-Based Stress Reduction (MBSR), 35–36
miscarriage, 59–60
misogynoir, 24, 38–39, 95, 169
Modern Language Association, 85
Moorland Spingarn Research Center (Howard University), 82
Morgan, Joan, 136

Morris, Susana, 142
Morrison, Toni, xii–xiii, 2, 32, 102, 107–10, 189, 200
Mossell Alexander, Sadie Tanner, 24, 85
motherhood, 108–9
Muhammad, Khalil Gibran, 163–64
multitasking, 5–6, 69
Murray, Pauli, 82
music, 13, 19–20, 70, 127, 200–203
Mvula, Laura, 177
Myers, Josh, 198

Nap Ministry, 170
Nash, Jennifer, 76, 128, 198
National Association of Colored Women (NACW), 138
National Black Women's Health Project, 67
National Council for Black Studies (NCBS), 138–39, 142–43
National Council of Negro Women (NCNW), 137–38
National Women's Studies Association (NWSA), 130
Naylor, Gloria, 102
Neal, Mark Anthony, 198
Negi, Lobsang Tenzin, 35–36
networks, networking, 39–40, 62–64, 126–27, 142, 144, 146, 178, 182–83. *See also* community
Nicholas, Howard, 169–70
No More Martyrs, 43–44, 127

Oberlin College, 127
Odetta, 2
Okazawa-Rey, Margo, 15–16, 167–68
Oldways, 94, 127
100 Black Women Professors Now (100BWPN), 126–27
oppression: academy and, 15–16, 57–58, 61, 164; Black feminism

and, 4–5, 49, 61, 90, 94–96, 108–9, 128, 164, 191–92; challenging, 6–8, 26, 36–39, 49, 68–69, 94–96, 128, 164, 168–69, 188, 192–92, 204; wellness and, 34, 38–39, 68–69, 204
organization, organizing, 17, 74–75, 95–96, 99, 101, 103, 185
Ormrod, Jeanne, 104
outline, 42–43, 74–75, 100–102
Owens, Deirdre Cooper, 85

Painter, Nell Irvin, 34, 135
Palestine, 7, 167–68
panels, 153
Parker, Allison, 135
Parker, Pat, 36
Parks, Rosa, 34, 93
peace, 23, 30, 35, 39, 49, 54–56, 61, 108, 117, 168, 172, 175, 189, 193, 217
peer review, 2–3, 9–10, 32–33, 39–41, 73, 105, 111–15, 118–21, 125, 131–32, 134–37, 141–42, 145, 185–86
Perkins, Linda, 91
Perry, Imani, 198
Perry, Keisha-Khan Y., 129
Phi Beta Kappa Honor Society, 127
Phillips, Mary, 142, 196–97
Piervil, Esther, 194
plagiarism, 99, 121, 131–32
pleasure, 2, 13, 61, 146–47
Pluto Press, 101–2
podcasts, 121, 129
politics: academia and, 3, 113–14, 125–26, 131–32, 158–60, 163, 165; Black women and, 26–27, 38–39, 49, 75–76, 99, 159–60, 196; literacy and, 47–48; wellness and, 6, 15–16, 23–24, 50, 196; of writing, 17, 32, 38–39
Pope, Alexander, 3
Portwood-Stacer, Laura, 101

positionality, 136
power: academia and, 145, 177–78; Black feminism and, 31–32, 36, 60, 91–94, 167–68, 170, 190, 196–97; of community, 32; literacy and, xiv, 47–48; political, 162; wellness and, 52–53, 190, 196–97
practice, 17–18, 181; formal, 99–100; liberatory, 25–26, 157; mindful, 24; personal, 17, 55–56, 185; political, 17, 185–86; private, 47; problem-solving, 169; professional, 17, 185; public, 17, 185–86; publishing, 17, 185; referential, 73–74; regenerative, 200; relational, 125; rising, 185–86; wellness, 200; of writing, 33, 38
predominantly white institutions (PWIs), 48–49
Pressley, Ayanna, 204
Priest, Maxi, 71
Prince, 200
prison abolition, 196–97
Pritchard, James, 92–93
privacy, 47
problem-solving, 90, 92, 96, 169, 181
productivity, 27–28, 30, 113–14, 198
professional development, 32, 126
professional organizations, 39, 43–44, 77–79, 85, 112, 127–31, 138–39, 143–45
promotion, xiv, 9–10, 13–14, 51, 110, 113–14, 132, 136–37, 148–49, 165, 185. *See also* tenure
proposal, 100–101, 103–7, 116–18, 164–65
prospection, 29
public engagement, 17, 111, 121, 123, 125–31, 137, 139–40, 144–45, 153, 158. *See also* community
publishing: diversity in, 3, 100, 104, 107, 132; ethics of, 99, 105, 118–19, 131–37, 145; flourishing

publishing *(continued)*
in, 1–2; labor of, 3, 105, 113–14, 117–18, 146, 153; navigating, 3–4; as practice, 17, 185; process of, 2–3, 12, 52, 91–94, 100–107, 113–23, 126, 131–37, 140–41; "publish or perish," 51; stress and, 2–3, 120–21, 147, 177–78; time of, 41, 105–6, 120–21

queer and transgender women, 1–2, 25–26, 50, 61, 107, 112, 166, 169, 171, 182
queer and transgender studies, 81, 112, 161, 163–64
questions, 14–15, 18–19

race and gender studies, 42, 79–80, 112, 129–31, 160–66, 169, 177. *See also* Black Studies; Black Women's Studies; Women's Studies
Radcliffe Institute (Harvard University), 142
radicalism, 8–9
Ramsey, Sonya, 139
Randolph, Sherie M., 82–83, 128, 198
Ransby, Barbara, 112
Rappaport, Helen, 75
reader reports, 12, 69, 118–19, 140–41
reading: agency and, xiv, 47–48, 59; Black feminism and, xi–xii, xiv, 31, 47, 112; deep, 87–88; of history, 59–60, 91–92, 97; politics of, 47–48, 76; writing and, 12, 14, 47, 55–56, 99–100
Reagon, Bernice Johnson, 9
REAL BAD NEWS, 172–75
Reason Foundation, 161
Reese, Ashanté M., 129
reflexivity, 17, 69–70
regeneration, 29–31, 44, 80, 110, 193, 200

regenerative writing, 15, 23, 44, 110, 182, 213, 220
relationship building, 116–21. *See also* community
Rent, 197–99
Repko, Allen, 80
resilience, 35–36, 47, 55, 95, 185
resistance, 8–9, 11; Black feminism as, 37, 61, 68–69, 95, 204; wellness as, 30–31, 36, 204
rest, 170, 185
retrospection, 29
review process, 10, 106–7, 113, 120–22
rhythm, 32–33
Rice, Condoleezza, 75
Rihanna, 200
RISE (Rest, Immerse, Study, and Engage), 185–86
Robinson, Bernice, 162
Robinson, Randall, 93
Rockquemore, Kerry Ann, 1
Rogers, Nile, 177
Ronald E. McNair Scholars Program, 58, 88–89, 144
Ross, Rosetta E., 135
Rouse, Jacqueline, 135
Routledge, 102
royalties, 105
Rushing, Andrea, 27
Russell, Michele, 11

sabbatical, 5–6
Saffold, Jacinta, 129–30
Sage Publications, 102
Sanchez, Sonia, 48–49, 81–82, 102, 110, 113, 193
Sankofa, 20, 23, 220, 282
Sapolsky, Robert, 52, 62
Savage, Barbara D., 75, 80–81
#SayHerName, 128
Scheherazade, 93

Schomburg Center for Research in
  Black Culture (NYPL), 82
Schoolhouse Rock, 58
science, technology, engineering, and
  math (STEM), 42
Scott, Hazel, 13
Scott, Jill, 96–97
Scott, Patricia Bell, 81
Seacole, Mary, 75
self-awareness, 54–55
self-care, 15–16, 23–28, 34, 44, 50, 55,
  60–61, 71, 139, 157, 189–97, 200.
  See also wellness; *under* care
self-compassion, 8, 15
self-determination, xii, 15, 27, 61,
  137–38, 157–60, 167–68, 194
self-education, 37, 47, 88, 99–100,
  110, 157–58
self-publishing, 57, 66, 74, 100,
  112–13
self-reliance, 15, 27–28, 33, 107,
  182–83
Sertima, Ivan Van, 92–93
service, 1–3, 5, 13–14, 43, 51, 68–69,
  92, 97, 165, 181–82
Sesa Wo Suban, 16–19
Shange, Ntozake, 32
Sharpley-Whiting, Tracy, 126–27, 187,
  198
Simone, Nina, 2, 202
Simpson, Georgiana R., 24, 85
sisterhood, 61–62, 64, 81, 146–47,
  154
Sisters of the Academy (SOTA), 128;
  Research BootCamp, 140–44
Skills for Scholars (Princeton
  University Press), 103–4
Smart-Grosvenor, Vertamae, 32
Smith, Barbara, 9, 24, 81–82, 122–23
Smith, Christen A., 25, 129–30, 198
social justice, 3, 13–14, 60, 139,
  159–60, 162–63, 168–72, 189, 193

Social Justice Café for Girls, 43–44,
  127
social location theory, 15–16
social media, 129, 186–88
Social Sciences and Humanities
  Network Online (H-Net), 111
solidarity, 63, 167–68
solitude, 35–36
Sood, Amit, 55, 89
sororities, 127, 131
soul, 1–2, 19–20, 44, 63, 181, 199–204
sources, 69, 75–76, 101, 106, 121–22,
  142, 185–86; diversity of, 37,
  80–81, 125–26, 131–32; REAL BAD
  NEWS, 172–75. *See also* citation
Southern Christian Leadership
  Conference (SCLC), 162
space: in academia, 8, 26–27; of Black
  feminism, 25–27; demanding, 5;
  for healing, 19; for pleasure, 13;
  relational, 9, 30
Spencer, Robin, 198
spirituality, 2, 34, 52–53, 63, 129,
  171–72, 182–83, 196–97
standpoint, 26, 94
State Policy Network, 161
Stevenson, Brea, 194
stress: Black women and, 4–8,
  50, 59–60, 62, 87, 192–93,
  204; community and, 10–11;
  contextualizing, 6–8, 15–16;
  education and, 57, 59–60, 68–71,
  84, 87; publishing and, 2–3, 120–
  21, 147, 177–78; time and, 68–69;
  in United States, 49–51; wellness
  and, 35–36, 52–53, 55, 59–60,
  62–64; white supremacy and, 3;
  writing and, 4–5, 15, 70–71, 94–95.
  See also wellness
structure, 17, 100–101, 103
style guides, 85
Succession, 49